D0982534

The Hidden Power

The Hidden Power
Brian Inglis

JONATHAN CAPE
THIRTY-TWO BEDFORD SQUARE LONDON

First published 1986
Copyright © 1986 by Brian Inglis

Jonathan Cape Ltd, 32 Bedford Square, London WC1B 3EL

British Library Cataloguing in Publication Data

Inglis, Brian
The hidden power
1. Psychical research   2. Scientists—Attitudes
I. Title
133   BF1045.S35
ISBN 0-224-02284-9

The author and publishers are grateful to Duckworth & Co.
Ltd and A. D. Peters & Co. Ltd for permission to reproduce
the extract from *The Modern Traveller vi* on p. 53

Phototypeset by Falcon Graphic Art Ltd
Wallington, Surrey
Printed in Great Britain by Butler & Tanner Ltd
Frome and London

Contents

Illustrations

FIGURES   *page*

A new truth has to encounter three normal stages of opposition. In the first, it is denounced as imposture; in the second – that is, when it is beginning to force its way into notice – it is cursorily examined, and plausibly explained away; in the third, or *cui bono* stage, it is decried as useless, and hostile to religion. And when it is fully admitted, it passes only under a protest that it has been perfectly known for ages – a proceeding intended to make the new truth ashamed of itself, and wish it had never been born.

Herbert Mayo, *Letters on the Truths*
Contained in the Popular Superstitions,
1851 (see p.204)

The Menace of Scientism

I was brought up to regard science almost as a religion. It was not preached to my generation; it was taught us as the truth. A few mysteries remained; scientists, we were assured, would soon clear them away. Mistakes had been made, but the great virtue of the scientific method was that they were inevitably recognised, sooner or later, and put right, as Lamarck's had been by Darwin. Science's basic structure was presented to us as if secure for all time, founded as it was on the laws of nature. We should take it for granted, much as we took Jesus's divinity for granted.

For most of us, the shedding of belief in Christianity served only to increase our respect for science. We had no idea that the quantum physicists were undermining its materialist foundations. We assumed that any criticism of Darwin could only be the work of one of those crazy Creationists. Only gradually did it begin to dawn on those of us who began to study certain aspects of it more critically that we had been the victims of a confidence trick. We had not been taught science. We have been taught scientism.

The sociologist James McClenon defines scientism as 'the body of ideas used by scientists to legitimate their practices'. Long smarting under the lash of the 'hard' scientists, sociologists are now beginning to enjoy their revenge by exposing just how illegitimate some of those practices are. They are based not on facts, but on faiths, which have to be supported by the methods that religions traditionally use. In particular, scientism cannot tolerate the suggestion that some of its dogmas – Darwinian theory, say – may be only partly true.

Scientists 'act like the defenders of the One and only Roman Church acted before them', as Paul Feyerabend, the fiercest of their critics, has lamented. 'Church doctrine is true, everything else is pagan nonsense.' This would matter less, he argues, if they faced competition, as the Churches do. The science establishment is a state-supported, state-funded, self-perpetuating monopoly. It can impose its dogmas and deal ruthlessly with heretics.

Defenders of the scientific faith insist that there is a difference. They are rationalists. The public's continuing respect for science is in fact largely derived from the belief that, unlike religion, it enshrines reason. Here, though, Sir Peter Medawar has put his finger on the flaw, in *The Limits of Science*.

Although he is a rationalist, he admits he is sometimes unwilling to declare himself one because of the neglect of the distinction 'between the *sufficient* and the *necessary*'. The exercise of reason 'is at all times unconditionally *necessary* and we disregard it at our peril'; but 'I do not believe – indeed I deem it a comic blunder to believe it – that the exercise of reason is *sufficient* to explain our condition and where necessary to remedy it'.

Scientists have been responsible for the comic blunder, and its consequences have not been comic. Too often scientists have tended to assume that science is, or could be, sufficient to explain everything. So long as its materialist foundations seemed secure this was not entirely unreasonable. When the quantum physicists began to erode those foundations, scientism was already too well entrenched to admit it could be wrong.

Its reaction to the threat to its survival has been to grasp at academic straws, much as some Popes have reacted to the spread of liberal ideas by insisting upon a return to more rigidly ultramontane principles and practices. Positivism had led the way (with logical positivism to follow). Others have been neo-Darwinism, reductionism, behaviourism, sociobiology, structuralism, and recently neo-Marxism. Their common denominator has been a longing to restore the certainties that materialism promised. Each has been taught by its hot-gospellers to students as a received truth. Each for a time has appeared to offer salvation within its academic discipline. In the long run, all of them have been shown to be fulfilling the role of pit-props in a mine gallery threatened by subsidence – by the flow of anomalies which cannot be explained, so they have to be explained away.

Ten years ago Alan McGlashan observed that science was 'in the awkward position of a young woman who has inadvertently become pregnant and wonders how long she can continue in her job'. At the time nobody had noticed, people being 'far too preoccupied with their own affairs'. The condition can now no longer be concealed. And it is becoming clear that what scientists will have to face is the prospect of a return to the principle that materialism displaced: vitalism.

In its simplest form vitalism was described by Alfred Russel Wallace, explaining how he differed from Darwin over the evolutionary hypothesis they had independently reached. He agreed with Darwin about the way the human body had evolved, but he did not believe that man's moral and intellectual qualities could be satisfactorily accounted for by natural selection. They were not material. Other evolutionary processes must be at work.

The idea of an evolutionary 'life force' was explored by the neo-vitalists, as they came to be called: Henri Bergson, William McDougall, Hans Driesch. Respected though they were, they could make no impression on scientism. It could not incorporate the mind – the 'ghost in the machine' – let alone anything as metaphysical as a force undetectable by any known methods.

Had vitalism simply required an admission that a Shakespeare or a Mozart, and our appreciation of them, would require a slight bending of the rules, it might have made more headway. Many a dedicated materialist, after all, has continued to say his prayers, assuming God will not intervene in the lab. The problem has been that the ghost in the machine insists on talking and playing games – as Wallace was disconcerted to find. It was not an abstraction. It had emotional and physical side-effects.

When Wallace's insatiable curiosity led him to investigate mediumship he was treated to a flow of information which appeared to be clairvoyant, along with percussive noises, materialisations, levitations and other seance phenomena, in light good enough for him to check that no human agency was responsible. Worse, whatever invisible agent *was* responsible seemed to be controlled by an intelligence capable of answering questions by raps or movements of the seance table.

Action or communication at a distance without any physical explanation had been outlawed by materialists as contrary to the laws of nature. Wallace held that as observed facts cannot be supernatural, the laws were at fault. There must be a force flowing through people capable of providing the action and the communication. Camille Flammarion coined the term 'psychic' for it. We now call it paranormal – though parapsychologists prefer the neutral blanket term 'psi', covering both the forces involved and the phenomena.

Psi cannot be pinned down in a simple definition. It reflects a hypothesis that a force exists capable of biological action and communication at a distance, and of interacting with known forces such as gravity. Its manifestations – ESP, psychokinesis (telekinesis), poltergeists, divination and so on – have been reported from every era, from every part of the world. No other accumulation of experiences, attested by so many people from all walks of life, has ever been rejected.

Beliefs long and firmly held, it is argued, have often eventually been shown to be false. Agreed: but psi phenomena are not beliefs. They are experiences. Various beliefs have been and still are being attached to them, which posterity will have to sort out. Experiences are facts, as Wallace and several other eminent scientists insisted, and cannot be dismissed on this count.

Paradoxically these facts, though they provide concrete evidence in favour of vitalism, are one reason why vitalism's restoration will be bitterly opposed. To have to concede that there are unexplained psychic forces influencing evolution will be bad enough. To accept the existence of discarnate intelligences with the power to make objects move in defiance of gravity would be horrendous.

As a result scientists have been all too ready to accept the support of camp-followers, rationalists and sceptics, who assure them that psi does not exist, and that the phenomena are fraudulent. The 'reason' which the rationalists claim to rely upon is in fact irrational – the 'hasty, dogmatical self-satisfied type' which Hazlitt denounced in his *Table Talk* as 'worse than idle fancy or bigoted prejudice' because it is 'ostentatious in error, closes up the avenues of knowledge, and "shuts the gates of wisdom on mankind" '.

The sceptics, too, are not sceptical in the proper sense of the term. 'They are not seeking theories and causes to account for observed facts', as Aristotle said of the Pythagoreans; they are trying to accommodate their observations 'to certain theories and opinions of their own'. This has made them unreliable allies, as scientists are just beginning to realise.

The collapse of materialism has been making some scientists re-examine the case for vitalism. This in turn necessitates a fresh look at the case for psi. I have tried to present that case as Wallace insisted it should be presented, citing J.S. Mill's 'an argument is not answered until it is answered at its best'; but there are weaknesses in the experimental evidence, in particular, which parapsychologists admit to, and which should not be brushed aside.

I have tried, too, to show how dishonest the campaign to discredit psychical research has been. As the philosopher C.J. Ducasse pointed out, even if the sceptics have been right, and the phenomena do not occur, the sheer quantity and quality of the reports, and the fact that many of those who experienced or witnessed the phenomena have been people of high intelligence and integrity, 'is exceedingly interesting from the standpoint of the psychology of perception, of delusion, illusion or hallucination, of credulity and credibility and of testimony', and needs investigation. If psi effects *have* really occurred, on the other hand, 'they are equally important from the standpoint of the psychology of *in*credulity and *in*credibility – or, more comprehensively, of orthodox adverse prejudice, such as widely exists'.

I do not 'believe in' psi, in the sense that many a scientist believes in reductionism. I accept it, in the sense of recognising that certain phenomena exist and need investigation. I have written, therefore, from the standpoint of one who accepts the reality of the phenomena not from personal experience, still less from any 'longing to believe' they exist, but from the conviction that they cannot all be put down to delusion and deception. And if they exist, the implications are surely too important to be ignored.

It is going to be difficult to persuade scientists to abandon scientism and mechanistic attitudes, and even harder to persuade them to look again at psi. The fact that only two British universities applied for the Koestler bequest, which was offered to fund a Chair of Parapsychology, has indicated the continuing strength of the resistance movement. Will it, then, be public opinion that leads the way – as it has begun to do in connection with medical science? Between 70 and 80 per cent of the population, to judge from opinion polls, accepts the reality of paranormal phenomena.

Public opinion has little power except when, as in medicine, it can back a change of allegiance by paying for what it wants. Big Business is better placed. A few firms have been taking the advice of the late Sir Val Duncan, Chairman of Rio Tinto Zinc, and exploring the possibility of divination to find seams of ore, or oilfields.

The most lavish, though not entirely welcome, paymasters for psychical research are government agencies. In Russia and America they have been active, funding research to test individuals who can exercise psychokinetic powers or display extra-sensory perception, in the hope that their talents can be exploited.

Still, perhaps the positive results which have been obtained and 'leaked' may teach both sides caution in case their plans are being given away as Syria's were to the Israelites. 'Who is the spy in my entourage?' the king of Syria asked. 'None, my Lord, O King,' a servant told him. 'Elisha the prophet, that is in Israel, telleth the king of Israel the words that thou speakest in thy bedchamber.'

I

THE EVIDENCE FOR
PSI

The first question which presents itself is why, given that there has been so much evidence for psi in all ages, and in all parts of the world, has it not been accepted that there is a powerful case on its behalf, which ought not to be dismissed out of hand?

Physics

Acceptance of psi has been blocked in a number of ways, chiefly by the influence of eighteenth-century rationalism, which has remained strong. David Hume laid down that a miracle constitutes a violation of the laws of nature – laws derived from the 'firm and unalterable experience of mankind'. As it came to be assumed that action at a distance, other than through the agency of some known force, and communication at a distance, other than through the known senses, were contrary to the laws of nature, they were put in the 'miracle' category, and dismissed as superstition. Extrasensory perception and psychokinesis (PK) did not happen, because they could not happen.

Historians of science have tried to show that this rejection of ESP and PK was based on a misunderstanding of Newton's theory of gravity. Pope's verdict, in his *Epitaphs*,

> Nature, and Nature's laws lay hid in night:
> God said, *Let Newton be!* and all was light.

has been too uncritically accepted. Nobody knew better that all was *not* light than Newton himself. He regarded it as inconceivable that 'inanimate brute matter' should act upon other matter without contact, unless something else, not material, was responsible. That gravity should be innate, 'so that one body may act upon another at a distance through a vacuum without the mediation of anything else', he wrote to the Revd Richard Bentley, was 'so great an absurdity that I believe no man who has in philosophical matters a competent faculty of thinking can ever fall for it' – an opinion which encouraged Bentley in a sermon to assert that gravity must be a manifestation of divine energy. Newton's theory was actually denounced by Leibniz as presupposing some 'senseless occult quality', unless Newton could point to some physical means by which the attraction was produced. Occult it remains to this day.

Gravity is accepted because it has to be – its effects are there for all to feel, and witness – and because, unexplained and inexplicable though it has remained, it obeys certain rules. Its effects can be quantified. So can those of magnetism, though its action at a distance has erratic features. Psi has remained an outlaw not because it is unexplained, often though that is used as an excuse for rejecting it, but because it cannot easily be pinned down for purposes of scientific measurement.

Half a century ago the 'laws of nature' were found wanting. The quantum physicists showed that their materialist basis had been fallacious. More than that, their new model introduced intimations of psi. The first came when it was discovered that nuclear particles sometimes seemed to be in two places at once. Psychical researchers had long known the phenomenon of bi-location (graphically illustrated in Goethe's description of the occasion when he had met and talked to a friend in the street who, at the time, was sitting in Goethe's living room). Particles, too, appeared to be able to move from one orbit to another without traversing the space in between, the phenomenon known to psychical researchers as teleportation, frequently featuring in accounts of poltergeist hauntings.

Quantum theory also took in communication at a distance, to Einstein's alarm. He had accepted 'Mach's Principle' that everything in the universe is interconnected (Bertrand Russell thought it 'savoured of astrology'), but jibbed at the quantum physicists' notion that 'twin' particles, if separated, would continue to act as if linked, because it implied telepathy. A few years after his death, the proposition was formally presented in mathematical form by J.S. Bell of the CERN Institute at Geneva. If two particles which have interacted are shot off in different directions, interference with the 'spin' of one will affect the 'spin' of the other, no matter how far apart they may be. The proposition has since been confirmed by tests.

Its interpretation poses a major problem, Arthur Koestler observed in *Janus*, as it *does* seem to imply 'a sort of "telepathy" between the particles'. Koestler was careful to point out that these discoveries do not mean that physics is about to provide an explanation for psi phenomena. Nevertheless the baffling paradoxes of physics 'make the baffling phenomena of parapsychology appear a little less preposterous'. Although the analogies may prove to be treacherous, 'it is encouraging to know that if the parapsychologist is out on a limb, the physicist is out on a tightrope'.

Most physicists still shy away from quantum theory's implications, for the same reason as Einstein. They resent the way psychical researchers appear to be trying to extricate themselves from banishment by clinging to quantum's soft underbelly, much as Ulysses and his comrades clung to the bellies of sheep to escape from the Cyclops' cave. Some, however, have admitted that Hume's 'laws of nature' argument against psi is dead, and ought to be buried. 'The notion that certain things are impossible is tied to an assumption that the universe is made of real things, and that things are separated in a well-defined way', Geoffrey Chew, Head of the Physics Department at the Lawrence Berkeley Institute in California, has stated in an interview on the relationship of psi to quantum physics; 'all sorts of possibilities open up'. A few have gone further. 'Relativistic quantum mechanics is a conceptual scheme', Costa de Beauregard of the Poincaré Institute in Paris claimed after Bell's theory was vindicated, 'in which phenomena such as psychokinesis or telepathy, far from being irrational, should on the contrary be expected.'

Physicists who accept the evidence but decline to accept its implications argue that, so far, it is entirely based on a mathematical model of what happens at micro levels. This may have no counterpart in the macro world in which we live. One possible exception – other than the reports of the psi phenomena themselves – is the way in which crystals develop. Researchers hoping to obtain new crystals from solutions, much as ice crystallises from water, have found that it can be maddeningly difficult. Yet as soon as a crystal emerges for the first time, a chain reaction appears to start up. Crystals emerge elsewhere until the procedure seems simple. Nobody understands why. The explanation usually given is that microscopic dust particles are carried to other solutions, 'infecting' them – a typical example of the way in which implausible 'natural' explanations are accepted, rather than have the door left open for unexplained action at a distance.

An alternative hypothesis, which Rupert Sheldrake has presented in *A New Science of Life*, is the existence of 'morphic resonance', analogous to the sympathetic vibrations of stretched strings to the appropriate sound waves. Morphic resonance implies action at a distance without transmission of energy – in other words, psi. This heresy so disturbed the editor of *Nature* that he reacted after the manner of a Grand Inquisitor, denouncing the book as 'the best candidate for burning for many years', though he admitted that he no longer had the authority to order an *auto-da-fé* – an interesting reflection of the way in which *Nature*, once the most respected of scientific journals, has come to regard itself primarily as the Defender of the Faith: of scientism.

Botany

The morphic resonance theory straddles the frontier between animate and inanimate territory that Jagadis Chandra Bose began to explore a century ago, with illuminating results. They were so well demonstrated and presented that, at the time, they convinced his fellow-scientists. Yet they were so disconcerting that they were not followed up, and are today rarely mentioned in academic journals.

Bose had graduated at Cambridge in physics, botany and chemistry before being appointed Professor of Physics at the Presidency College, Calcutta, where his initial investigations enabled him publicly to demonstrate wireless transmission in 1895 – even before Lodge and Marconi. This brought him immediate fame as a physicist: the editor of the *Spectator* was intrigued and impressed by 'the spectacle of a Bengali of purest descent lecturing in London to an audience of appreciative European savants upon one of the most recondite branches of modern physical science'.

Bose's next line of inquiry, into metal fatigue, might have brought him fortune as well as fame; he discovered that certain metals could recuperate, if given a rest. Graphs of fatigue and recovery, he pointed out, showed striking similarities between metal and animal tissues: in both 'fatigue could be removed by gentle massage or by exposure to a bath of warm water'.

Although this was dangerous ground, Bose was actually able to demonstrate that his 'treatment' worked. It happened, too, that at the time, the turn of the century, many physicists seriously believed that they would soon be able to provide all the answers to the problems of other disciplines, including physiology and botany. Bose could consequently be congratulated for having advanced the boundaries of physics. Even

when he went on to compare plant reactions with animal
reactions, though he encountered some suspicion as a man
who was moving far from his academic base, he had acquired
a sufficient reputation to be able to overcome it.

The Neoplatonist philosopher Plotinus had surmised that
plants· 'aspire to contemplation'. Gustav Fechner, the
nineteenth-century founder of psychophysics, went further
and claimed that they have souls. He did not mean, he
explained, that they had souls individually; simply that they
had a kind of psychic identity, as well as their material
properties. They had a richly developed life of the senses, he
argued, in certain respects more developed than the sensory
range of animals.

Bose confirmed this view by showing that plants react to
'irritation' or to 'blows' in much the same way as animals.
Again he was able to carry the physicists with him by
explaining that the response was 'electrical' and by demonstrating it with the help of a gadget, a 'crescograph', with
which he silenced his critics. In 1917 he received the accolade
of a knighthood. Had he not carried scientific research into
areas unexplored before, and used impeccably scientific
methods to back his findings?

After Bose's death, doubts set in. How could a plant, with
no nervous system of the animal kind, react to irritation or
blows in the same way as an animal? When Bose's writings
were examined, they showed that his explanation was not
physical, but psychic. There was a 'pervading unity' of the
kind described by the Hindu philosophers of old. When his
own work brought him to the same conclusion, it had led him
to appreciate the force of words written 3,000 years earlier:
'They who see but one, in all the changing manifoldness of
this universe, unto them belongs Eternal Truth – unto none
else!'

Mystical concepts such as a pervading unity were anathema to conventional botanists, physiologists and psychologists
alike. They could not very well overturn Bose's findings.
Instead, they resorted to the equivalent of sending him to
Coventry. His work was treated as if it had never existed.
When, nearly half a century later, it was repeated with similar
results, the research was deemed to be in the domain not of
physics but of psi, and, as such, not to be taken seriously.

Cleve Backster was a leading American expert on polygraphs; he had been called upon to advise a Federal Commission of Inquiry into their forensic use as lie detectors. Curiosity prompted him in the 1960s to try experiments on plants to find out whether they would react to threatening situations and, if so, whether their reactions would leave tracings of the kind shown on polygraphs. Attaching an electrode to the leaf of a plant, he immersed another leaf in hot coffee. Nothing happened. He then decided to try a more dramatic measure. He would light a match, he decided, and actually burn a leaf. At the instant he made this decision, 'at thirteen minutes, fifty-five seconds of chart time, there was a dramatic change in the tracing pattern'. It had been only the *idea* of using the match – suggesting to him that the thought must have been the trigger. If repeatable, this result would 'tend to indicate the existence of a perception capability in plant life'.

It was the measure of the extent to which Bose had been forgotten that Backster's paper, when it was published, appeared in one of the journals devoted to psychical research. Significantly, too – at least concerning parapsychology's condition by the 1960s – though it was greeted with interest there were reservations: particularly about his claim that as his experiments had been carefully controlled and randomised, their results had shown that plant reaction 'can be independent of human involvement'. Parapsychologists were sadly aware that success in one set of randomised controlled trials provided no guarantee of success in the next. Nor did they, on this occasion. A repeat performance by another research team gave negative results, to the delight of sceptics. As has frequently happened, parapsychologists tended to feel ashamed of themselves for having been taken in.

A report of a recent research project suggests that they should now feel ashamed of themselves for having dismissed Backster's work so lightly. In the first major survey of psychical research to come out of Russia, A.P. Dubrov and V.N. Pushkin have described how they undertook trials along lines similar to Backster's, but using electroencephalographs. They found that plants reacted to alterations in the emotional condition of human subjects.

Sceptics pointed out that the responses on the graph might be due to the effect of chemicals on the subject's skin, or perhaps to body heat. Fresh trials were set up, to test these hypotheses. It was suggested to subjects under hypnosis that they should identify with one plant or the other, the suggestion being designed to arouse strong feelings. The recordings revealed that each plant reacted 'only when the emotion of the subject had been directed to it, while there was no response from the other plant'. Neither chemical changes nor changes of temperature, in short, could account for the responses. The plants could only be responding to emotional changes: action at a distance.

In any case, that plants have certain powers which defy conventional explanations can hardly be disputed. In *Plants as Inventors*, published half a century ago, Raoul Francé listed a number of them. In particular, he pointed out, plants can move mountains, almost literally. 'Trees can split rocks into fragments with their growing roots, and dislodge houses' – as countless householders have reason to lament.

'I have seen a tree root burst a rock face on a mountain', Loren Eiseley, Professor of Anthropology and the History of Science at the University of Pennsylvania, recalled in his much acclaimed *The Star Thrower*, 'or slowly wrench aside the gateway of a forgotten city' – a cunning feat, he added, which we 'take too readily for granted'. Botanists, confronted with it, had called it 'osmotic pressure' – the ability of plant cells to behave in a way which reminded Francé of the effect of stoking in the boiler room on a ship. But when water pressure builds up, steam escapes. In a volcanic eruption, lava bursts forth. The roots of trees, far softer than rock or concrete, force their way through. How?

The ability of fungi to perform similar feats has been reported from many parts of the world. In Siberia a century ago, Vladimir Bogoraz reported that growing mushrooms could split open a tree, or even a stone. In 1984 an account appeared in the *New Scientist* of tumescence under the tarmac of an English street which grew 'with astonishing speed'; disturbing passers-by, before bursting open 'like John Hurt's chest in *Alien*. Forcing its way into the light came a mushroom, a perfectly edible, pink-gilled mushroom.' The witnesses were still stunned by the event, the report concluded, 'asking each other unanswerable questions'. How can a mushroom, which a passing pedestrian could have crushed, hardly knowing he had stepped on it, burst through tarmac? 'Clearly we have much to learn', the *New Scientist*'s commentator observed, 'about the electrophysiology of plant growth.'

However far advanced, electrophysiology is unlikely to explain certain other mysteries of plant growth – though along with speculation about chemical effects, it is still adhered to, as preferable to such unwelcome alternatives as the one Joseph Sinel offered in 1927. He described how a friend of his had set up an experiment to monitor the ways in which a climbing plant finds suitable 'holds'. If growing against a wall, he had discovered, the plant would grow towards the nearest nail: 'if there are two nails near each other, it will select the more suitable one, an old rusty and crooked one having the preference'. Experiments of this kind, Sinel argued, surely confirmed that things can be perceived without the use of any of the five senses; 'if so, the contention of those who oppose clairvoyance on the grounds that there can be no perception without the operation of one or other of these senses seems to me to break down'.

Sinel's 'long and honourable life' had been passed 'in the continuous pursuit of truth', Macleod Yearsley, a Fellow of the Zoological Society, observed in a foreword to Sinel's *The Sixth Sense*. His contributions to biology, geology and prehistoric archaeology were well known: 'whether his contentions are right or wrong I cannot presume to decide, but that they are based upon careful observation, scientifically carried out, I am quite sure'. Yearsley was very far from being a devotee of psychical research. To him, the value of Sinel's work was that any scientist who read it with an open mind would realise that it dealt 'to "Spiritualism" and the "occult" the shrewdest blow that has ever been struck'. In other words, he hoped scientists would realise that clairvoyance is a natural phenomenon, which they could and should investigate without worrying that they might be tainted with occultism. But by the 1930s clairvoyance was too deeply suspect in orthodox eyes for the advice to be heeded. In any case Sinel, however deserving of Yearsley's eulogy, was a naturalist, a species no longer taken seriously in academic circles.

Sinel posed other questions to which botanists have yet to find a satisfactory answer; such as how the common insectivorous bog-plant sun-dew, whose sticky hairs ordinarily are upright, ready to seize any fly alighting on them, turns upside-down when insects are unavailable, as if seeking nourishment in the bog below. Flies, Sinel had found, were more desirable: 'If a dead fly is now stuck upon the point of a needle and fixed an inch or two away from the plant, a decided movement of the leaves will commence. They will move in the direction of the fly, those nearest striving to reach it.' Not only had the sun-dew a sense of direction; it could tell what is, or is not, edible, the leaves ignoring inedible substances put on the needle. To Sinel this, too, looked like 'an incipient faculty of "clairvoyance" and, I hold *it is the same*, differing only in degree of complexity from that in humanity itself'.

The ability of the Venus fly-trap to snap shut when a fly is inside has attracted some attention from physiologists, puzzled by the plant's ability to exert what resembles a powerful muscular reaction, such as closing one's fist, with no muscles to account for it. The need to offer a 'natural' explanation led to what the *New Scientist*, in a note on the subject in 1981, described as 'the classic textbook model of rapid changes in motor cell turgor', based on the fact that plant cells maintain their shape through 'turgor' – water pressure. The trap, according to the model, was closed simply by rapid jettisoning of water from the appropriate cells. As reductionist models go, it had sounded plausible. The only snag, as Stephen Williams of Lebanon Valley College, Pennsylvania, eventually pointed out, was that the major cells, far from getting smaller as they jettisoned their load, actually increased in size. Having consigned the 'classic textbook model' to the wastepaper basket, Williams offered his alternative: electric signalling. Even supposing this to be correct, it has left the queston unresolved. On receipt of the signal, how is the trap closed?

A number of orthodox commentators, looking at what has been discovered about insectivorous plants, have admitted that they are 'not satisfactorily accommodated in the omnibus of evolutionary doctrine', as C.W. Wardlaw noted in his *Organisation and Evolution in Plants*. They are not accounted for by invoking psi, either; but at least psi would make them easier to explain.

There is now more direct evidence of psi involvement. Controlled trials have been carried out with the help of 'laying on of hands' by a healer, to find whether it could influence the rate of growth of seeds.

The healer was a former cavalry officer in the Polish Army, Oskar Estebany; the tests were conducted in the early 1960s by Dr Bernard Grad of McGill University, Montreal. It was not even necessary, Grad found, for Estebany to hold his hands above the seeds, for the seeds to develop faster than the controls. They developed significantly faster if watered with a solution from a beaker he had held between his hands. Tests with other individuals, 'double blind' – neither they nor the investigators were allowed to know which trays of seeds were 'treated', and which were the controls, until the trials were complete – have since produced confirmatory results at McGill. They have also been successfully repeated elsewhere.

These results were ignored. When in 1973 Peter Tompkins and Christopher Bird examined the case for plant psi in *The Secret Life of Plants*, a balanced survey of the evidence from history and from research, the book was gleefully disparaged by the academic establishment. The editor of *Science*, Philip Abelson, suggested it should be put on the equivalent of the Vatican's Index, as unsuitable reading. In *Natural History* Arthur Galston, Professor of Biology at Yale, was similarly dismissive, singling out for derision the evidence about inter-communication between plant species, and their reactions to sound.

Ten years later an article in the *New York Times*, recalling how the book's heretical notions had 'incensed a major portion of the scientific community', described how two separate teams of plant biologists had just found that some trees appear to be able to pass on warnings about impending insect attack, enabling defensive chemical action to be taken. That plants can, and do, react to sound has also since been demonstrated. Even more embarrassingly for the botanical establishment, the 'natural' explanation for the way in which plants react as if they have the same nervous system as animals has been shown to be a fudge, hastily invented early in the century to account for Bose's findings.

Generations of students have been taught that the explanation is 'phytohormones', that is, plant hormones. Today, 'the deceptively simple question being asked is "do plants really have hormones?"' and the response of some scientists is challenging theories that have dominated research and teaching for more than half-a-century', according to Dr Jonathan Weyers, of the Department of Biological Studies at Dundee University. The issue is not academic, as it 'has profound implications for agricultural and horticultural practice'. Much remains to be discovered, Weyer admits, but 'what chance is there of success if the concepts underlying the research are unclear and the methods weak?'

Keen gardeners will often say of a colleague or rival that he has 'green fingers' though they may be unwilling to say it in public, because rationalists have for so long insisted that there is nothing more to it than applied knowledge and hard work. Erwin Schrödinger, Nobel Laureate and one of the most admired of the leading physicists in recent times, was not so sure. 'The genius of Gustav Theodore Fechner did not shy at attributing a soul to a plant', he recalled in a lecture in Cambridge in 1950. He could not himself fall in with such fantasies; 'yet I should not like to have to pass judgment as to who has come nearer to the deepest truth, Fechner or the bankrupts of rationalism'.

Ethology

'The first and simplest kind of locomotory behaviour is what is called kinesis', W.H. Thorpe, Professor of Animal Zoology at Cambridge, observed in *The Origins and Rise of Ethology*. The first it may be; the simplest it is not, as he went on to illustrate. Kinesis guides primitive creatures to a source of nourishment or of light in spite of the fact that they have no organs of hearing, sight, smell, taste or touch. In other words, it is extra-sensory – in the common meaning of that term. In humans such guidance would be described as psychokinetic. This is only another way of indicating that nobody has found how bacteria, say, seem to know where to go for sugar, and move in its direction. They must have another sense. For all we know they may have several senses, as yet undiscovered. The important point is that there is some form of guidance.

That ethologists should be uneasy about the source of the guidance is understandable. They have wanted to secure academic status for their discipline, which has not been easy. The term 'ethology' was originally introduced by J.S. Mill to describe how character is built, as distinct from psychology which was concerned with mental process. Psychologists, refusing to accept the distinction, appropriated the study of character formation for their own discipline. Konrad Lorenz, Niko Tinbergen and others have only recently re-established ethology as the study of animal behaviour, with the help of Thorpe at Cambridge and Sir Alister Hardy, Professor of Zoology at Oxford.

Hardy tried to make his colleagues face the mystery of kinetic guidance. Single-celled amoebas are extremely rudimentary organisms, he reminded his audience at the Hibbert lectures in 1965; yet their near relations, the Foraminifera, 'build houses which are little short of marvels of

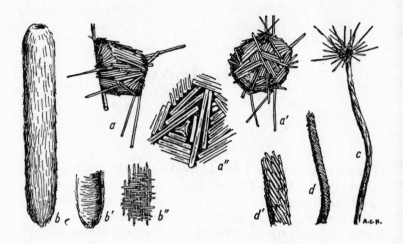

Figure 1   Illustrations from Hardy's *The Living Stream* of foraminifera
architecture and building. How did they learn their skills?
Surely, he argued, there must have been a psychic element
involved.

engineering and constructional skill'. He was using the term
'skill' advisedly, he insisted. Foraminifera, he felt, present a
serious challenge to conventional biology. Here are minute
creatures, with no discernible sense organs, 'appearing as
mere flowing masses of protoplasm, yet endowed with extraordinary powers'. Not only do they select specific objects from
all the jumble on the sea-bed, 'they build them into a design
involving a comparison of size. They build as if to a plan.'
How did they learn to be not merely builders but accomplished architects? 'The mystery', he concluded, 'surely concerns the relation of this "psychic" life of the animal to its
mechanical body.'

It must have been the first time that many of Hardy's
academic colleagues had heard the term 'psychic' used in a
scientific context. Although Hardy's standing as a zoologist
was such that he could get away with it, he could not arouse
his fellow ethologists to follow the course he himself had taken,
exploring the possibility that psychical research might be able
to uncover the secret of kinetic guidance, displaying itself as it
does at so many levels of development. It has been left to the

'pop ethologists', as they have been described, Lyall Watson in Britain, Robert Ardrey and Lewis Thomas in the United States, to keep on posing the question: who, or what, is the guide?

Take the best known of all the mysteries of primitive organisms: the behaviour of the slime mould. 'At first they are single amebocytes swimming around, eating bacteria, aloof from each other, untouching, voting straight Republican' – Lewis Thomas has explained. 'Then, a bell sounds, and acrasin is released by special cells towards which the others converge in stellate ranks, touch, fuse together, and construct the slug, as solid as a trout.' Within the 'slug', the amoebas abandon individuality and take on specialist functions, the aim being eventually to form a capsule full of spores and launch it from the top, the spores floating away to renew the cycle as individual amoebas.

The discovery that a chemical rings the bell, the assembly signal for the amoebas to congregate, has tended to be presented as if it were the explanation for the behaviour of the slime mould. As well might psychologists explain what goes on in churches by calling attention to the ringing of church bells for morning service. How did the amoebas come to congregate in this way? Through chance mutations? The idea is comically far-fetched.

The Living Computer

It becomes even more far-fetched as an explanation of the behaviour of termites, observed and lovingly chronicled by the South African naturalist Eugène Marais in the early 1900s. Because his observations pose embarrassing questions that ethology has been unable to answer without recourse to psi, his work is now rarely mentioned. Yet it is of crucial significance.

Termites are blind. What fascinated Marais, among other things, was the skill with which they constructed the storerooms in their termitaries. Groups of termites start to build two adjacent pillars. When the work is complete, a termite carries a grass stalk to the top of one of them, attaching one end of it with sticky fluid in such a way that the far end slips gently across and down on to the other pillar.

There, a termite is waiting to stick it down to form a crossbeam, on which tiny pebbles can be plastered 'until a perfect arch results'.

Sometimes, Marais observed, the result is not perfect. The work is then completed by inclining the two pillars towards each other until they meet. How, he wondered, had termites, low as they are on the evolutionary slopes (Marais regarded himself as a Darwinian), developed so sophisticated a technique – even if it sometimes failed? The stock explanation of the time was 'instinct'. This, Marais felt, was 'like trying to explain the nature of wind by saying it is *wind*'.

Exploring further, Marais took a steel plate, higher and wider than the termitary, and drove it through the middle, effectively cutting off builders which were putting up one pillar from those which were putting up the other. Nevertheless both continued the operation; and when he withdrew the plate, he found that the two halves of the arch fitted perfectly. It would be absurd, he felt bound to admit, to assume that the individual termites involved had all known their individual and collective duties. They must all be directed, he surmised, by what for want of a better word he called a group soul.

He was not, of course, thinking of 'soul' in the religious sense that Christians have come to use. He thought of it in its original meaning, as a 'vital principle'. This variant on the vitalists' 'life force' did not commend itself to biologists. Nor did his explanation that a termitary was 'a separate and perfect animal, which lacks only the power of moving from place to place'. Termites, he argued, are regulated much as blood corpuscles are in the human body, rushing to do their duty wherever the nervous system directs them. The fatal flaw in this reasoning, from orthodoxy's viewpoint, was that for Marais it constituted 'the strongest possible proof that it may be possible for the psychological influence to have effect on an organism at a distance'. Worse, he thought the group soul is as mysterious 'as telepathy, or other functions of the human mind which border on the supernatural'.

This was not an original idea. It was implicit in works such as Alfred Espinas's *Des sociétés animales*; and made explicit by Charles Riley, Entomologist to the US Department of Agriculture and first President of the Washington Entomological Society. 'There can be no doubt that many insects possess the

I & 2 How do insectivorous plants such as the sun-dew and the
Venus fly-trap capture their prey? Rather than allow psi any
possible role, materialist hypotheses are occasionally
presented; but, so far, none has carried more than temporary
conviction.

3 A fully developed termitary. Eugène Marais was certain termites possessed a 'group mind', the founder of sociobiology E. O. Wilson, in his *The Insect Societies*, that they did not.

4 Laurens van der Post was convinced of the extra-sensory powers of the Kalahari bushmen, who could find water in parched desert. In recent years many of these powers have been lost.

power of communicating at a distance', he had asserted in 1894, 'of which we can form some conception by what is known as telepathy in man.' The power, he thought, 'would seem to depend neither upon scent nor upon hearing in the ordinary understanding of those senses, but rather on *certain subtle vibrations*, as difficult to apprehend as is the exact nature of electricity'. He went on to defend the proposition by saying that although he had no sympathy with spiritualist notions, he was 'just as much out of sympathy with that class of materialist scientists who refuse to recognize that there may be and are subtle physical phenomena beyond the reach of present experimental method'.

Riley's advice was not heeded. Nor was the warning of the eminent American zoologist, Henry Morton Wheeler, given in a lecture to biologists in 1910. Biological theories must remain inadequate, he argued, so long as the study of complex organisms, such as ant colonies, was left to 'psychologists, sociologists and metaphysicians', because of 'our fear of the psychological and the metaphysical'. This fear, he thought, was 'all the more ludicrous from the fact that even our so-called "exact" sciences smell to heaven with the rankest kind of materialistic metaphysics' – a barbed reference to the way in which physicists, still confident that materialist science would eventually provide all the answers, had fallen back on metaphysical concepts to fill in the gaps.

Not being a vitalist, Wheeler wanted some alternative to 'soul'. He suggested 'superorganism'. Although it did duty for some years, it explained nothing, and gradually the term was dropped. 'It is not just that the idea has been forgotten,' Lewis Thomas commented, noting its disappearance. 'It is as though it has become unmentionable, an embarrassment.' Besides, it was no longer so necessary to have any term, because unwelcome curiosity could be fended off with the help of what at first glance is a plausible scientific explanation of the way termitaries organise themselves: pheromones.

Pheromones – free-floating molecules carrying scents – have been shown to provide the stimuli which prompt termites (and animals of many kinds) to action, say, to abandon one task in order to take up another for which the need is more immediate. Marais had speculated that scent might be the means by which alarm or other signals are transmitted within a termitary. He had realised, however, that scent signals could not conceivably account for the complexity of the work undertaken by termite builders, let alone for the termitary's elaborate architecture. And this mystery has nagged at some 'pop ethologists' to this day.

'A solitary ant, afield, cannot be considered to have much of anything on his mind,' Thomas has remarked. 'Indeed, with only a few neurons strung together by fibers, he cannot be imagined to have a mind at all, much less a thought.' Yet four or ten ants together round a dead moth 'begin to look more like an idea' – though a fumbling one; and when you watch sufficient numbers of ants, they 'seem to reach a critical mass, a quorum, and the thinking begins'. The termitary turns out to be 'a kind of live computer, with crawling bits for its wits'.

Where does the 'thinking' come from? Scientists, as Thomas realised, have continued to evade this problem, because they remain uneasy about collective societies which behave as if they were single organisms. Yet in a sense Thomas evaded it, too. He did not take his observations to their logical conclusion – that a live computer, like an inanimate one, must be programmed. Unless programmed, how do termites collaborate not simply as part of a collective but also, when the need arises, through individuals performing specialised tasks?

In present-day terms, Marais's group soul might be thought of as a computer programmer. Smells or sounds may be the way in which the programme is fed into the computer, to get the desired results. They cannot explain how neurons strung together by fibres know how to react, let alone how the instructions are composed. The presumption must be that the forces involved are acting directly on the termites. Something, or somebody, is in effect not merely conducting the orchestra, but also playing all the instruments, and composing the score.

Scientists have had little difficulty in evading this issue. This is partly because the habits of termites do not impinge on the everyday life of the community (except occasionally as nuisances in the garden); partly because of the public's vague notion that all has been explained by pheromones, or, if not, soon will be by the next advance in biology or biochemistry. It is only recently that suspicions have been aroused that no such advance along conventional lines can provide the answer. The reductionist approach will continue to come up

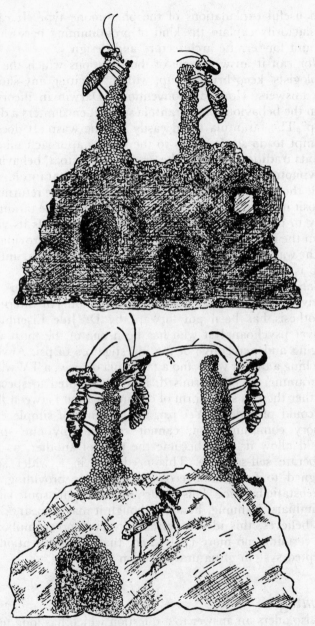

Figure 2 The drawings of termite builders at work in Marais's *The Soul of the White Ant*.

with useful explanations of the pheromone type. It cannot satisfactorily explain the kind of programming necessary to account for termite architecture and design.

Nor can it answer some of the questions which the 'pop ethologists' keep bringing up, without eliciting any satisfactory answers. How can conventional Darwinian theory explain the behaviour of a tarantula when it encounters a digger wasp? The tarantula could easily kill the wasp. It does not attempt to do so. It reacts to the wasp's approach much as rabbits traditionally do in the presence of a stoat, behaving as if hypnotised into passive immobility. The tarantula waits while the wasp digs a hole ten inches deep, before returning to deposit its sting in precisely the correct spot in the tarantula's body to paralyse, not kill it. The wasp then stuffs its victim down the hole, where it survives long enough to provide food for the wasp grub, placed on the tarantula's stomach, until the grub is a wasp ready to fly away.

Can it seriously be maintained that these encounters have survival value for the tarantula? It cannot. An alternative hypothesis has been put forward by Dr Jule Eisenbud, a Denver psychoanalyst who has been one of the most wide-ranging and perceptive of the investigators of psi. Anybody watching a digger wasp and a tarantula on, say, a TV wildlife programme, he has surmised, may be tempted to speculate whether there is some form of communication between them. Psi could provide it. Yet psi, in the sense of simple extra-sensory communication, cannot explain why one species should allow itself to become the prey of another, as if by deliberate self-sacrifice. This needs psi in a wider sense, designed to fulfil some ecological purpose providing, say, homeostatic balance. This in turn would require some kind of preliminary planning. Fanciful though it may appear, Eisenbud believes, this idea is 'essentially no more complicated, and certainly no more far-fetched, than the conventionally-accepted system of natural selection'.

Homing

Psi also offers an answer to a question which has long teased naturalists and zoologists, an answer less far-fetched than the ones they have provided. How do individual members of species which through chance or human intervention are carried far from their normal base find their way back to it? Everybody knows that pigeons can, and do. That other species – even crustaceans – can 'home' is less generally realised. A fisherman friend of Joseph Sinel's in the Channel Islands who used to keep alive the lobsters which he caught, lost a batch of them in a storm: 'great was my friend's astonishment when, three months later, he found no less than five of his captives among his catch', identifying them by some twine he had used to keep them separate in their confinement. They had travelled at least four miles, he told Sinel, 'over rocks – frequently intersected by steep gullies – with certainly no landmark to guide them'.

There must be hundreds of such anecdotes, and although few can be verified, they have been supplemented by experiments on species ranging from limpets to the deer mice of Wyoming. In the 1930s O.J. and A. Murie took five of these mice a mile from their nests, before releasing them. The mice, which ordinarily never ventured more than about fifty yards from their nests, soon found their way back. The younger they were, too, the more rapidly they seemed to be able to return, as further trials showed. One which was only five weeks old was taken two miles away. It was back in two days.

Yet as the naturalist Bingham Newland complained in 1916 in his *What is Instinct?*, the stock explanation for homing of this kind was (as a newspaper correspondent had just asserted) 'sight and memory' – *not* instinct. The orthodox theory was that even homing pigeons found their way back to the loft, or coop, by acquiring enough knowledge of the countryside in their early flights to be able to pick up the landmarks which will later guide them home. Had pigeon racing been a more fashionable sport this notion could hardly have survived, but communication between pigeon fanciers and the academic world must have been rare.

Incredibly, the 'sight and memory' explanation survived even the Second World War, in spite of the exploits of some of the homing pigeons that were brought into service with the RAF. Should an aircraft have to ditch in the North Sea, returning from a raid over Germany, the navigator would make an estimate of its position at the time, attach a note to the pigeon, and release it. If it managed to return to its loft an air/sea rescue operation would be mounted. With luck the inflated dinghies would be found, and the crew picked up. How could sight and memory have brought this pigeon home across the North Sea?

The final blow to the sight and memory theory was dealt not by pigeons, but by albatrosses. When jet engines were introduced at the end of the war, there was always the danger that birds would be sucked into them. With an albatross, the danger was not just to the bird. The large albatross population on Midway Island in the Pacific was an obvious menace. The US navy, aware that mass slaughter would have enraged public opinion at home, decided to banish them.

As a preliminary experiment it was decided to take some of the birds far outside the normal range. Although a few were never seen again, most returned. Of four which had been taken to Puget Sound, two were back within a fortnight – having flown over 3,000 miles, without any landmark between the mainland and Hawaii, through adverse weather conditions. As the writers of the official report mildly commented, 'we suggest that existing theories of bird navigation do not fully explain their behaviour'.

The episode might not have attracted much attention had Robert Ardrey not used it as one of his case histories in his best-seller *The Territorial Imperative*, a scathing denunciation of scientific obscurantism. It reminded him, he wrote, of the musical comedy *Jumbo* in which Jimmy 'Schnozzle' Durante, arriving on stage with an elephant he had stolen, and being asked by a policeman where he had got it, replied 'What elephant?' 'What elephant?', Ardrey lamented, 'is the harried, half-demented reply of the sciences these days, when you ask them how animals find their way home.'

As a populariser, Ardrey was an easy target for academic disparagement, but his range of experience through field work and knowledge of what was happening in research made him a formidable adversary. The evidence which he produced, even if his territorial imperative hypothesis to account for it did not carry conviction, was worrying. Ethologists were also disturbed by the news that at Duke University Gaither Pratt, one of J.B. Rhine's assistants in the parapsychology department, was working on the theory that psi might be a component in homing. With the sight and memory assumption discredited, they were confronted with the urgent need to find some alternative, any alternative, which could be put up to refute psi.

At Cambridge one of Professor Thorpe's graduate students, G.V.T. Matthews, took on the task. Initially he expected he would be able to show that pigeons' homing ability is not innate. He took young pigeons out from their loft to distances well beyond the range of their flights around it. They were not allowed to see where they were going; they were even gently tumbled, as if in a spin-drier, to disorientate them. Once released, they flew straight back to their loft.

Another man might have been satisfied with the prestige of having been the first to demonstrate that the homing sense of pigeons *is* innate. As this would have left open the possibility that they use psi – that they are guided back to the loft by PK, automatically adjusting their flight path – Matthews continued his research in the hope of finding a plausible alternative. He did. Bird navigation was a subject that had 'attracted the attention of parapsychologists recently, quite unnecessarily as we shall see', Matthews claimed at a CIBA symposium on ESP in 1956. 'There is no need for any recourse to ESP here. The orientation depends intimately on the sun.'

There could be no doubt to whom he was referring. Gaither Pratt was actually there, in his audience. One of the shrewdest of the parapsychologists who had trained under Rhine at Duke, Pratt had never imagined that homing ability is regulated solely by psi. On the contrary, he had been collaborating with Dr Gustav Kramer of the Max Planck Institute in Wilhelmshaven, who had been conducting experiments to find out whether migrating birds use the sun as a navigational aid. The verdict was that birds do use it, to keep on course. This was not the same, however, as using it to *set* course. Migrating birds usually fly in predetermined directions. A homing pigeon may be released from any point of the compass relative to its loft.

Matthews's hypothesis had been mainly based on his discovery that pigeons home less easily when the sun is obscured. For this, there could be other explanations, such as weather conditions. Pratt hit upon a simple experiment to settle the issue. Matthews had explained that pigeons orientate themselves, where necessary, by circling after their

release until they have checked out the sun's position relative
to their loft. They would learn to do this, he explained, in their
flights around the loft before they were taken out for their first
homing exercise. Pratt divided his pigeons into two groups,
one of which were exposed to the sun in their cages, the other
kept in shadow. If Matthews were correct, the 'sun' group
should be able to take off for the loft on release, while the
'shadow' group would need to circle. The experiment showed
no difference between the two. Pigeons might use the sun as a
point of reference while on course; but they did not need it to
set course. When Matthews attended a conference at Duke, to
present his case, it was promptly demolished. He had 'gone
out on a limb of speculation', Pratt commented with understandable satisfaction, in view of Matthews's contemptuous
attitude to the research at Duke – and 'the limb had been
sawed off behind him'.

Had Pratt been an academic ethologist, his contribution
would have had to be taken seriously, but few scientists were
likely even to hear about the proceedings at a conference held
at Duke, already notorious for its link with ESP research.
Matthews's findings, for which he had been awarded a
doctorate, continued to be accepted. Further research, after
all, might confirm his theory (a view occasionally expressed to
this day). His main achievement, however, turned out to be
that his work helped to make research into homing academi-
cally respectable. Teams were soon at work, looking for other
possible 'natural' explanations.

Magnetism was the first to be put forward. Pigeons, the
hypothesis was, navigate by aligning themselves to the earth's
magnetic field. 'Animal magnetism' had been out of favour
since Mesmer's time, and as late as 1971 W.A.H. Rushton,
Professor of Zoology at Cambridge, had laid down that
magnetism 'does not act on any of our senses'. Suppose,
though, that bio-magnetism were to be found – an additional
sense in its own right? It was duly found. Magnetic tissue was
traced lying between the eyes and the brains of pigeons.

As with navigation by the sun, navigation with the assistance of the earth's magnetic field presented a problem. Did
pigeons really have built-in navigational equipment of a kind
rivalling that installed on airliners, capable not merely of
following a magnetic or a sun-guided course, but of computing

with its help how to reach the loft from whatever point of the compass they were released?

A rival theory soon emerged. Italian researchers claimed to have solved the mystery; pigeons home by their sense of smell. Implausible though it sounded – how could pigeons pick up the smell of their loft if it was downwind? – the research team could point to the result of an earlier experiment which had appeared to show that when adult salmon return to the river where they were born, in order to spawn, they use their sense of smell. Professor Arthur Hasler of the University of Wisconsin had caught 300 salmon moving up two arms of a river in the State of Washington. He had blocked the noses of half of them with cotton wool, before putting them back in the river below where it divided. Salmon left with their sense of smell took the correct fork; those deprived of it were hopelessly confused. So were homing pigeons, the Italian team found, in similar circumstances.

By this time rival teams of ethologists were on the watch for flaws. Blocking birds' noses, critics argued, might be sufficient to disorient them, regardless of whether smell was involved. Soon, yet another contender appeared. In 1981 two Cornell physicists claimed to have found that pigeons can hear and detect changes in sound too distant and too low in pitch to be heard by humans. Infrasound, they suggested, provides pigeons with their guidance.

Migration

Meanwhile a parallel line of inquiry was in progress. How do birds and other species find their way when they migrate? Might this not throw light on the allied problem of homing?

The old assumption had been 'observation and memory', as Bingham Newland had found when he began to study the subject early in the century. The young birds 'were conducted by their parents, or others who have made the journey before'. This was manifestly untrue, Newland pointed out, in the case of cuckoos. Far from guiding the young cuckoo back to the south at the end of the summer, the parents deserted it to be reared by non-migrating species, themselves leaving weeks in advance. Yet the young cuckoo, flying singly, could find its way from Norway to Africa.

The explanation, Newland suggested, was clairvoyance – using the term in the loose sense often employed then, roughly equivalent to ESP today. Lacking any plausible alternative, the scientific establishment preferred to ignore Newland. Like Sinel, he was only a naturalist. Still, his exposure of the weakness of the 'observation and memory' idea was disturbing, especially as it applied also in the case of migrating butterflies. 'One generation of the Monarch butterfly migrates outward to a breeding ground, mates, lays eggs, and dies', as Renée Haynes pointed out in *The Hidden Springs*. 'Those eggs hatch into caterpillars which feed, weave cocoons, emerge as butterflies and return to the home of the parents they have never seen.' Furthermore they return again and again to the same roosting spots.

Surveying the evidence and the theories for the way insects orientate themselves while migrating, C.B. Williams, a Fellow of the Royal Society and the world's foremost authority on the subject, felt compelled to admit in 1958 in his *Insect Migration*, 'we are left with the unsatisfactory conclusion that we know neither the external cause nor the internal mechanism'. He had shown that none of the stock hypotheses offered by entomologists could serve. That the migrating butterflies might be using psi apparently did not enter his calculations.

In the late 1950s the German zoologists Dr Frank Sauer and his wife unexpectedly came to science's rescue with the help of experiments on blackcaps, conducted in a planetarium. Switching the stars around at the migrating season, they found, confused the birds, so that they started out in the direction which the stars in the planetarium rather than the stars in the night sky indicated. Birds appeared to be using celestial navigation, like sailors of old.

In daytime, the Kramer team at Wilhelmshaven found, they made use of the sun. With the discovery of the bio-magnetic component, this could be added to the list of explanations. It was becoming a little confusing until, gratefully, ethologists were presented with a way out of their dilemma: 'back-up'. 'Like many well-designed systems they have *many* mechanisms available to them – they can navigate using landmarks, a sun compass, geomagnetism, smell and possibly even low frequency sound', Jeremy Cherfas has argued, surveying the evidence in the *New Scientist*. They use whichever system is appropriate to their need; 'the smart money has always said it would be a pluralist approach, with multiple back-up systems in case of failure' – on the analogy of an airliner.

Always? Scientists have short memories; Cherfas had forgotten that little more than a quarter of a century before, science's money had still been on 'sight and memory' as the explanation. In any case, to invoke pluralist back-up is to present another problem. The epithet 'bird brain' is designedly pejorative. Again, can it seriously be maintained that birds have bio-sextants and bio-compasses, in addition to extremely sophisticated organs of smell and of hearing? Do birds' minds have computers into which the information coming from the back-up is fed, prescribing the course they are going to fly? As for butterflies . . . If parapsychologists had put up so far-fetched a notion, it is easy to imagine the derision which would have been heaped upon it.

In the circumstances, it is not surprising that some ethologists have been casting longing eyes back to the time when simple sight and memory ruled. In *The Evolutionary Ecology of Animal Migration* R. Robin Baker has been able to show that a few species become familiar with a wider area of territory than had been realised, and this has encouraged some sentimental wishful-thinking. 'Homing (even from several thousand miles away, as in the Manx Shearwater) may thus be achieved by memory of spatial clues,' the *New Scientist*'s reviewer gratefully concluded. 'If this hypothesis is true (and by now I'm more than half-convinced that it is) a major mystery will have been solved.'

Will it indeed! What about the cuckoos, and the butterflies?

Sex

To explain how males of a species manage to find a distant female in her mating time has presented science with even greater difficulties than homing or migration. Obviously the route towards the female cannot be determined by bio-sextants or bio-compasses. For want of any explanation other than psi, entomologists have clung to the hope that the males are attracted by smell – an assumption that long predated the discovery of pheromones, so great was the need to ward off psi's intrusion.

But there was a snag. The pioneering entomologist Jean-Henri Fabre described how one evening after he brought a chrysalis home and put it in a box in his study, a servant reported that his study was 'full of big flies'. A female moth, Fabre found, had emerged from the chrysalis, and the 'flies' were males – males, too, of a species not ordinarily seen in that neighbourhood, which meant that they must have flown from a distance. This, and the fact that the female had been enclosed in a box, made smell an unlikely guide. Besides, Fabre found when he released males to the north of the female while the wind was from the north, they still came to her, whereas 'if they were guided by odoriferous particles dissolved in the air, they ought to arrive from the opposite direction'.

In 1935 the similarly named Russian entomologist L.A. Fabri repeated Fabre's experiment, with slight variations. He put out a female butterfly in a wire cage, caught and marked sixty-four male butterflies which arrived at the cage, and carried them away to distances of between six and eight kilometres. The speed of their return left no doubt that it was the attraction of the female which had brought them; yet some arrived when there was no wind to carry scent, and others came downwind.

The discovery of pheromones, however, made it inevitable that scent would again be invoked as the explanation for sexual homing. What happened as a result has been entertainingly narrated by Philip Callahan, Professor of Entomology at the University of Florida, in his *Tuning in to Nature*, describing the hypotheses which have been put forward to account for the way in which male moths rush to a female 'on heat'. First, in the 1950s the British entomologist Dr H.B.D. Kettlewell was able to demonstrate to his own satisfaction that Fabre had been in error. Male moths *do* assemble around a female, he asserted, by picking up her scent. He was upstaged by Dr F.H. Wright, a physical chemist, who had evolved a theory which, although it would keep smell in the forefront, gave it a different twist. Wright had come to the conclusion, as Callahan put it, that moths 'decode odor (he has never said how) by identifying what is called *osmic* frequencies from odor molecules' – the frequencies being established by 'intermolecular vibrations'.

The entomologist was saying that the insect antenna detects scent; the physical chemist was saying that it detects infra-red radiation *from* scent. That a physical chemist should muscle in on entomological territory was bad enough; worse was to follow. Eric Laithwaite ('a brilliant electrical engineer', as Callahan described him), Professor of Electrical Engineering at the Imperial College of Science in London, presented yet another hypothesis, directly contradicting Kettlewell's. Laithwaite, like Fabre and Fabri, had observed a moth species flying downwind to the female, and had decided some form of electromagnetic infra-red radiation from the moth was involved.

Having poked gentle fun at the battling British, Callahan presented his own hypothesis, which suggested that Kettlewell and Laithwaite were right *and* wrong. It was all a matter of back-up – though Callahan did not himself use that term. An infra-red signal, he had found, is emitted by the female moth, along with pheromones. The males, he believes, fly along the path provided by the stream of pheromones and the strongest of the infra-red signals, in much the same way as he himself had flown along a radio range as a Second World War pilot – the infra-red signals providing the direction in which to fly, and the strength of the pheromone signal indicating the distance still to be covered.

Plausible though this hypothesis sounds, thanks to Callahan's lucid presentation, it means rejecting the observation that had prompted Laithwaite to evolve his theory of navigation by infra-red signals: 'he must have been very wrong about his moths flying with the wind, as was Fabre, for the wind must carry the little emitting satellites to the antenna'. *Must* carry them? Fabri, after all, whom Callahan does not mention, had also observed that the wind was sometimes in the wrong direction. The observations of Fabre and Fabri had already, in fact, been subjected to a test. The common vapourer moth was used, for convenience, as the female is wingless and the males fly and mate by day. Males were captured, taken to a distance, and released. Although a ten-mile-an-hour breeze was blowing, the males were easily able to find the female whether released up- or downwind;

suggesting, as Laithwaite mildly put it, 'that scent alone is an insufficient explanation'.

As radiation alone does not appear to be sufficient explanation, either, the door remains open for psi. Callahan, in fact, does not dispute that psi may be involved, though he is reluctant to incorporate it in his own theories until more is known about it (researchers interested in ESP, he suggests, should attempt to find out how it works instead of trying 'to prove that it exists').

The Occam's Razor principle – the principle of accepting the fewest possible assumptions – has often been invoked to rebut psi. Here, it needs to be introduced on psi's behalf. Assuming psi's existence, a powerful case can be made for it as the *first* sense – the kinetic sense, which a programme initially instilled in primitive organisms. Out of this, the hypothesis goes, developed psychokinesis as we now think of it, along with the various forms of ESP – clairvoyance, telepathy, precognition. These, incidentally, can be classified as back-up, too, along with the five senses – and any others which may be uncovered, such as a bio-magnetic sense. So even if it could be proved that the sun, magnetism, smell and hearing can now account for homing or migration, this would not eliminate the psi component altogether, any more than our use of our eyes disposes of the case for second sight. If ESP were 100 per cent effective, we would surely continue to use our eyes when crossing the street. In our case, back-up has taken over.

Similarly tests such as the one with salmon do not eliminate psi from the reckoning. Psi's impact is called 'extra-sensory' because it does not reach consciousness through the normal channels of hearing, sight, smell, taste or touch. Yet as has often been pointed out, the term is a misnomer. Psi experiences use one – sometimes more than one – of the five. For example, people who have encountered apparitions, and there are scores of well-attested cases, are for a few moments convinced that the person they see is really there. If they shut their eyes owing to fright, as frequently happens, the apparition disappears.

Psi, in other words, uses sensory channels as back-up. Psychic odours have been reported throughout history, and are the commonplace of seances. If a sitter has cotton wool stuffed up his nose, he would not detect the odour. The salmon which had their nostrils blocked may have become confused because they were deprived of a psi component in their computer programme.

Flocks

Of all the problems presented to conventional science by the behaviour of species, one of the most baffling has been the ability of flocks of birds and shoals of fish to fly or swim as if part of a perfectly drilled three-dimensional *corps de ballet*. It has been the more irritating in that even the most casual inspection of a flock of starlings shows that whatever game it is that they play, whirling around the sky, it does not resemble Follow My Leader; a point which struck Edmund Selous when he began to investigate the phenomenon around the turn of the century. The signal for the changes of direction, though they might have no discernible purpose, appeared to direct the movements of all members of the flock instantaneously – a spectacle he recorded again and again in his diary. 'Each mass of them turned, wheeled, reversed the order of their flight', he noted on October 8, 1901. They 'changed in one shimmer from brown to grey, from dark to light, as though all the individuals composing them had been component parts of one individual organism'.

Selous was perhaps the first ornithologist of note to devote himself, 'with extreme tenacity of purpose', Professor Thorpe has recalled, 'simply to observing and noting down with great thoroughness exactly what birds were doing in the field when undisturbed'. Not surprisingly, as a consequence, he was 'largely neglected or despised by the stuffy museum ornithologists of his day', though he was to have considerable influence on later researchers, notably on Julian Huxley – and, it may be surmised, on Thorpe himself.

The museum ornithologists did not object to Selous solely on account of his all-weather dedication to field work. They were also appalled at the conclusions to which his study of birds in flocks led him. Following his account of the flight of the starlings, 'a marvellous thing to witness', he commented: 'again I asked how, without some process of thought-transference so rapid as to amount practically to simultaneous collective thinking, are these things to be explained?' If thousands of birds were able to perform identical movements at virtually the same instant, must there not be some link? 'The universally distributed effect requires a universally distributed cause', Selous argued, and boldly entitled the book in which he cited his diary entries *Thought Transference, or What? in Birds*.

The standard assumption at the time was that the birds kept station in flocks much as fighter pilots were soon to be trained to do: visually following their leader. To Selous this was palpably absurd. It would give rise to hopeless confusion. Despite occasionally spreading and closing up again, the birds never seemed 'unduly pressed together', never impeded each other. Besides, 'how is it possible', he asked impatiently, 'for an extended troop of hundreds of birds to rise together from the ground, at one and the same instant, as though threaded on a labyrinthine wire, except through an impulse acting upon them in their entirety?' Again, he felt there must be thought-transference. Yet this, he was beginning to realise, was not enough. The birds would be in different states of receptivity, some asleep, some feeding. Perhaps there was more to it? The impulse to action must come from a flock 'brain' – a near parallel to what his contemporary Marais was beginning to deduce from his study of termites.

The museum ornithologists ignored Selous, and those who, like Bingham Newland, followed his line. Flocks of plover, Newland reported, went through similar manoeuvres. Although they were 'executed at incredible speed, there are no collisions, no bungling, as must surely occur if each out of, say, 200 birds is acting on his own and endeavouring to fly even conformably with a leader'. Yet as late as 1967, when a correspondent wrote to the *Daily Telegraph* describing how a flock of about a thousand starlings had run into a concrete wall, killing a hundred of them and temporarily stunning the rest, Dr Maurice Burton, a recognised pundit in such matters, explained to the *Telegraph*'s readers that, in flocks, birds fly on the 'follow my leader principle'. It was not necessarily the same leader, he admitted, but if the starling who happened to be in the lead made a mistake, all the rest would follow. Asked on what research this assumption was based, Burton admitted that he did not know of any. Observation, he claimed, had shown that species which form flocks 'are visually aware of

5 Homing pigeons return to their coops – but how?

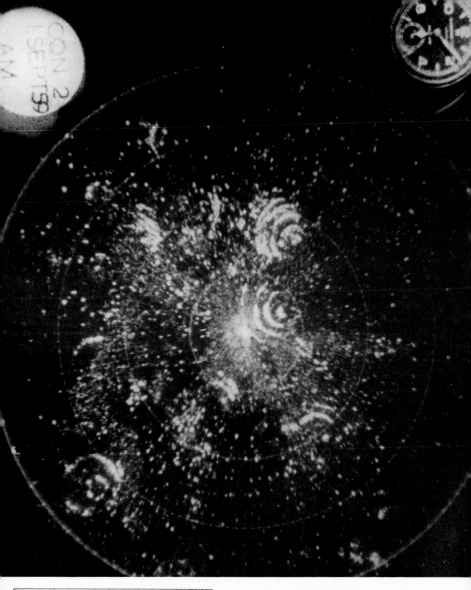

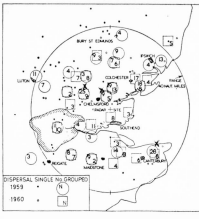

6 The rings of 'angels' which the early radar operators found each day on their screens, above the Home Counties. What is the programming that unites the flocks of starlings which are responsible for the rings?

their fellows and tend to follow suit as the others move', the first to show the 'intention movement' becoming the *ad hoc* leader.

So manifestly contrary to the facts, even to the general public, is the follow my leader explanation that lately some attempts have been made to qualify it. A recent paper in *Nature* by Wayne Potts of the University of Seattle has claimed that the evidence from frame-by-frame analysis of filmed sequences suggests that flocks follow the same procedure as lines of chorus girls. An individual bird starts to back into the mass of the flock, followed by others only fractions of a second later but relatively slowly enough to enable those birds which are more distant to observe what is happening and adapt to it.

Even the *New Scientist*, usually quick to poke fun at *Nature*'s eccentricities, took this theory seriously as preferable to the earlier 'bizarre' alternatives, such as Selous's. Yet it is clearly inadequate. Chorus lines are necessarily two-dimensional in their movements; they are choreographed; they are directed; they follow a musical beat. Without such aids starlings in a flock have to keep station not only with those ahead and on each side of them, but also with those above and below them. Yet high-speed film has revealed that thousands of birds in a flock may all change direction in a tiny fraction of a second – quicker than even the best drilled chorus line is expected to do.

In default of any more plausible theory, ornithologists have tended to fall back on the notion that birds must have some yet to be discovered 'radar' apparatus on the lines of the one which bats have been found to use to capture moths. The discovery of bats' echo-location system has often been cited as an example of how misguided it is to allow psi to creep in to the reckoning in seeking an explanation for biological mysteries. It used to be believed that bats used clairvoyance, the Harvard psychologist Edwin Boring has recalled. 'Then research succeeded in finding a sensory explanation, and clairvoyance evaporated.' Yet, marvellously ingenious though it is, the radar system cannot completely account for the speed and selectivity of bats' reactions, as a paper in *Nature* pointed out in 1968. Bats can choose insects in a swarm, consuming two in a second, or scoop up fish, as some do, from below the surface of a pool. Nor, for that matter, does the method they use to find and catch their prey explain how they avoid bumping into each other in their caves. Films taken in a Texan cave with the help of infra-red light have revealed thousands of bats swirling around so closely packed that space could hardly be detected between them, with never a sign of a collision.

Still, the notion has been implanted that the discovery of bat 'radar', even if it does not solve all the problems relating to the ability of gregarious species to perform complex man-oeuvres while keeping station, provides the starting point from which conventional science will in the foreseeable future provide the solutions, leaving psi in the role of a superstition.

Even if the 'radar' theory should turn out to have some relevance to station-keeping in flocks, it cannot account for the way in which the movements of the flock as a whole appear to be programmed. A flock does not perform like a team of pilots giving a display of aerobatics. They could not manoeuvre in the same way even if, thanks to some new invention, the correct distances between the aircraft could be maintained by some automatic signalling system. A closer analogy would be to an aerobatic team all of whose intricate movements are not only programmed, but radio-controlled from the ground, with all the aircraft on auto-pilot, and the auto-pilots all plugged in to a central controller.

Admittedly the analogy becomes difficult to sustain if it is carried too far. Flocks of starlings do not behave as if controlled by any rational intelligence. Often they whirl around the sky as if for the pleasure of showing off. Yet an element of orderliness regulates the movements not just of individual flocks, but of all flocks within an area.

When radar operators first began to monitor the sky above London, on the look-out for unidentified aircraft, they found that at precisely the same time every morning ripples began to run outwards across their screens, as if the sky were a pool over the city into which a stone had been dropped. At precisely the same time every evening they returned, as if the morning's ripples had been filmed, and the film was being played backwards. The radar operators, baffled, gave the ripples the name 'angels'. The angels turned out to be the dense flocks of starlings, flying out to the countryside from Trafalgar Square and other roosting points, and returning to them with military precision.

Vitalism Revisited

From the findings of conventional scientists, even without reference to the work of psychical researchers, there is ample evidence of the existence of a force, or forces, resembling gravity's action at a distance, yet apparently acting only through animate species. If there are neutrinos, mysterious particles capable of streaming through us and through the earth, detectable only when they collide with other elementary particles, may there not also be 'psychons' – the term suggested by the psychical researcher Whately Carington – in space, detectable only when they interact with, or are exploited by, living creatures?

'If one applies the term to perception by processes unknown to us', Niko Tinbergen has suggested, 'then extra-sensory perception among living creatures may well occur widely.' A number of phenomena, after all, which used not to be understood, were 'extra-sensory in this sense'; he cited bats' echo-location systems. The discovery of echo-location is recalled with pride. Why should scientists not hope for a similar breakthrough in connection with ESP?

There are two main reasons. The discovery of psychons would not pull psi out of the paranormal category, so much as draw physics and other disciplines towards it. And the acceptance of psi would cause massive disturbance in the other disciplines, as biologists are uneasily aware, thanks to the advance warning given by Sir Alister Hardy, with his proposal that changes of habit should be allowed a role in evolution, alongside chance mutations.

From time to time, Hardy pointed out, members of a species may change their feeding habits owing, say, to a drought, or the discovery of a new source of nourishment – as tits did when they realised they could get at milk left on doorsteps by pecking through the plastic bottle-tops. Individual tits with beaks better designed for this act would have an advantage, much the same as men and women with Roman noses would enjoy in an era when Roman noses happen to be fashionable. Although Hardy remained a staunch Darwinian, this came close to rehabilitating the Lamarckian theory of evolution through acquired characteristics, as Erwin Schrödinger pointed out. After winning his Nobel prize for his contribution to quantum physics Schrödinger became interested in exploring the relationship between physics and metaphysics, which led him on to an interest in evolutionary theory. Behaviour, he asserted in a lecture he gave in Cambridge in 1950, 'plays a relevant part, nay, plays the most relevant part in evolution'. It was 'almost the same as if Lamarckism was right, only the "mechanism" by which things happen is more complicated than Lamarck thought'.

Lamarck, in other words, may turn out to have been right, though for the wrong reasons. This is not something that neo-Darwinians care to contemplate. They have ignored Hardy. They are now finding it increasingly difficult to ignore their critics, a few of whom used the occasion of the 1982 centenary of Darwin's death to pose some unwelcome questions. Nor will they find it easy to answer the case presented in *Evolution: A Theory in Crisis* by Michael Denton.

A microbiologist, Denton dismisses Lamarckism, vitalism and Creationism as occultist. His objection to Darwin's evolutionary model is that it is not scientific enough – in the sense that it requires a massive act of faith to swallow it whole. Yet in its present form, commonly described as neo-Darwinism, its evangelists' insistence has been that it must be swallowed whole – as Jacques Monod illustrated with his assertion 'Chance alone is at the source of every innovation'.

The neo-Darwinian dogma has laid down that natural selection can occur only when chemical changes in the genes, of the kind which can be caused by, among other things, radiation, cause mutations. The mutations are random, but if one occurs which benefits the species, it will be preserved. Therefore 'pure chance, absolutely free but blind, is at the root of the stupendous edifice of evolution', Monod argued. This was not just one hypothesis among many. 'It is today the sole conceivable hypothesis, the only one that squares with observed and tested fact'. On the contrary, Denton replies, the neo-Darwinian theory suffers from four serious and debilitating weaknesses. It relies upon an implausible hypothesis for the way life began on earth. It glosses over the fact that mutations 'provide change, not progress'. (As Pierre Grassé, Professor of Evolution at the Sorbonne, pointed out: 'they do not create evolutionary novelties'.) It has been unable to account for the gaps in the fossil record, which leave ugly holes in the evidence for the gradual development of species. And it does not begin to explain certain observable phenomena, such as mimicry.

Obviously mimicry in plants or animals can have survival value, and does. It is used by many species as a protection or as a lure to trap victims or to facilitate procreation. The problem is to explain how species have become perfect mimics through chance mutations, because the initial stages before the mimicry was perfected could have brought no benefit.

Hardy cited the case of orchids which so clearly resemble the female form of certain insects in colour, shape and smell that the males are sexually attracted: 'the excited spouses who

Figure 3 Mimicry. In the centre is a typical Ascilid fly. To the left
(a) is a South American bee and, below, its Ascilid fly
mimic; to the right (d) is an African bee, and its Ascilid fly
mimic (from *The Living Stream*).

come for the creative act unwittingly, by carrying pollen,
complete instead the sexual process for the flowers'. Difficult
though it is to imagine how this complex process (and there
are even more complex examples) could have been accomplished by chance mutations, what benefit could the necessary
mutations have provided in the preliminary stages, before the
resemblance was perfected? Aspiring comedians have to wait
until they have got their act together before they mimic a
celebrity. What can have prompted the orchid mutations
during the aeons required before the resemblance was perfected?

Darwin himself realised this represented a threat. 'If it
could be demonstrated that any complex organ existed which
could not possibly have been formed by numerous successive,
slight modifications', he conceded in the sixth edition of *The
Origin of Species*, 'my theory would absolutely break down.'
Chance mutations could possibly bring about perfect mimicry, but the improbability is so obvious that orthodox biologists
have continued to be disturbed by it ever since. C.H. Waddington, Professor of Genetics at Edinburgh University,
bluntly claimed that to attribute the evolution of so many
'wonderfully adapted biological mechanisms' to blind chance
is like suggesting that 'if we went on throwing bricks together
into heaps, we should eventually be able to choose ourselves a
most desirable house'.

More than once, Waddington went to the brink of heresy
with statements of this kind. He could however never quite
pluck up the courage of his lack of conviction, and publicly
concede that the dogma of natural selection, in the form it has
taken, is simply untenable. A protagonist of psi need no longer
feel constrained because it does not fit the conventional
mould. On the contrary, psi can go a long way to account for
the deficiencies in Darwinian theory, as Hardy realised:
'behavioural selection, due to the "psychic life" of the animal',
he believed, '*whatever we may think of its nature*, is now seen to be
a most powerful creative element in evolution'.

Neo-Darwinians have taken comfort from the realisation
that life on earth stretches back further than used to be
thought. It would have to be stretched far further still to take
account of evolution by chance mutations alone, even if
Grassé's warning that they provide only change, not progress,

is disregarded. Yet evolutionary development could be considerably speeded up, Hardy realised, if there is 'a general subconscious sharing of a form and behaviour pattern – a sort of psychic "blueprint" – shared by members of a species', leading to a telepathic spread of habit changes. May not the rapidity with which the tits' habit of breaking through milk bottle-tops spread suggest that psi, rather than copying, is the explanation?

This was as far as Hardy was prepared to go. He did not wish to overturn natural selection by random mutations, only to supplement it: 'the psychic stream of a shared behaviour pattern in the living population would flow on in time, parallel to the flow of the physical DNA material'. Hardy, too, was thinking of telepathy primarily as a method by which members of a species picked up useful habits from others. Yet thought-transference of this kind, Selous had warned, does not fully account for what he observed. 'Thought-transfusion', he felt, came nearer to it. Simple transference of information from one bird to others would not account for the unison of starlings in flocks. There must be some collective force at work.

To contemplate the rehabilitation of Lamarck was unnerving enough for evolutionists in the Darwin tradition. To have to take seriously the notion of a group soul was even more unpalatable. Yet how else could mimicry be explained, if chance mutations proved inadequate? Although telepathy might account for the speeding-up of a process once it had begun, how could animals, let alone plants, realise in advance the benefit that mimicry would confer, and proceed to take the required steps to attain to it?

Various explanations have been offered. The Creationist version, taken uncritically from Genesis, can only be treated like other myths as an attempt to explain history in terms acceptable to the chronicler and his readers (Darwin's theory, as distinct from his observations, is also in this category). A more plausible case can be made for what can best be described as creationism with a small 'c'. A recent exponent, Michael Pitman in his *Adam and Evolution*, has scored a minor triumph by obtaining quite a respectful review in the *New Scientist*. Pitman's creationism resembles deism, assuming the existence of a creative force without allowing allegiance to any particular god. The most fancied of the rival candidates, though, is neo-vitalism – admittedly a vague concept, yet one with respectable antecedents.

As William McDougall defined it (though he preferred the term animism) the theory is that a living human is distinguished from a dead one, and from inanimate matter, because of the 'operation within him of something which is of nature different from that of the body, an animating principle generally, but not necessarily or always, conceived as an immaterial or individual being, or soul'. This, materialists complain, is a metaphysical concept, lacking any scientific foundation. As materialism has lost its own scientific foundation, it is hardly a convincing argument.

The animating principle is commonly linked to entelechy, an idea of Aristotle's revived early in this century by Hans Driesch. Evolutionary advances, the theory was, occur not by chance but because the life force is purposive. It seems imbued with an innate desire to improve itself, as if guided by precognition. It sometimes has to work *against* natural selection, because when the survival of the fittest produces too successful a species, the species' sense of purpose may be lost, much as when a talented artist finds a profitable line in portraits and settles for it.

Though they may dislike entelechy as a concept, neo-Darwinians have been compelled to flirt with it, as Arthur Koestler sardonically showed in *Janus*. Even Monod, while repeating that chance and chance alone is the source of all creation, has felt constrained to admit that although the corner-stone of the scientific method is the systematic denial that 'true' knowledge can be obtained by interpreting phenomena in terms of 'purpose', 'objectivity nevertheless obliges us to recognise the teleonomic character of living organisms'. By teleonomy, Monod explains, he means that in their performance living organisms 'realise and pursue a purpose'. What is the difference, Koestler asked, 'between Monod's teleonomy and the good old Aristotelian teleology, the view that developments arise through the purpose or design that they serve'? Does not Monod's concession 'remind one of the Lamarckian heresy, according to which evolution is nature's response to the organism's needs'?

Acceptance of entelechy, teleology, teleonomy, or whatever

else purposiveness in nature may be called, involves acceptance of neo-vitalism. Neo-vitalism can without difficulty
incorporate action and communication at a distance as well as
communal programming of the kind which Selous and Marais
suggested. It was no accident that the three leading neo-
vitalists in the early part of this century, who struggled in vain
against the materialist tide – Henri Bergson, William
McDougall and Hans Driesch – accepted the reality of
psychic phenomena. All three served a term as President of
the Society for Psychical Research.

One question, often asked, remains. Suppose, for argument's sake, that the case for psi as an evolutionary force is
conceded. Living creatures ordinarily regarded as low on the
evolutionary ladder once enjoyed the advantage of action and
communication at a distance, retrocognition (instinct) and
precognition (entelechy). If psi was so invaluable then, why
did it gradually fade out? Surely it ought to have brought
benefit to the species which exploited it?

If entelechy is admitted, the explanation presents no difficulty. Programmed action at a distance, controlling all those
involved, was eminently suited to life in a termitary. If
evolution incorporated a drive to more sophisticated ways of
life it ceased to be so useful, retarding as it would do the
emergence of individuality. 'For a solitary animal egoism is a
virtue that tends to preserve and improve the species', as
Schrödinger put it. 'In any kind of community it becomes a
vice.'

The development of the five senses as a back-up to psi also
meant that even in species which remained as communities,
one or other of the senses, and especially sight, could provide
more immediately useful information than ESP, as Robert
Thouless, Reader in Educational Psychology at Cambridge,
illustrated in a survey of the state of psychical research in
1942. If a deer had to rely upon ESP to make it aware of the
threat from an approaching tiger, a warning signal could be
useful before the tiger came in sight; but the signal might be
too vague to provide precise information as to, say, whether it
was going to pass by at a safe distance. 'The deer would be
incomparably better off if it trusted to the strictly limited sense
of vision and hearing, when it would be left peacefully feeding
until a tiger was near enough for it to be necessary to do

something about it', Thouless argued. 'The risk that sometimes the tiger would be too near for escape before it was seen
would be a small price to pay for the relief from a tendency to
react which might in the majority of cases be set off by a
situation in which the danger was remote in space or time.'

Increasing reliance upon the senses led to a loss of innate
know-how, with consequences for more highly developed
species which Marais illustrated in an account of one of his
experiments. He took a newly-born otter from a nest, rearing
it with a bitch along with her puppies; and a newly-born
baboon, which he himself reared with a feeding-bottle. When
both animals were three years old, he took them to their
natural habitats. Although the otter had never seen a river, it
hesitated only for a moment before plunging in; within half an
hour it had 'caught a crab and a large carp and devoured
them on the rocks'. The baboon not merely did not know how
to forage; it tried to pick up a scorpion, and would have eaten
a poisonous mountain fruit – accidents which do not happen
to baboons in the wild.

The baboon learned what to do, and what not to do, and
survived; nature had 'given him a psyche which is able to
acquire individual causal memories', but at the same time had
'done away with his inherited race memory'. Nature, Marais
concluded, 'demands payment for all she gives'; both the
baboon and man have paid a heavy price for their new type of
psyche. Nevertheless he was sure that race memory is not
destroyed; it is simply dormant, in 'a kind of permanent
inhibition' and can still be artificially stimulated into action.

Shamanism

As we can watch the behaviour of amoebas, ants and starlings, the evidence for psi which they provide is more trustworthy than anything we have about the first humans.
Anthropology has been able to tell us little. The most valuable
source of information has been the reports of explorers,
travellers, missionaries and traders who came into contact
with tribal communities which had had no experience of
civilisation. Although reports are often maddeningly inadequate because of the writers' preconceptions and fears about
what most of them took to be supernatural influences, they
present a reasonably clear picture of the different ways in
which psychic forces were interpreted and exploited.

When reasoning ability improved, humans had to learn to
bring many types of instinctive behaviour under better control. As soon as individuals threatened by a predator could
decide whether it would be safest to hide, to run, or to climb
the nearest tree, they would want to make that decision *as*
individuals, unimpeded by any remaining group reaction of
the kind which still influenced herds. Although instinct occasionally took over in emergency – as it still can do, in moments
of panic, when our limbs refuse to obey the mind's instructions – in ordinary circumstances its commands were resisted.

In the most primitive tribes – primitive, that is, in the sense
that they appeared to be most backward to the explorers who
encountered them – the ability to exploit psi appears to have
been common. Until very recently, as Sir Laurens van der
Post has described, the Kalahari bushmen retained their
extra-sensory faculties. According to David Unaipon, one of
the first Australian aborigines to win respect among the white
settlers in Victoria, his people used to light fires to make
smoke signals, not to convey specific information, but to invite

all who saw them to tune in, as it were, for the transmission of telepathic messages. Among the Zulu, Bishop Callaway found that people who lost some valued possession would attune themselves to find it by second sight. It was as if communication at a distance was in the process of being relegated to the sixth sense, which could be called upon only when the need arose.

In more advanced tribes – again, in the eyes of the explorers – the ability to communicate at a distance had largely been lost, along with many another benefits which instinct had formerly provided, such as the ability to know, as if by clairvoyance, which berries were edible, which were poisonous. That this loss was considered serious could be judged from the fact that, almost without exception, tribes employed a shaman, witch doctor or medicine man to remedy the deficiency. He was commonly chosen (most, though not all, shamans were male) because in his childhood he had shown signs of developing extra-sensory powers, and he was put through often extremely rigorous training to perfect them. In the course of it he would learn to shake off consciousness, going into convulsions and entering a trance in which he could 'see' what was happening at a distance, or 'hear' advice – from the spirit world, it was believed. Sometimes the words came through him. It was as if he were being possessed by the spirit, so that it could talk direct to the tribe.

Whatever the source of the shaman's information, its main object was to provide for the tribe what instinct would have provided, had it not been lost. Should a member of the tribe fall ill, the shaman in his trance would diagnose what was the matter and prescribe a remedy. Should food or water be hard to obtain, he would 'see' where to go. Should an enemy tribe approach, he would 'hear' whether to fight or fly. It was as if he could tune in to the appropriate wavelength, as ants do, though to a more sophisticated programme. Some shamans could even employ psi for psychokinesis – for action, as well as communication, at a distance. The shaman's main function, though, was to be the tribal seer.

Unluckily, by the time anthropology was establishing itself as an academic discipline shamanism was disintegrating. The impact of civilisation was having a catastrophic effect. Missionaries, fearing shaman powers were diabolic, had done

their best to have them stamped out. When belief in the devil
evaporated, it was supplanted by rationalist disbelief in
magic, except in the form of conjuring tricks. Colonial officers
regarded shamans as a threat to their authority, and they had
the last word, as Belloc observed in *The Modern Traveller*:

> Whatever happens, we have got
> The Maxim Gun, and they have not.

The Maxim Gun lessened the tribe's confidence in the
shaman, and his own confidence in his visions and voices. At
the same time, shamans were finding it more difficult to tune
in to them. They had begun to need drugs to enter their
trances, and what emerged was often confused, needing
interpretation. Some had to employ aids to divination, often of
a kind water-diviners still use, a forked twig or a pendulum,
providing guidance. Or they would cast bones on the ground
in front of them, in the hope that the pattern they formed
would trigger off clairvoyance, much as fortune-tellers came to
use tea-leaves.

When anthropologists were seeking to show they were
deserving of academic status, in the second half of the
nineteenth century, they were faced with the need to sort out
the inchoate mass of material which the explorers, travellers,
missionaries and traders had provided, as well as the more
detailed information arriving from colonial officers. Shamanism was only one of the problems; but as Edward Tylor
realised when he was preparing *Primitive Culture*, the first
major survey of the whole range of information about savages
(as they were still usually described), it was the most disquiet-
ing.

Manifestly the tribal shaman had been, and sometimes still
was, an important figure. He owed that importance to the
tribe's belief in his ability to harness the supernatural.
Accounts by the hundred had described how shamans used
their second sight, or their magic. Some of the writers believed
the power was genuine, some admitted themselves baffled,
some attributed it to trickery. As a rationalist, Tylor was
naturally reluctant to accept that shamans could have genuine
magical powers. On the other hand, his reason told him that
shamans the world over could not have been successfully
deceiving their fellow-tribesmen with the same repertory of

conjuring tricks for thousands of years. They must believe in what they were doing. 'Magic has not its origins in fraud, and seems seldom practised as utter imposture.'

If magic were not imposture, how to account for it? This presented Tylor with an even more worrying question. The 1850s and 1860s, while he was preparing the book, had seen the table-turning craze at its height, and the emergence of spiritualist mediums claiming extra-sensory and telekinetic powers. From what he had heard and read, and perhaps from what he had witnessed, Tylor was not disposed to reject the evidence out of hand. Yet to accept it would add to his difficulties in dealing with shamanism, and might damage anthropology's prospects in academic circles.

Shamans might not engage in table-turning, but the descriptions of their magic were often virtually interchangeable with the descriptions of what occurred at seances. That both shamans and mediums attributed the phenomena to spirits was to Tylor unimportant. Fallacious interpretations, he knew, often linger, or are periodically revived. It was the similarity of the phenomena that disturbed him. Could it be, he wondered, that 'the Red Indian medicine man, the Tatar necromancer and the Boston medium share the possession of a belief and knowledge of the highest truth and import which, nevertheless, the great intellectual movement of the last two centuries has simply thrown aside as worthless?' He could not believe that this was what had happened; but he felt compelled to admit that if it *had*, 'the savages on whom some ethnographers look as degenerate from a higher civilisation may turn on their accusers and charge them with having fallen from the high level of savage knowledge'.

The Rotten Bough

Tylor left the issue open. Not so James Frazer, who laid down in *The Golden Bough* in 1890 that tribal magic was wholly fraudulent. It was based, he claimed, on two principles. One was 'homeopathic' – like produces like. This accounted for such practices as making an image of an enemy and sticking pins into him, to destroy him. The other was 'contagious' – things which have once been in contact continue to act upon each other, accounting for such practices as collecting an enemy's nail-parings and burning them, to destroy him. Both homeopathic and contagious magic were manifestly bogus, Frazer asserted. Magic was 'a false science as well as an abortive art'.

Frazer had done hardly any field work, certainly none which qualified him to pontificate on tribal magic (as Mary Kingsley was later to testify, *The Golden Bough*, which she had assumed would be her guide when she set out on her travels in Africa, was useless). Frazer was simply wrong. Tribesmen did not believe that sticking pins into an image of an enemy would kill him in the same way as sticking a knife into his body. They believed that they were invoking a psychic force, action at a distance, which could kill him. The function of the image, or the nail-parings, was simply to act as a focus of attention – much as some psychics like to hold a watch or a handkerchief belonging to a missing person they have been asked to find.

Needless to say, this interpretation would have meant nothing to Frazer, who did not accept the existence of psychic forces. As Tylor was not disposed to make a public issue of tribal magic, it was left to Andrew Lang to reply. A remarkable polymath – author, historian, biographer, translator of Homer, the leading authority on folklore and legend – Lang drew on his wide reading in anthropology to take *The Golden Bough* apart, revealing it to be not so much a synthesis of the available source material, as a succession of fantasies erected on flimsy foundations. In connection with tribal magic, Lang went back to Tylor's question: what was the reason for the resemblance between shamanism and spiritualism? For Lang, spiritualism was a word 'of the worst associations, inextricably entangled with fraud, bad logic and the blindest credulity'. Yet the phenomena fascinated him. Some he had experienced. Others had been described by observers he respected. Granted that there were fraudulent imitations of magic, he asked, why should human folly 'everywhere and always suffer from the same delusions, undergo the same hallucinations, and elaborate the same frauds?' Why should educated people have the same delusions as Eskimos and Maoris?

Lang bespattered the pages of his *Cock Lane and Common Sense* with parallels. Spirit rappings? They had been heard by Australian aborigines; they were referred to in ancient Egyptian papyri; the Greek Neoplatonists had experienced and recorded them – much as they were being recorded in London suburbs. Cold breezes? They had riffled Swedenborg's papers. Insensibility to heat? Fire-walks had been reported from many parts of the world. Second sight? In the Western Isles of Scotland it was still common, and had been endemic. Levitations? They had been seen by the Neoplatonist philosopher Iamblichus, 'by a great company of ordinary witnesses in all climes, ages and degrees of culture', and, in Lang's own time, by 'certain scientific, and (as a layman might suppose), qualified persons' – among them William Crookes and Alfred Russel Wallace. As for table-turning, if in Tibet a lama wished to trace an object he would sit in front of a small table, resting his hands on it; at the end of half an hour, when he raised his hands the table would levitate, and then float in front of him until it fell to the ground, giving the direction in which to proceed. A witness who described the process, M. Tscherepanoff, claimed that he watched it fly for about forty feet.

Apparitions, too, were an everyday occurrence in some tribal communities, particularly of an individual who had just died. His appearance, as soon as it was realised that it had been a hallucination, was taken by his relations as a sign he *had* died. In the 1880s apparitions of the dying had been reported by the score to the Society for Psychical Research in reply to a questionnaire – reported, too, by respected men and women who had no obvious motive for inventing their stories.

Lang was even able to cite anthropological and historical parallels for certain practices associated with spiritualist mediumship which had aroused most suspicion; in particular, the use of a curtain, a 'cabinet', behind which the medium was supposed to accumulate psychic energy. Jesuit missionaries working among the American Indians had found that their medicine men used a chimney-shaped 'lodge', inside which they sat until the spirits arrived to give them messages.

Could it be, then, that the phenomena were genuine? Certainly they were often faked: 'but that ignorant modern knaves should feign precisely the same raps, lights and movements as the most remote and unsophisticated barbarians', Lang reiterated, 'and as the educated Platonists of the fourth century after Christ, and that many of the other phenomena should be identical in each case, is surely noteworthy?' Lang could not help wondering, greatly though he admired Tylor, why Tylor had not asked 'are these tales true, and if so, what do they mean?' Yet surely it was evident that if clairvoyance occurred, 'and if appearances of men at the hour of their death are, verily, beheld at a distance, then a savage's philosophy had more to go on than mere dreams'.

Tylor still refused to be drawn. *The Golden Bough* came to be regarded almost as anthropology's bible. When R.R. Marett, Tylor's successor in the Oxford Chair, ventured timidly to suggest that the resemblances between spiritualist and shamanist phenomena were so striking that they ought at least to be made the subject of investigation, Frazer replied that even if they were, anthropologists were not qualified to undertake it. Shamanism was a form of insanity, and as such should be left to psychiatrists.

Although *The Golden Bough* is no longer taken seriously by anthropologists, its legacy remains. As recently as 1963 Jacquetta Hawkes was echoing it; tribal magic, she asserted, is 'based on the two misapprehensions that things which are alike are the same, and things which have been connected continue to affect one another'.

In any case, field workers have been discouraged from taking shamanism seriously as a subject for investigation. Anybody who at the start of his or her career decided to conduct research to try to find out whether, say, the clairvoyant or telekinetic abilities of a shaman were genuine would have been regarded as a little odd. If the outcome was that the abilities *were* genuine, a report to that effect would have been as good a way as any to banish any prospect of academic advancement. With a handful of exceptions, aspiring anthropologists have avoided the issue.

Of the field workers who applied to join van der Post in his expeditions among the Kalahari bushmen some, he found, wanted only 'to measure bushman heads and behinds, others to measure his sexual organ, and one to analyse his spit'. Asked if they were not interested in the mind and the spirit and the personality of bushmen, they replied, 'that is not our department of science'. The bushman had been destroyed, van der Post feared, 'without our ever bothering to find out what sort of person he really was'.

And not only the bushman. On his deathbed, in 1879, the explorer William Howitt warned that tribal communities were being transformed so rapidly by contact with civilisation that his successors must not fall into the error of imagining that the aborigine communities which they would be investigating would necessarily resemble those he had found and described. All over the world, the chance of investigating tribal divination and magic has been lost because shamanism has been under pressures which have corrupted it, where they have not actually destroyed it – missionaries being the chief destroyers, as Arthur Grimble showed in his *Pattern of Islands*.

Grimble, van der Post and a few others have been convinced by their experiences that tribal magic and divination ought not to be rejected out of hand. The world's leading authority on shamanism, Professor Mircea Eliade, agrees. Periodically individual anthropologists pluck up the courage to tell their colleagues they ought to pay more attention to the role of psi. 'A significant revolution which concerns us all is taking place quietly but surely in a related branch of science', a former President of the American Anthropological Association claimed in 1952, referring to parapsychology, 'and it is not being met in an honest, truly scientific manner'. Seven years later C.W. Weiant, in an academic paper on the subject, expressed his strong belief that 'every anthropologist, whether believer or unbeliever, should acquaint himself with the techniques of parapsychological research and make use of these, as well as any other means at his disposal, to establish what is real and what is illusion in the so-called paranormal'; if the believers should turn out to be right 'there will certainly be exciting implications for anthropology'.

Unluckily, few psychological researchers have had either the training or the opportunity to do the necessary field work. A few tests have been carried out of the card-guessing type in tribal communities, with positive findings. There is also a substantial body of anecdotal evidence of the kind Robert Van de Castle has collected, including accounts of the powers of the celebrated Shoshone medicine man, 'Rolling Thunder', with his ability to exercise psi effect. An admirer who wanted to photograph him with a Polaroid camera was told to go ahead, but that none of the negatives would come out; and three exposures were duly wasted. At this point Rolling Thunder relented; the next one, he said, would be all right. It was.

Ironically, the works which have done most to revive interest in the magical element in shamanism have been Carlos Castaneda's series about 'Don Juan' – the irony being that Don Juan, the Mexican shaman, has turned out to be, if not a fake, a composite character owing much to Castaneda's vivid imagination. One of the works in its original form was for a postgraduate thesis at the University of California. It was accepted only after he had added a 'structural analysis' which impressed his examiners but was in fact a spoof – a hilarious parody of the structuralist method spawned by Claude Lévi-Strauss.

Structuralism

'No anthropologist has ever secured greater fame than Claude Lévi-Strauss', the commentator on his work in Sturrock's collection of essays on structuralism has claimed. The assertion reveals just how completely, for a few years, structuralism took over anthropology. The damage it did was incalculable. Structuralism's basic principle, in so far as it can be said to have had one, was that what are important are not the facts, but relationships which can be established between them. The nearest it came to dealing with psi was in connection with tribal medicine, as in *Culture and Curing*, subtitled 'anthropological perspectives on traditional medical beliefs and practices', a collection of papers by anthropologists holding academic positions in America and Britain, and ostensibly dealing with spiritualist or magical healing in different parts of the world.

With a single exception, none of the papers considered whether the magical healing methods do, or do not, work. This was not what structuralism was about, as the contributors made clear. What was important was that it had facilitated the comparison of medical systems in different cultures, so that, as one of them put it, 'points of congruence and divergence along the similarity-difference continuum' could be studied. What little could have been learned from the studies was fogged over by similarly excruciating jargon: 'components in any synchronic recitation may include mythic symbols'; 'the diachronic nature of oral processes manifests itself in the combination of these kinds of elements'; 'personality etiologies postulate at least two levels of causality'; and 'the person, in Fipa theory, is a structured entity which analysis shows to be homologous with various supra-personal dimensions of the Fipa cosmos'.

Such jargon, David Lodge, Professor of English at Birmingham University, has argued, was necessary to structuralists to provide them with 'the power to intimidate their personal peers'. Had they spoken and written in everyday language they would have been rumbled long before – just as they would have been if they had been compelled to answer Lang's question, 'do these things actually happen?' The structuralists were able to escape the need to deal with realities by fudging. 'According to them oracles, rain dances, the treatment of mind and body *express* the needs of the members of a society, they *function* as a social glue, they *reveal* basic structures of thought', Paul Feyerabend has observed; interpretations which are 'hardly ever the result of critical thought'.

Howitt's fears were justified. It is now too late for much to be learned from tribal communities. A better prospect lies in India and other eastern countries where the tradition still holds that the journey to enlightenment will often be accompanied by psychic phenomena, ranging from second sight to levitation. They are not regarded as important in their own right. At best they are seen as an indication that progress is being made. But some individuals – the despised fakirs – having progressed to that stage, go no further, and use their psychic abilities to earn their living.

A guru may continue to display his psychic powers to impress disciples and potential disciples, while insisting that the phenomena are not important in themselves – as Jesus did. And one other strand of shamanism remains unbroken in some parts of the world by civilisation's destructive impact. As the medical profession assumed that its theory and practice were immeasurably superior to tribal medicine, the shaman in his role as a diagnostician, prescriber and therapist was not regarded as a menace to be put down, as he had been by priests. One of his methods, in particular, caused no worry because to conventionally trained doctors it was assumed to be useless: the therapeutic use of trances – altered states of consciousness, as psychologists now prefer to call them.

Psychic Healing

In his trances, 'seeing' what should be done or 'hearing' the spirits' advice, one of the shaman's traditional functions was to diagnose and prescribe for illness. When witchcraft was held responsible – say, by the materialisation of a foreign substance in the sick person's body – the shaman would dematerialise it by magic.

In a few countries, notably Brazil and the Philippines, shamanism has been fused with spiritualist ideas, as well as some from conventional medicine, into what has now come to be known as psychic surgery. The best-known practitioner in Brazil, José Arigo, had a spirit 'control' who claimed in his lifetime to have been a doctor. He diagnosed in medical terminology (surprisingly up-to-date it was, according to doctors who investigated him) and prescribed drugs or surgery. The drugs might be conventional; the surgery was not. Arigo would use a kitchen knife, taking no precautions to prevent septicemia. Although the surgery appeared to witnesses to be rough and ready, the patient would feel no pain, and the gash left by the knife would quickly close up without stitches, leaving hardly a trace.

In the Philippines the psychic surgeons do not use knives, claiming that they can enter the patients' bodies without them. This type of 'surgery', too, is ordinarily painless, and leaves hardly a trace, even when a tumour, say, has been extracted.

Has a tumour been extracted? Or are such operations simply examples of clever sleight-of-hand? From time to time a sceptical investigator or the producer of a television crew has seized the substance and submitted it to examination. When it has been found not to be a human organ, the operator, and by implication psychic surgery, has been denounced as fraudulent.

The issue is not quite so simple. Anthropologists who took the trouble to investigate healing in tribal communities often reported 'surgery' of a similar nature, and their accounts show how it developed. When the spirits diagnosed the existence of a foreign substance materialised by witchcraft, the demater-ialisation process was psychic, accompanied by ceremonial – mumbo-jumbo, as doctors thought it. *Their* surgery was often so impressive that shamans, fearing they would be outfaced if they could not compete, began to imitate it in their ceremonial. From this it was a short step to using sleight-of-hand, palming a 'tumour' and producing it at the end of the operation to show it really had been removed.

In *If This Be Magic* Guy Lyon Playfair recalls how Loren Parks, a successful business man with academic qualifications in psychology, decided to investigate psychic surgery in the Philippines, and came away satisfied that it was genuine. Later he heard that he had been deceived; the surgeon had been detected using sleight-of-hand. Returning to investigate further, Parks came to the conclusion that although sleight-of-hand was indeed used, it was in a sense not fraudulent, because it worked. 'There is no stronger suggestion I know of than believing that someone with divine powers can enter the body with bare hands and close up the incision without leaving a scar and with no infection', he decided. 'It really works, yet it is as phony as a three dollar bill. *It is the fastest, most effective form of healing that I know.*'

How does it work? Clearly auto-suggestion is a prerequisite, but can it be held responsible for closing up an incision without leaving a scar? Or is some form of psychokinetic energy involved, generated between healer and patient? Or is it perhaps a combination of the two?

That some cases of sleight-of-hand have been detected has made it easy for scientists to dismiss psychic surgery as bogus, particularly as the transporting of patients with terminal diseases from California to the Philippines had threatened to become a profitable commercial racket. Scientists are finding it less easy to reject another phenomenon traditionally associated with shamanism, and assumed to be fraudulent: the shaman's ability to induce in himself and others an altered state of consciousness in which protection is afforded to the body from extremes of heat or cold which ordinarily would be unendurable, and even fatal.

Incombustibility

'Mastery of fire, insensibility to heat and, hence, the "mystical heat" which renders both extreme cold and the temperature of burning coals supportable' are indications, Mircea Eliade has observed, that the shaman 'has passed beyond the human condition'. The ability to demonstrate that mastery over heat or cold has been achieved is one of the ways in which aspiring novices prove themselves. Travelling in Tibet, Alexandra David-Neel found that on a frosty, windy night they would be required to sit cross-legged and naked on the ground by a river; 'sheets are dipped in the icy water, each man wraps himself in one of them and must dry it with his body' – the winner being the one who has dried the largest number of sheets before dawn. The size of the sheets varied, she admitted, and sometimes they were so small that they were almost symbolical; but she had seen some contestants 'dry a number of pieces of cloth the size of a large shawl'.

Demonstrations of incombustibility – the ability to withstand extreme heat without pain or injury – are more familiar, presumably because it is easier to make a fire than to make ice. Historically the most familiar form is the fire-walk, well-attested in classical literature and frequently encountered by travellers to this day. The procedure varies: wood or coals are set alight in a prepared pit, and left to burn down to a level, or stones are heated over fire. The shaman, or guru, then walks across barefoot, followed by his flock and by anybody else who cares to volunteer.

Fire-walking happens to be one of the few features of shamanism which has survived for long enough to be witnessed and tested. Trial by ordeal, in which suspects are allowed to try to prove their innocence by performing tasks which would normally leave them blistered and scarred, but which leave them unscathed, has all but disappeared; but the colonial officer and magistrate Frank Melland, investigating it in Rhodesia early in this century, was impressed by the fact that it was sometimes invoked in relatively trivial cases. Suspects would hardly have offered to handle red-hot iron or to dip their hands in boiling water if they knew that they had no hope of passing the test.

The reality of 'incombustibility', as it has come to be known, can no longer seriously be disputed, except by the rearguard of resolute sceptics. Yet the realisation has been slow to dawn that tribal communities must have been far ahead of us in their ability to discover a way in which to provide some as yet unexplained form of protection from the

effects of extreme heat. The familiar Old Testament tale of
Shadrach, Mesach and Abed Nego surviving unscathed in
Nebuchadnezzar's burning fiery furnace, myth though it may
be, may have had a nugget of truth in it, after all.

History

Early Civilisation

Although the evidence about psi in early civilisations is even scantier and less reliable than in the tribal communities which preceded them, it is clear that the practice of magic and divination by shamans was corrupted in much the same way as it was to be corrupted under colonial rule. Tribes were brought under the control of central governments, as the Israelites were in the period of the Babylonish captivity. In early civilisations the 'prophet' – the shaman – gradually decomposed into the priest, who dispensed doctrine, and the diviner, who increasingly relied on formulae. Divination came to rely on indications such as the positions of the planets, or omens, such as claps of thunder or the direction of the flights of birds overhead. Inevitably the diviner was tempted to interpret the evidence to suit the will or the whim of whoever was in authority over him.

Yet intimations of psi are always and everywhere to be found. Some, admittedly, remain almost total mysteries: notably the evidence of abilities which cannot easily be accounted for in communities which flourished in what is commonly regarded as pre-history. They were uncommonly advanced in certain respects, as they were capable of quarrying huge chunks of stone, bringing them great distances to centres such as Stonehenge, and setting them up there with a mathematical precision that suggests they must have been installed either as part of a well-established religion, or to explore the heavens – perhaps for astrological purposes – or both.

That there were civilisations with sophisticated equipment comparable to today's is hardly likely; indications would surely have been found of their existence. Extra-terrestrial visitors, too, would surely have left more recognisable traces of their handiwork. A plausible hypothesis has been put forward by Frank Wilson in *Crystal and Cosmos*: that some communities acquired and used faculties 'unadulterated by the material preoccupations of civilisation', which 'could have transported them from their undeveloped state to one which was conducive to revelatory experiences'. These faculties were lost with the onset of civilisations of a more materialistic type, though the tradition may have been preserved among the practitioners of kabbalism, alchemy, and astrology.

Whatever their function, megaliths have presented archaeologists with problems which are still either unresolved or have been too glibly rationalised away for comfort. They have emphasised, for example, that transportation would have been possible using the primitive means that were at man's disposal, given sufficient manpower. The question still has to be asked, John Ivimy has pointed out in *The Sphinx and the Megaliths*, how supposedly illiterate barbarians could have become 'so ingenious, so emancipated, so intellectually and socially mature that they were able of a sudden, first to conceive the abstract idea of building such a structure, next to make the considerable mental effort needed to plan it in detail without making drawings and finally, to organise themselves so as to make the colossal and prolonged physical efforts that were needed to cut and move the stones and set them up on the site'.

The search for a way to account for such mysteries has led to conflicts between rival academic disciplines. The discoveries of the astronomer Sir Norman Lockyer about the alignment of stone circles, presented in his *Stonehenge and Other British Stone Monuments* in 1906, might have been expected to command respect, as he was an FRS, Director of the Solar Physics Laboratory, and founder of *Nature*, which he edited for half a century. A few mistakes he made, however, were seized upon by mainstream archaeologists, who declined to believe that primitive ancient Britons could have known about astronomy. 'The idea has led a generation of antiquaries to waste much time and ink', Sir Mortimer Wheeler, President of the Antiquaries Society, complained.

When further research continued to point to Lockyer's case being correct in principle, even if not in details, Dr Glyn

Daniel, editor of *Antiquity*, asked Professor Fred Hoyle to investigate. Hoyle came to the conclusion that the alignments of the standing stones were 'just the ones that would have served far-reaching astronomical purposes'. It was an unwelcome verdict, and Daniel announced in 1967 that a further inquiry would be undertaken by an archaeologist, Jacquetta Hawkes. Although her qualifications were not immediately obvious, as she had no training in astronomy, the choice was understandable, as she had already ranged herself on the side of Wheeler and Daniel. The standing stones had been erected as temples, she had assumed. 'I see no argument strong or consistent enough to change our previous belief', her verdict ran.

The belief – rationalisation would be closer to the mark – has now been challenged from a different quarter: the results of research carried out by members of the Dragon Project, a research venture begun in 1978 by a scientist, Don Robins. Robins had become curious about the stone circles dotted around Britain and many other countries. Might there be some way, he wondered, to allow the stones to 'speak' for themselves, rather than remain the subject of speculative controversy between archaeologists and 'off-archaeologists', as Glyn Daniel had contemptuously described them? Starting from the premise that, as folklore suggested, some unexplained forms of earth energy might be associated with them, he began to explore with the help of two instruments, an ultrasonic detector and a Geiger counter.

Both methods indicated that there are indeed earth energies of some kind, in connection with the stone circles. The instruments revealed 'energy anomalies', as Robins cautiously described them. Dowsers' gadgets – forked hazel twigs or pendulums – were also affected but Robins, anxious to keep the Dragon Project within conventional scientific boundaries, concentrated upon providing scientific evidence for the anomalies. He was relieved when his account, appearing in the *New Scientist* in 1982, did not produce a hostile reaction. The mystics were happy to have scientific verification of their belief in earth energies. Members of the archaeological establishment were silenced by the scientific presentation of the facts. Eventually it dawned on Robins that 'we had actually become respectable. Science fact had merged with science fiction, and I could actually discuss this work with archaeologists in a sane and reasonable manner.'

When Robins's *Circles of Silence* came out in 1985 the Dragon Project was still at the anomaly-testing stage. It has not solved the mystery of why and how the circles came to be built. It has a long way to go before it will begin to explain how the various energies – ultrasound, radiations, the dowsing component – interact. Yet it lends suppport to the idea that cosmic energies are involved. If the people who quarried the stone and transported it to the selected sites were illiterate barbarians, it is not easy to accept that they were moved only by religious zeal. Perhaps Frank Wilson's notion is right: that in those days consciousness had not taken people's minds to the point where they could no longer pick up evolution's messages guiding them to courses of action. May they not have been programmed in ways comparable to those which Marais found in termitaries, taking advantage of humanity's additional resources of hand and brain?

The Christian Tradition

In the earliest era of recorded history some insoluble problems remain. No clear distinction can be made between history and myth. We cannot tell for certain which episodes in, say, the Old Testament (or even the New) were accurately recorded. The preconceptions of the chroniclers render their narratives suspect; the interventions of the gods in Homer, or of the Lord in the Bible, are twisted to suit prevailing beliefs. Yet there is a measure of consistency in the records which E.R. Dodds, Regius Professor of Greek at Oxford, found significant.

In 1971, surveying the evidence about psychic phenomena in classical times, Dodds commented that although he could not vouch for its reliability, he was impressed by the way it fused with the evidence from other eras, and from other parts of the world. Some of it, he admitted, could be accounted for by lingering oral tradition. Ghost stories can beget other ghost stories. Nevertheless the fact that the descriptions of the phenomena were much the same then as they have been since provided what he felt was a useful check. If they were no longer encountered, the presumption (unless there were some obvious reasons) would be that they were myths.

Mircea Eliade has made the same point. In this field, he insists, the historian is not bound to pronounce on the authenticity of specific cases. 'For our purpose, what is important is to underline the perfect *continuity of paranormal experience*.' There is 'not a single shamanic "miracle" which is not also well-attested in the traditions of the Oriental religions and in the Christian tradition'.

The Christian tradition, and the writings associated with it, provide the bulk of the historical evidence for psi. Not that it is lacking in, say, the Buddhist tradition. It was assumed that anybody who attained a certain level of spiritual development would be able to be in two places at once; to become invisible; to pass through solid matter; to levitate; to walk on water, and much else besides. But these, Buddhist teaching emphasised, were side-effects. Buddha's 'characteristically dry comment', Aldous Huxley recalled, on one of his disciples' feats of levitation was 'this will not conduce to the conversion of the unconverted, nor to the advantage of the converted'.

Jesus, too, deplored the publicity his miracles brought him, according to the gospel writers. Most of them were in the shamanic tradition, adapted to his and his disciples' needs: changing the water into wine; multiplying the loaves and fishes; calming the storm. Miracles have gone out of fashion, and Christians tend to forget how deeply their religion is indebted to them, in particular those which occurred after the crucifixion; for without them the disciples would hardly have had the heart to carry on Jesus's work – miracles such as Jesus's materialisation, and the disciples' possession (as they regarded it) at Pentecost by the Holy Spirit, creating gusts of wind and cloven tongues of fire, and starting them speaking in languages they did not know.

Christianity was originally based on the assumption that divine forces emanating from God and distributed by the Holy Spirit could enable those possessed to work miracles. As time passed, however, and the Church settled into an organisation with a hierarchy, a bureaucracy and settled dogmas, spirit possession became suspect, along with its associated miracles, except when performed by holy men and women in circum-stances where it was unlikely that the devil was up to his tricks. As a result, the bulk of the evidence for miracles is distorted either by hagiography or, where they were attri-

buted to the devil, by the fact that the confessions were
extracted under torture.

Still, some of it is hard to reject out of hand. Far from being
impressed by miracles when they were performed by the
living, the Church authorities tended to view them with
suspicion as in all probability diabolic. That the levitations of
St Teresa of Avila were reported in her lifetime, and that she
was actually able to set them down in her autobiography
without fear of retribution for the sin of pride, was unusual.
More characteristic of the authorities' attitude was the treatment of Joseph of Copertino, a Franciscan who frequently
levitated, sometimes during Mass. He was banished from the
chapel, even from the refectory, and investigated by the
Inquisition. His levitations, though, happen to be uncommonly well-attested, as so many people witnessed them, from the
local peasants to the Pope. Even so shrewdly sceptical a
commentator as Eric Dingwall, after studying the accounts,
came to the conclusion that they cannot be dismissed as
hagiography.

Nevertheless hagiography makes many other remarkable
case histories suspect, and outside the Church the accounts
tend to lack attestation. Poltergeists are the main exception;
their activities, upsetting furniture, breaking crockery, causing showers indoors, are well chronicled. There are some
reliable-sounding instances, too, of divination.

'I know of no country, either so polished and learned, or so
rude, barbarous and uncivilised', Cicero wrote, introducing
his treatise on the subject, 'where it is not allowed that some
persons are gifted with an insight into the future, and are
endowed with a talent to predict.' This talent has often been
displayed by individuals of the highest mental and moral
calibre, among them Socrates and Joan of Arc.

At his trial, Socrates told his judges that he had always
relied for guidance on his inner voice, the voice of his daemon,
which would break into his thought, even into his conversa-
tion, to warn him if he were about to make some error, even a
trifling one. Joan, at her trial, described in detail what her
voices and visions had done for her, including glimpses of the
future which were attested by those who were present when
she described them.

'Even if one believes that Joan's voices were not supernatural and objective phenomena, but the private projections of her imagination', Marina Warner has claimed in her recent biography, 'it must be accepted that she herself never heard them except as external, separate entities who were independent of her and over whom she exercised no control at all.' As some earlier biographers have also emphasised, the strength of Joan's testimony about her voices and visions lies in her insistence that they were real, to her, in spite of the fact that this insistence was one of the two main counts against her. There is also independent testimony to their psi content, from her clairvoyant perception of the sword which lay behind the altar in the Church of St Catherine of Fierbois, to her precognition of how and where she would be wounded when the time came to raise the siege of Orléans.

Joan's description of her voices, and the resolution with which she maintained their divine source, were to seal her fate. Teresa and Joseph, in their Orders, were able to convince the authorities not just that the miracles were genuine, but also that they were divine. Outside the Church, and not seldom within it, individuals who tried to exploit psi, along with tens of thousands of men and women who did not, but who were accused of doing so, were charged with witchcraft, tortured until they confessed, and burned at the stake. Except at the humblest of social levels, where village 'wise women' could continue to practise using charms and incantations, or in places where the witch-hunters' writ did not run, such as the Western Isles of Scotland where second-sight was endemic (impressing Samuel Johnson), divination and magic were driven underground.

The Renaissance
Towards the end of the fifteenth century a new word was added to the English language: supernatural. The Christian assumption had been that all phenomena were natural. Some, however, occurred only when angels were acting on God's behalf, or demons acting on Satan's. God could also intervene in person. Only God, Thomas Aquinas argued, could perform real miracles. Still, as levitations and other such phenomena looked the same whether the source was divine or diabolic, and as the decision as to who was responsible for them was

made by fallible humans (who might change their minds, as they did over Joan of Arc), the term 'supernatural' came to be adopted to cover miraculous events in general.

Hardly had the term come into colloquial use when the advance of science prompted the need for a companion term to make the distinction between phenomena attributable to divine or diabolic intervention, and those which could more reasonably be put down to some natural cause, yet to be discovered. Magnetism was one example. For a time, mariners using the loadstone had risked being charged with witchcraft. Early in the fifteenth century Pietro Pomponazzi, the prototype of later sceptics, suggested that most of what had been regarded as supernatural could be explained in natural terms: astrological influences, he thought, would be traced to some emanation from the planets. For forces of this kind, and their effects, the term occult came into circulation.

Occult implied a kind of neutrality. 'Occult or hidden qualities are those which are not immediately known to the senses,' Daniel Sennert explained in his survey of natural philosophy early in the seventeenth century. They were known only through their effects; 'their power of acting is unknown. So we see the loadstone draw the iron, but that power of drawing is to us hidden.' Gravity was in this category. So, too, was alchemy.

Occult, in short, had a very different meaning from the one it was destined to have later. This was to confuse many historians and biographers, who were inclined to treat the interest which Newton and Boyle had in alchemy as curious aberrations, pardonable only because they had redeemed themselves in the long run thanks to their scientific achievements. Only recently, in the 1980s, has Keith Hutchison of the University of Melbourne cleared away this misconception. Belief in the occult, he has shown, did not involve belief in the supernatural. On the contrary, involvement in alchemy or astrology – or in Joseph Glanvil's case, ghost-hunting – could indicate a desire to find a scientific explanation for what had been regarded as supernatural.

Newton was emphatic in his assertion that there must be some explanation for gravity, because to believe that one body could act on another at a distance unless some force was involved was an absurdity. The fact that he was unable to find what constituted the force was to lead to the change of meaning that 'occult' suffered, as churchmen did not hesitate to insist that the only possible explanation was the power of God. Even Newton sometimes felt disposed to agree. It was because the occult could be exploited in this way, Hutchison points out, that Leibniz criticised Newton. People who claimed gravity was occult were right 'if they mean thereby that there is a certain mechanism unknown to them, by which bodies are impelled towards the centre of the earth'. If their implication was that no such mechanism existed, Leibniz asserted, or that God was responsible, then their occultism was 'senseless'.

Hutchison's thesis is not merely of etymological interest – not just 'a vacuous matter of words' he insists. It is in fact crucial to the understanding of the reason science degenerated so quickly into scientism. Anxious to banish superstition, scientists elevated theories that worked, like Newton's, into laws of nature. Gravity and magnetism could be accepted because they were sufficiently consistent in their operation, and because the effects could be demonstrated at will. Arbitrarily they were pulled out of the occult category, although they remained inexplicable. Psi effects were inconsistent and could rarely be demonstrated at will. Worse, they suffered from guilt by association with angels, demons, witches, ghosts and the denizens of folklore. Besides, so-called miracles were still being produced and hailed within the Church to delude the gullible faithful! Instead of being left as anomalies awaiting an explanation, psi effects in general were sentenced to the secular equivalent of excommunication. 'Occult' went, too.

By the mid-eighteenth century, excommunication had been replaced by what amounted to a death sentence, pronounced by David Hume in his essay on miracles. As they broke the laws of nature, he argued, and as the breaking of those laws was contrary to the uniform experience of mankind, miracles did not occur. From this time on, therefore, scientism could not afford to ignore evidence which contradicted Hume. It had to be demolished, or the laws would be in jeopardy.

What scientism failed to allow for was the possibility that natural forces existed – occult, in the original sense, undiscovered and unexplained, yet capable of affecting and even defying gravity or magnetism, much as a magnet, lifting iron, defies gravity. 'Reason has taught me that to condemn anything positively as false and impossible is to claim that our brains are privileged to know the bounds and limits of God's will, and of mother nature's power,' Montaigne had observed. 'There is no more patent folly in the world than to reduce these things to the measure of our own power and capacity.' In their folly, this was what eminent scientists began to do.

Their first mistake is in retrospect so ludicrous that it should have been a warning. When several people in a French village in 1768 saw a meteorite descend nearby, and told the local abbé, he sent a piece of it to the Academy of the Sciences. It was not a meteorite, the Academicians who investigated it – Lavoisier was one of them – asserted. Stones could not fall out of the sky. Belief in meteorites was a superstition dating back to the times when Jove was supposed to hurl his thunderbolts. It must be part of a stone on the ground, struck by lightning. Jean Deluc, one of the founders of meteorology for weather forecasting, claimed that if a meteorite fell at his feet he still would refuse to believe in it.

Perhaps the most revealing of all the symptoms of scientism's growing arrogance came when another meteorite fell in France in 1770, and was witnessed by the mayor and the city council. The reaction of the celebrated chemist Comte Claude Louis Berthollet was to complain, 'How sad it is that an entire municipality enters folk tales upon an official record, presenting them as something actually seen, while they cannot be explained by physics or by anything rational.' As a result of such pronouncements, all over Europe the curators of museums shamefacedly got rid of their collections of meteorites. It was not until the early years of the nineteenth century that books about them could be taken back off the shelves marked 'Superstitions' in libraries.

'If you think of it, for 18th century minds meteors were no easier to swallow than UFOs for us', Arthur Koestler commented. 'Hence the same choking and spluttering reaction.' The choking and spluttering has continued in connection with those types of communication or action at a distance which have a biological or psychological component, and consequently do not behave with the consistency of gravity or magnetism. Mesmer's 'animal magnetism' hypothesis was rejected mainly because it assumed the existence of a fluid emanating from the planets – though also because members of the medical profession declined to accept the trance state. It was a hangover, they insisted, from the old belief in diabolic possession. Mesmerised subjects were only pretending to be entranced – a view that remained orthodox for more than a century. By the 1840s the mechanistic view of the universe was firmly entrenched. The shock was all the greater when the occult made a come-back so striking that, as Conan Doyle was to recall, it appeared as though 'some psychic cloud had descended from on high'.

The Psychic Cloud

Of the many intimations that the prevailing belief in the laws of nature was ill-founded, one from this period remains of particular interest because it involved what came to be known as exteriorisation – a type of action at a distance unconsciously generated by an individual or a group, as if they are acting as transformers of psi energy into physical energy.

One morning in 1846 the furniture in a house in the village of Bouvigny, in the Department of the Orne, began to behave as if it had taken an aversion to Angélique, a 14-year-old. Wherever she went, objects moved away from her as if by repulsion. Even in the mid-nineteenth century, diabolic possession would in all probability have been diagnosed; but the local landowner, thinking electricity might be responsible, recommended a scientific examination. After investigations locally, Angélique was despatched to Paris for tests by the Academy of the Sciences.

Had Angélique been presented as a purveyor of supernatural phenomena, the Academy would certainly have had nothing to do with her. They had already decided to have no more investigations of Mesmer's animal magnetism, because it was deemed contrary to natural law. Electricity was another matter. There were, after all, electric eels; just possibly . . .

The preliminary investigation was carried out by Dr Tanchou. He was left in no doubt that whatever the force might be, it was extremely powerful. The heavy sofa on which he was sitting moved, with him on it, when she came to try to sit down on it. When held by his assistants, chairs were forcibly wrenched from their grasp. Tanchou accordingly called in

François Arago, astronomer, physicist and statesman, one of
the ablest of French scientists, and a dedicated rationalist.
With three colleagues, Arago witnessed the same effects as
Tanchou. Still in the belief that some form of electricity must
be responsible, a committee was formed, the apparatus required to test the hypothesis was set up and trials were begun.
Some static electricity was found; nothing out of the ordinary.
Then, suddenly, objects ceased to move at Angélique's
approach. It was as if the current had been switched off at
source. There was nothing for it but to wind up the investigation, and send Angélique home.

In retrospect her story regains significance, showing as it
does how necessary it was by that time for scientists to have
some possible explanation at hand to account for phenomena
which, if they had not actually witnessed them, they would
have dismissed as supernatural, and therefore spurious. 'Electricity' sufficed for that purpose. Later, when it had begun to
dawn on sceptics that electricity could not have been responsible, trickery was retrospectively alleged. As Guillaume
Figuier had to admit, in his reconstruction of the case, the
allegations did not stand up to critical scrutiny.

Other startling manifestations were recorded in the late
1840s, including perhaps the most remarkable poltergeist case
of all time, reported in the official police gazette in Paris. After
work began to open up a new street near the Sorbonne, heavy
paving stones began to rain down on it as if being thrown 'by
no mortal hand'. As the public was tempted to attribute them
to occult influences, elaborate measures were taken by the
gendarmerie to track down the offenders, without success.

The actual psychic cloudburst, as it might well be called,
also began in a poltergeist infestation, at the home of the Fox
family in Hydesville, near Rochester, New York. Although as
such hauntings go it was a mild affair, it had startling
repercussions, reverberating to this day.

It began conventionally with rappings and bangings, but
when two of the Fox children, Margaret and Kate, were able
to persuade the rapper to identify himself, by means of a
simple 'yes' or 'no' code of raps, as the spirit of a man who had
been murdered in the house years before, the publicity
launched the children on an unprecedented career. Like
Angélique, they exteriorised, but in a more controlled fashion.

Not only could they produce bangs from all around a room, investigators – often hostile – reported; they could make heavy tables rap, shudder, shift position, rear up on end, and sometimes float. Soon it was found that the sisters' presence was unnecessary. Over the next five or six years 'table-turning', 'table-tilting', or 'table-rapping', as it was variously described, became an international craze of a kind which had never been seen before, and has not been equalled since.

The Table-turners

The enlivening of wood by human contact was not new. It had been reported from tribal communities, in classical literature, and by travellers in India and Tibet. In the seventeenth century a Jewish sect had practised a form of table-turning as part of their religious ritual, very similar to that in which the Victorians now engaged. A hostile critic at the time had noted that the table would rise in the air even when laden with many hundredweight. To the great majority of those who sat down, evening after evening in the mid-nineteenth century, it was simply a new pastime, though a baffling and on occasion a frightening one.

Any article of furniture would do, but tables were convenient to sit around in a circle; finger-tips on the table, hands touching those of neighbours to form a loose linkage. Sitting in near-darkness, the company would wait, often for an hour or more, for the first indication that the psi forces were beginning to operate: raps, and shudders. Then the table would begin to swivel (hence 'table-turning') or rear up on one side. Eventually, in some seances, it would leave the floor altogether, so that the sitters had to become standers, reaching up to keep their fingers on the top, and eyeing each other from under it – incidentally satisfying themselves that nobody was applying any physical 'lift'. 'I have no doubt that there are *thousands* of tables turning every night in London', Sir David Brewster observed in the spring of 1853, 'so general is the excitement on the subject.' Correspondents assured him that the same excitement had spread through the capitals of Europe.

The table-turning craze presents important evidence for the reality of psychokinesis – much more important than psychical researchers themselves have realised. The case histories have attracted relatively little attention because they have not been regarded as providing sufficiently good scientific evidence. To the historian, the sheer quantity and consistency of the accounts would ordinarily carry complete conviction, were it not for the reluctance to accept PK. The occasional practical joker there must have been, making the raps with his knuckles and lifting the table with a foot. Yet dozens of accounts make it clear that nobody could have been physically responsible for the tables' movements.

It is not as if the people who left the accounts were believers. Thomas Babington Macaulay and his group could hardly bring themselves to credit the evidence of their own eyes. In the Royal Palace of Osborne, Queen Victoria decided that magnetism or electricity must be responsible. Some of the most convincing accounts came from country rectories, where the vicar, his family and domestic servants watched in manifest bewilderment tables behaving as if the devil was in them (some came to fear he probably was), having been conditioned to believe that the existence of such forces had long since been discredited.

'The facts are undeniable', von Humboldt, science's elder statesman, had to admit. 'It now becomes the task of science to explain them.' A handful of scientists agreed with him. In Geneva, the Comte de Gasparin and his friend Professor Marc Thury began a careful investigation with monitoring instruments and a variety of precautions designed to prevent, or at least detect, the use of physical force. They found that some people could coax no movement out of the table; for others, it would behave as if obeying their instructions. If two people for whom it would not move put their hands on the table, and two others for whom it *would* move laid their hands on the hands of the first two, the table moved, though the first two felt no pressure. (Significantly, this is a common experience in connection with water-divining. Many people who obtain no reaction holding a forked hazel twig, when they are walking over an underground stream, feel it 'kick' strongly in their hands if a water-diviner has his hand upon one of them.)

De Gasparin's testimony is the harder to ignore because of his reputation. Then, and since, psychical researchers who have reported results which cannot readily be attributed to trickery on the part of subjects – psychics, mediums, or others involved in tests – have themselves come under suspicion for rigging the experiments. Evidence of good character has been rejected on the excuse Horatio Donkin put forward to counter the claim that the known integrity of Henry Sidgwick and his fellow-founders of the Society for Psychical Research should lift them above suspicion. 'In all scientific inquiries', Donkin laid down, 'the good faith of individuals concerned should form no part of the data on which the conclusion is to rest.'

In many areas of science, a case could be made for this attitude. The real test of a scientist's honesty, Donkin was arguing, should be provided in repetitions of his experiments to find if the same results are obtained. Manifestly this should not have applied to tests of phenomena such as table-turning, where the results might depend upon the psychic energies of a group, coming from some as yet undiscovered source, erratic and undisciplined. It was, and remains, necessary to check the credentials of a researcher if, as in de Gasparin's case, the accounts leave no doubt that if there had been trickery, he must himself have been the perpetrator.

What would have been de Gasparin's motive? He had an honoured name as a liberal statesman who had chosen exile rather than be false to his principles. Although a freethinker and a long-time opponent of ultramontane Catholicism, he was not sorry to have the opportunity to tease the Vatican, which had condemned table-turning as having truck with the devil; yet he could have done this more effectively by finding an explanation for the movements of the tables which would fit the scientific preconceptions of the period. His book makes it clear that he and Thury were careful, dispassionate investigators, compelled by what they witnessed to accept that it could not be accounted for by any of the known physical forces.

There is another reason why, in connection with psychical research, the good faith of investigators needs to be scrutinised. It may turn out that *bad* faith is involved, arising out of the strong feelings which the subject generates.

Most men and women who engaged in table-turning thought of it simply as a pastime. Others, following the method improvised by the Fox sisters, asked the table questions, and sometimes found it would reply by making rapping sounds, or lifting a leg – once for yes, twice for no. Occasionly the answers appeared to demonstrate that they came from the dead. Out of this grew spiritualism: originally simply as recognition of life of some kind after death; later, with a capital 'S', as a religion.

Michael Faraday had grown up as a member of a fundamentalist Protestant cult. 'Spirits' were an abomination to him. If tables moved, he felt sure, it must be because of some physical force. He realised he could not claim that conscious physical force was being used. Too many of his friends and acquaintances would have resented the slur. Faraday fell back on a hypothesis put forward by the physiologist William Benjamin Carpenter – 'quasi-involuntary muscular action'. Table-turners were moving the tables with hands or feet without being aware of what they were doing.

It would not be enough, Faraday realised, to present this explanation unless he could support it with evidence. Accordingly he set up an experiment which demonstrated to his satisfaction that if a group sat around a table with a loose top, they might move the top without being aware that they were exerting pressure.

To advance this as the explanation for table-turning was irresponsible. It did not begin to account for the way in which tables, as distinct from table-tops, were reported as moving. But Faraday was at the height of his career. Scientists who shared his views felt they did not need to investigate for themselves, as they could cite his experiment. It is still often cited, to this day, as if it had been a genuine test.

Faraday may be acquitted of deliberate dishonesty; not so Sir David Brewster. He had made his name in the field of optics, and is credited with the invention of the kaleidoscope, but he was best known, much as the American science writer Martin Gardner is today, as an assiduously sceptical critic of what he considered to be pseudoscience of any kind.

Brewster had picked up the technique from Eusebe Salverte, who in *The Occult Sciences*, published in 1829, had re-examined many well-known instances of the miraculous in history not, he insisted, to discredit them, but to suggest that the priests or magicians responsible for them had been using scientific methods in secret and 'with the greatest care, concealing that knowledge from all other men'. Priests, for example, must have found a chemical which in the annual ceremony liquefies the blood of the martyr St Januarius on his saint's day. Naturally they were not going to let this be known to the faithful in Naples.

Although some of Salverte's speculations were reasonable, others were distinctly far-fetched. When he described how Apollonius, watching a Hindu procession wending its way to a temple, felt the ground moving under his feet like 'a boisterous sea', Salverte suggested that a gang of workmen had been employed underneath to lift and jiggle a platform of earth, on which Apollonius would be standing. To claim that such an operation could be 'readily effected with the aid of a mechanism' was hard enough to swallow; his argument that ostensibly supernatural events throughout history could be explained away by the existence of self-perpetuating secret societies, including priests and alchemists, was even less plausible. How could a secret involving gangs of workmen have been kept for so long?

Nevertheless Salverte's apparently well-researched survey was useful to those scientists who, like Arago, were seeking to extricate all the branches of science from the grip of the Church – still a powerful influence, owing to its hold on education. And it was also useful to David Brewster who, as it had not then been published in English, was able to draw on it freely in his *Letters on Natural Magic*, published in 1832.

Daniel Home

When the medium Daniel Dunglas Home arrived in London from the United States in 1855, Brewster was one of the first to make an appointment to witness his solo table-turning act. What he saw staggered him, as he told a number of his friends. It was 'quite inexplicable by fraud, or by any physical laws with which they were acquainted', he assured Lord Dunraven. Yet a few months later in a letter to the *Morning Advertiser* Brewster claimed that as he had not been allowed to examine the table, he would conjecture that its movements were 'done by the agency of Mr Home's feet'. He had seen enough to satisfy himself that they could all have been produced in that way, 'and to prove that some of them, at least, had such an origin'.

Dunraven, Thomas Trollope and others who had heard

Brewster on the subject of what he had witnessed at his sittings with Home protested, to no avail. A casual reader of the *Morning Advertiser*, knowing of Brewster's reputation as a scientist, would have been likely to assume Brewster's first remarks must have been misheard.

Not until after Brewster's death did an account appear which he had written at the time of the sittings, incautiously published by his daughter in a memoir of her father. In it he made clear that he had been given every facility to investigate both the medium and the table. It had made unaccountable movements, actually rising off the floor 'when no hand was upon it'. When a larger table was brought in, it made similar movements. A small hand-bell, placed on the carpet, rang when nothing could have touched it; it then 'came over to me and placed itself in my hand'. Disembodied hands appeared, which could be grasped, melting away under the grasp. 'We could give no explanation', Brewster admitted, 'and could not conjecture how they could be produced by any kind of mechanism.'

Evidently Brewster had quickly realised that if he were to stand over his initial judgment, his reputation as the leading hard-headed science writer would be jeopardised. That he should have been prepared to lie to protect his reputation is not in retrospect surprising. He had borrowed from Salverte to the point of plagiarism. Twice he was detected using his anonymous column in the *North British Review* to insist that Sir David Brewster should be credited with inventions for which he was not responsible.

Charles Wheatstone, who had been regarded as the inventor of the stereoscope – one of the articles claimed – had wrongly been given the credit. He had merely carried into operation 'the essential principle which had been enunciated by others'. Unluckily for Brewster, the article caught William Benjamin Carpenter's eye. Guessing who had written it, Carpenter exhumed what Brewster had written at the time Wheatstone's account of his invention first appeared, saying that the importance of Wheatstone's contribution was 'impossible to overestimate'.

Undeterred, Brewster used another of his anonymous *North British Review* articles to seek to appropriate the credit previously given to Robert Stevenson for having discovered the

type of lens which had been adopted for use in lighthouses:
'The hundreds of lives which were lost on the Scottish coast
from the imperfections of the lighthouses during the ten years
that the engineer refused to listen to Sir David Brewster's
recommendations of the lens apparatus lie at the conscience
door of the engineer.' On the strength of this recommendation
Brewster proceeded to petition the Treasury in the hope of
obtaining a grant.

Stevenson's sons had no difficulty in proving that the story
was a fabrication. Brewster did not receive a grant. Neither,
though, did his tactics bring him into discredit. They were
ordinarily employed, after all, against the common enemy,
resurgent superstition. His career ended not, as it might well
have done, with a gaol sentence for false pretences or perjury,
but with his installation as Principal of Edinburgh University.
A hall there still bears his name, and he is occasionally
referred to with respect – indeed with reverence. In 1985 a
book was published under the title *'Martyr of Science': Sir David
Brewster*, presenting him as (to quote one reviewer, R.V.
Jones) 'an outstanding product of the Scottish enlightenment'
and 'a true physicist, both good and prolific'. Prolific he
certainly was. Good he most certainly was not.

That sceptics should still cite Brewster – as Trevor Hall has
done in his biographical sketch of Home – to deride Home is
revealing. It shows just how difficult it is to find better
evidence against the medium. For a quarter of a century
Home gave sittings, sometimes two or three a week, year in
year out, except for occasional periods when his powers
seemed to ebb. Sometimes they were 'seances', in the usual
sense of the term. Home, himself a spiritualist, would give
information to sitters which they believed came from deceased
friends and relatives. More commonly he practised physical
mediumship: table-turning with (as Brewster had found)
additional effects, such as disembodied hands, or invisible
hands which played musical instruments (playing them,
according to most accounts, sentimentally but well).

Although effects varied from sitting to sitting, the movements of the tables were ordinarily the main feature. Rapping
sounds would be heard coming from the table or from
different parts of the room. The table would then begin to
shudder before moving around, rearing up on two legs, and

often floating. Occasionally Home himself would levitate.

Inevitably people who had not attended a sitting, and who found it impossible to believe what they were told by friends who had, were inclined to assume that Home must be an exceptionally brilliant conjuror. The dozens of accounts of the effects Home was able to produce render this explanation untenable. Even if he had been able to use both hands and feet, he still could not have moved, let along raised, some of the heavy dining room tables with which he was confronted. The use of gadgetry to lift them was ruled out by the fact that he was continually giving sittings in houses he had never entered, in rooms he had never before seen, and he had no assistant who might have helped him rig up the necessary contraptions.

Wealth could not have been Home's aim. He took no fee, and declined to pawn such presents as he accepted, even at those times when his powers left him, and he found it hard to make ends meet. By far the most impressive aspect of his career, though, was that his sittings, unlike those of the great majority of the mediums who followed in his wake, were given in light good enough for the eight or nine people present (rarely more) to see precisely what he was doing. Usually he was doing nothing, sitting dazed as if in a trance, at a distance from the table and the musical instruments (often brought by doubters, who suspected that Home must use his own, with musical boxes inside).

Most of the men and women who left accounts were doubters before their first sitting. Some had made no secret of their scepticism, and were astonished when Home urged them to take any precautions they might think necessary – though as the sittings were held in the light, precautions of the kind so often applied with mediums later, such as tying them up, were superfluous.

In one other respect the sittings differed from those of mediums in the late Victorian era: their social composition. They attracted a number of the great Royal Houses of Europe – Home was a frequent and, as the memoirs of the period show, an honoured guest both of the Emperor Napoleon and of the Tsar Nicholas – and a representative cross-section of the Establishment of the time: statesmen, members of the profes-sions, writers, journalists. When in the late 1850s he was 'taken up' socially by Mrs Milner-Gibson, wife of the President of the Board of Trade, the celebrities who came to her evenings included Robert Chambers (editor of the *Encyclopaedia*), Bulwer-Lytton, Edwin Arnold, Monckton Milnes, Landseer and Alexei Tolstoy. 'The piano played with no one near it,' Tolstoy wrote to tell his wife. 'Home was raised from the ground; and I clasped his feet while he floated in the air above our heads.' A disembodied hand had dissolved when he grasped it. A hand-bell had sailed around the room, ringing.

The effect, Tolstoy felt, was overwhelming. The accounts by other respected citizens in Europe and America tell the same tale. It was all very well for people who had never attended a sitting, Thackeray – who himself had attended in a deeply sceptical frame of mind – told one scoffer: 'Had you seen what I have witnessed, you would hold a different opinion.' All but a handful of those who attended came to the same conclusion. On no occasion, during a sitting, was anybody able to detect Home in any action which might have been interpreted as cheating.

Towards the close of his career, Home was investigated by scientists. Although he had agreed some years before to submit to tests by Faraday, Faraday had insisted as a precondition that he should not merely renounce his belief in the existence of spirits, but admit they were 'utterly contemptible'. Understandably Home refused. In Russia in the early 1870s he participated in experiments with Alexander von Boutlerow, Professor of Chemistry at the University of St Petersburg, in which he was able to increase the tension on a dynamometer by 50 per cent – also convincing one of Boutlerow's colleagues, Nicholas Wagner, who had attended 'with the greatest incredulity and disgust'. On his return to Britain, Home obtained similar results in tests by William Crookes, witnessed by William Huggins, subsequently President of the Royal Society, and the lawyer Serjeant Cox.

There was no lack of malicious gossip about Home in his lifetime, with suggestions as to how he was deceiving sitters with the help of a telescopic fishing rod concealed in his jacket and other devices. Compared with the eye-witness descriptions, they only serve to make the case that his powers were genuine look even stronger. Biographers and commentators since have similarly been unable to find any seriously damag-

Figure 4 Experimenting with this gadget, when Crookes put the
whole weight of his body on the mahogany board it
registered only 2 lbs on the balance. Daniel Home, with his
fingers on the table end of the board, was able to make the
other end oscillate 'as if by successive waves of the psychic
force', the balance registering a 'pull' of 6 lbs.

ing material. Perhaps the most eloquent testimonial to him is
Trevor Hall's, published in 1984. Although Hall's knowledge
of the peccadilloes of Victorian mediums is unrivalled, he has
been unable to find anything which can seriously damage
Home's reputation.

Table-turning sittings were later to fall out of fashion as a
pastime: partly because sitting around in the darkness, which
most mediums (unlike Home) required, waiting for things to
happen, was tedious; partly because the invention of the ouija
board meant that the services of a table to answer questions
could be dispensed with. Nevertheless table-turning has often
been tried out since by psychical researchers, curious to
observe what happens. One feature has particularly interested
investigators. The movements, Sir Oliver Lodge recalled, 'are
characteristic of the action of a living being'. The tables
behave oddly, 'but intelligently and capriciously, just as live
things do'.

In Belfast during the First World War Sir William Barrett
went to a sitting with the Goligher circle, then being investigated by W.J. Crawford, a lecturer in engineering at Queen's
University. In good light, Barrett and a sceptical friend of his

were invited to see if they could make a table which was floating a foot above the floor descend to floor level again. 'This both of us found it impossible to do,' he reported. 'Though we laid hold of the sides of the table it resisted our strongest efforts to push it down.' When he sat on it, it tipped him off.

Whately Smith, invalided out of the Royal Flying Corps after a crash, had a similar experience. A scientist, he had become curious about psychic phenomena, and was later to devote himself to meticulous research into ESP. In his report on the Goligher circle he explained that he, too, had tried to hold the floating table: 'by dint of great exertion I could prevent it from moving in any one direction and could keep it steady for a second or so, but it instantly moved in some other direction, the force changing with great rapidity'.

In 1964 Kenneth Batcheldor, principal clinical psychologist for a group of Devonshire hospitals, and some friends decided one evening to try to see if they could get results from table-turning sessions. In time they began to get movements, and tilts. They, too, found that the table resisted pressure. Eventually they obtained other effects, including levitations, and the table duly tipped off anybody who tried to sit on it. Over a period of more than twenty years the experiments have been carefully monitored, not to prevent the use of physical force but to detect it. A number of other groups working along similar lines have been obtaining similar results.

Scientists are ordinarily expected to provide an explanation for phenomena which are as well attested as table-turning. As Lodge put it in 1894, following his own investigation, 'any person without invincible prejudice who had had the same experience would come to the same broad conclusion, that things hitherto held impossible do actually occur'. The reports of recent trials conducted by people who are clearly motivated only by a desire to achieve a better understanding of the forces involved make scepticism progressively harder to sustain. Yet, as Crookes found from early on in his research, 'the power producing the phenomena was not merely a blind force, but was associated with or governed by intelligence'. Threatened by the revival of vitalism, biologists are in no mood to contemplate the probability that tables can move without physical pressure, and capriciously – as if alive – at that.

Psychical Research

Alfred Russel Wallace's reminder to sceptics who pointed to evidence that some mediums had been detected in fraud as their reason for dismissing the findings of psychical research – that an argument is not answered until it has been answered at its best – was one of the promptings which led to the founding of the Society for Psychical Research, in 1882, with Henry Sidgwick as President and Frederic Myers and Edmund Gurney as joint Hon. Secretaries. Its aim was to scrutinise and test the evidence so scientifically that doubtful cases could be excluded. Only the best would remain to be answered. In this it could soon claim some modest successes. Some of the positive results of investigations of psychics – individuals who claimed to have telepathic or clairvoyant abilities – have yet to be seriously challenged. Multiple personality, previously rejected as an occultist superstition, attained psychiatric status. Considerable progress was made towards a better understanding of apparitions. Yet the mainstream work of the SPR and its American counterpart – the investigation of mediumship – though it produced striking results, made little discernible impression on the public and none on orthodox science.

The research started with two obvious handicaps. David Hume's belief that the laws of nature were never broken had congealed into the dogma that they *could* never be broken. Communication and action at a distance, by this time being described as telepathy and telekinesis, consequently could not occur. 'Neither the testimony of all the Fellows of the Royal Society', Sir William Barrett recalled hearing the physicist Hermann von Helmholtz assert, 'nor the evidence of my own senses, could ever lead me to believe in what is clearly impossible.'

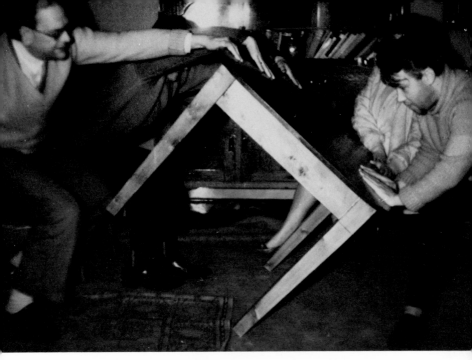

7 & 8 Convincing table-turning photographs are difficult to accomplish. Film with synchronised sound-track has recently been taken of Ken Batcheldor's sessions, and these are all but impossible to fake. *Above*, Batcheldor with Bill Chick, taken by infra-red light; *below*, more recently the pair are snapped by ordinary flash while working in total darkness.

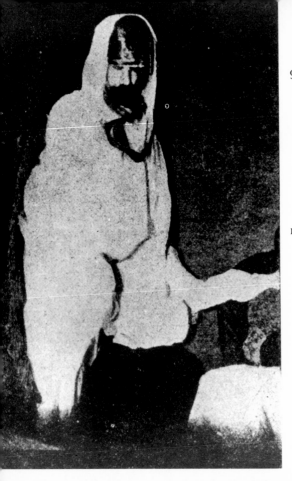

9 *Left*, witnesses saw the form of 'Bien Boa' actually materialising from the mouth of Marthe Béraud, and testified that there was no way in which an accomplice could have entered the room.

10 *Below*, Mirabelli could conjure up apparitions sufficiently consistently for this scene, of a dead poet seated between the two astonished witnesses, to be photographed.

Belief in this dogma was powerfully reinforced by disbelief in spirits. Spiritualism gave sceptics the excuse to follow the course Faraday had taken, and refuse to investigate the phenomena on the ground that to do so would commit them to taking seriously a palpable superstition. Some members of the psychical research societies felt the same way, and from time to time were given justification by the discovery of fraud. Nevertheless a few spiritualist mediums, two in particular, came through very careful investigation with records which still stand up to scrutiny.

Surveying the evidence for the Boston medium Mrs Leonora Piper in 1898 William James, who had initially been suspicious of her, had to admit that after fifteen years – during which many of her sitters would have been delighted to expose her, and detectives had been employed to catch her if she tried to collect information about them – 'not only has there not been one single suspicious circumstance remarked, but not one suggestion has ever been made from any quarter which might tend positively to explain how the medium, living the apparent life she leads, could possibly collect information about so many sitters by natural means'.

The investigation of Mrs Osborne Leonard, a London

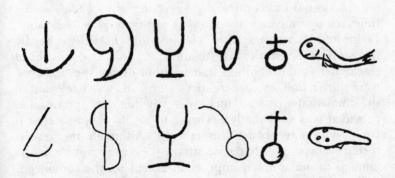

Figure 5 The drawings in the top line were the targets in a series of six; those in the bottom line were the guesses of the subject in a telepathy trial. They were published in the SPR's *Proceedings* in 1884.

medium, was even more thorough and more protracted. To ensure that she was not picking up information, consciously or unconsciously, from her sitters, enabling her to guess their thoughts, 'proxy sitters' were sent to her by the SPR. They did not know the individuals they were standing proxy for, and consequently could not give anything away which would help her. Yet her proportion of 'hits', correct pieces of information which came to her through her spirit 'control', compared to the 'misses' was consistently high – very much higher than the rate chance guesswork could have achieved – over a thirty year period.

Unluckily for their prospects of winning wider recognition, both women suffered from a common hazard of mediumship, the unpredictable behaviour of their spirit 'controls'. Most spiritualist mediums in their trances surrendered their own personalities to a 'control' or 'guide' who would often dictate the course a seance was to take, extending or terminating it at whim. On balance they were an unprepossessing crew. The best-known of them, John King, claimed to have been a buccaneer in his lifetime on earth. Mrs Piper's first 'control', 'Dr Phinuit', said that he had been a doctor in France. Inquiry revealed that no such person had practised at the time and place he had referred to, showing that the reliability of the information did not depend on the trustworthiness of the control.

Mrs Leonard's 'control' was a young girl, 'Feda', some-times co-operative, sometimes as capricious as the tables Lodge and Barrett described. Her infantile chatter was hardly the stuff of scientific investigation. A dedicated psychical researcher could maintain that whether or not the 'controls' were spirits, and if so, where they came from, was irrelevant to the immediate issue, which was whether the information provided was sufficiently accurate to justify claiming that it could only have come through psi. Although the results certainly bore out that contention, they were not dramatic enough to make much impression except on the convinced.

Physical mediumship was a very different matter. Even Helmholtz, if he could have been induced to attend, might have been shaken by the spectacle of a human body gradually forming out of a medium, becoming to all intents real, to the touch as well as to the sight, before vanishing again. The case

for ectoplasmic materialisations is in certain respects decidedly stronger than for mental mediumship. It is supported not
only by detailed records of experiments in which the precautions taken to prevent deception were described and testified
to by scientists acting as independent witnesses. There are
also a great many photographs to lend confirmation to the
testimony.

Many different types of materialisation were reported, from
the disembodied hands which Home's sitters saw and grasped
and felt melting away, to the 'apports' which would turn up at
spiritualist seances – objects which materialise as if out of thin
air, or appear to be translocated through walls from another
room. Understandably the kind which aroused most interest
were full-form human beings such as those which Kate Cook
produced for William Crookes and other witnesses in London,
and Marthe Béraud for Charles Richet in Algiers. The baffled
Richet, a physiologist and a staunch materialist, coined the
term ectoplasm for the material out of which they were made,
sometimes initially invisible, becoming diaphanous and eventually so closely resembling human flesh as not to be detect-
ably different to sight or to touch.

Inevitably sceptics claimed that the materialised form must
be the medium in disguise. As mediums usually retired behind
a curtained-off recess, the 'cabinet', at the beginning and end
of their performance, suspicion was inevitable. Kate's investigators – Crookes, Wallace, Alexander Aksakov – were sure
that there was no deception. The spirit form that emerged,
'Katie King', was taller than the medium and different in such
details as not having her ears pierced for ear-rings. 'Katie
King's' dresses, too, were different; yet within seconds of her
retiring behind the curtain Kate could be seen dressed as she
had arrived for the seance, with no trace of the dress worn by
the materialised form. Occasionally Kate and 'Katie' could be
seen at the same time.

The most convincing evidence for physical mediumship in
this period comes from the reports of the investigations of
Eusapia Palladino. She, too, quite often produced materialised forms, but they were not what most of her investigators
were looking for. Her speciality was telekinesis, action at a
distance.

From the lowest stratum of Italian society and illiterate,

Eusapia nevertheless was endowed with a power which 'attracts to her the articles of furniture which surround her, lifts them up, holds them suspended in the air', Ercole Chiaia, her first investigator, claimed in a challenge to Italian scientists to come and see for themselves. She could produce raps, notes on musical instruments and impressions of her hands in clay. Ordinarily the 'pseudopods' which emerged from her to move the distant objects were not visible, yet they could be felt by sitters, who would find themselves nudged or pinched as if by an invisible child, and a mischievous one – their shoelaces would be untied, their spectacles taken off their noses. Sometimes a pseudopod did become visible as an additional limb stretching out from her.

Cesare Lombroso reluctantly agreed to investigate. The leading psychiatrist in Italy, the founder of criminology, he was a follower of Comte, a hard-line rationalist. What he saw shook his scepticism. 'The facts exist', he felt compelled to admit, 'and I boast of being a slave to facts.'

For a quarter of a century Eusapia was subjected to investigation after investigation in a series of tests held in Italy, France and other European countries, attended by many of the most eminent scientists of the time. The records of some of the tests show just how stringent the precautions were. In a series conducted in Paris between 1905 and 1908 by eminent scientists – Arsène d'Arsonval, Gilbert Ballet, Henri Bergson, Pierre and Marie Curie, Jean-Baptiste Perrin among them – monitoring instruments were used which were designed not merely to register if physical force was applied, but which would register it in another room, so that it would make no difference if the sitters with Eusapia allowed themselves to be distracted. In these conditions she provided her stock repertoire of raps, the playing of instruments and the movements of distant objects. Playful invisible hands untied the scientists' cravats and pulled their hair. A stool from outside the circle advanced to Pierre Curie, and made as if to climb up his leg. A small table floated in over his shoulder making 'a pretty curve' as it did so.

Conjurors were by this time alleging that scientists were even more gullible than the public. Following the Paris tests three men well versed in conjuring, Wortley Baggally, Hereward Carrington and Everard Feilding, were despatched by the SPR to Naples, where they made no secret of their conviction that she was a disguised member of the profession, and they were going to prove it. They failed.

The great majority of the scientists who participated in the trials of Eusapia either accepted that the phenomena were psychic, or agreed that they could not be accounted for by any known forces. A few who admitted they had been unable to detect trickery maintained that it must have been used, as telekinesis was contrary to the laws of nature. Two investigators claimed actually to have caught Eusapia cheating. The accounts of their exposures are illuminating.

In 1895 a recently recruited member of the SPR, Richard Hodgson, claimed that he had detected Eusapia in tests at Cambridge releasing her hands and feet from the custody of her investigators, so that she might make use of them.

Even before he had witnessed a Eusapia session, Hodgson had claimed that this was how she did her tricks. Patiently, Lodge, Richet and others who had investigated her pointed out it was *not* how she made objects move. Certainly she would try to free her hands or feet from control, if she could. In her trances, she claimed, she had no conscious control over what she was doing, and it was up to her investigators to make sure she did not elude them. They had made sure, and in the process found that her hands and feet, if allowed to, made sympathetic movements. If she wanted to move an object at a distance she would 'make a little sudden push with her hand in this direction, and immediately afterwards the object moves', Lodge explained. When the accordion was being played, her fingers were moving appropriately. The process reminded him of 'the twitching of a dog's legs when he is supposed to be dreaming that he is chasing a hare'. Sceptics claimed that the movements were synchronous because Eusapia was using a very fine thread, which she had managed to attach to the objects she proposed to move. Apart from the difficulty of keeping even the finest thread invisible from investigators sitting beside her, no known type of thread could have been used for the pushing motion.

Hodgson knew, therefore, what to expect. Yet he allowed Eusapia to free her feet from control, insisting that this confirmed his view that she was a fraud. Sidgwick, repelled by materialising mediums, was quick to agree, adding that it was a rule of the Society that a medium once exposed should not again be investigated. Even Myers concurred, though on his own rather than the Society's behalf he later attended another trial, and agreed that fraud could not be the explanation.

The second 'exposure' was in the United States. Eusapia had been brought there in 1909 by Hereward Carrington, and a number of trials were arranged, including one presided over by Hugo Münsterberg, Professor of Psychology at Harvard. Münsterberg had made very clear his attitude to psychical research. 'The psychologist', he had asserted, 'insists that every perception of occurrence outside one's own body and every influence beyond one's own organism must be in-termediated by an uninterrupted chain of physical processes.' He had imagined it would be a simple matter to catch Eusapia out. He was disconcerted at their first session to witness a quick succession of events he could not account for.

Hardly three minutes passed before, 'in strong electric light', the table had begun to tilt, and eventually to rise into the air. Then, the room being darkened but with light enough remaining to see the faces of the sitters, 'a strong breeze blew suddenly from the cabinet' – the curtain, hanging a foot behind Eusapia's chair, actually bellied out over them. Throughout this part of the performance, Münsterberg in-sisted, her hands, knees and feet were controlled. Yet when the curtain was put back, a small table behind it 'was thrown up and fell down on the floor with a loud crash'. Later the table began to creep out from the cabinet into the sitting-room, the guitar gave out some tones, and Eusapia's immedi-ate left-hand and right-hand neighbours were touched, some-times on the arm, sometimes on the back.

Repeating the performance Pierre Curie had described, the table 'began to climb up from the floor and to reach as high as the elbow of one of us'. Münsterberg, who had stationed himself behind the medium, 'distinctly felt how the curtain bulged out with strong energy'. He was nonplussed. He knew she could not have an assistant working for her. The two men controlling her hands and feet were reliable, and a search had discovered no hidden gadgets. Still, he felt sure there must be some explanation. For the next session, he arranged that somebody would be allowed in secretly to install himself behind the curtain, to find out how the effects were obtained.

Münsterberg was to relate what happened in the *Metropolitan Magazine*, in an article entitled 'My Friends, The Spiritualists', brimming over with goodwill towards Eusapia and Carrington. He had allowed her an hour to give her performance, he explained. While she was giving it he sat beside her, making sure she did not loosen her hands to make use of them. Nevertheless his arm was pinched through the curtain, as if by a thumb and fingers – 'it was most uncanny'. Eventually the moment he was waiting for arrived. Eusapia gave 'a wild yelling scream'. The assistant behind the curtain had seen a foot stretching out under her chair, and had caught it. 'Her scream indicated that she knew that at last she was trapped and her glory shattered.'

Was it? Exhilarated by the success of his ruse, Münsterberg was ready to give Eusapia every credit. 'Her achievement was splendid', he went on. 'She had lifted her unshod foot to the height of my arm when she touched me under cover of the curtain, without changing the position of her body. When her foot played thumb and fingers, the game was also neat throughout.' After all, he benignly concluded, 'she is a wonderful woman'.

Wonderful indeed! A sceptic who read Münsterberg's article, Stanley L. Krebs, pointed out that if it was an accurate account of what had happened, not only would Eusapia's leg have to be 'articulated at the knee, upon a motionless hip, making a rotation of about 135°, as well as an elongation of about double its length'; the foot would have had to be transformed into a hand capable of grasping him between thumb and fingers. How, Krebs wanted to know, had she done so clever a trick?

Years later, James Hyslop, who ran the American Society of Psychical Research, confirmed that the 'exposure' had been a failure. Unable to accept the evidence for physical mediumship, Hyslop had refused to have anything to do with Eusapia, and had been unwilling to come out in her support at the time, but he had found that two of Münsterberg's colleagues on the investigation disagreed with Münsterberg's verdict.

Even without their testimony, Münsterberg's case against Eusapia falls apart. How could his arm have been pinched from behind the curtain, unless by a pseudopod? Far from exposing her, he had given her one of her most impressive testimonials – coming as it did from him. Yet the assumption that she was caught cheating has lingered, so that she has rarely been given any credit by parapsychologists.

Some of the allegations were based on a misapprehension. In the Paris trials one observer thought he saw a fine thread stretch between her fingers. He could not have been expected to know that what appeared to be filaments were continually being reported in investigations of psychics. They were visible, but not tangible, investigators had found, as if they were minute beams of light emanating from the hands. As for the charge that she was for ever trying to free her hands or feet, this was no more cheating than it is for a subject under hypnosis obeying when told to play some trick to cheat his neighbour – one of the stock devices used by club hypnotists to amuse audiences. Admittedly some researchers have argued that cheating is cheating even if, in a trance, it is committed unconsciously. The fact remains that as Eusapia's investigators were aware of what she would seek to do in advance, they were the cheats, if they took advantage of her.

Marthe Béraud, later better known by her pseudonym 'Eva C.', has also been retrospectively smeared. This has not been difficult, as the photographs of her materialisations, examined without reference to the accompanying records, appear bogus. Her 'full forms' look like people in fancy dress. It is natural now, as it was in her day, to suspect that she used to emerge from the 'cabinet' in disguise or that she had smuggled in an accomplice. In her later years, when the materialisations were often two-dimensional, they look like cardboard cut-outs. Yet nobody reading the reports and comparing them with the photographs can seriously maintain that she could have faked them unaided. The precautions taken, testified to by a host of scientists who were not themselves psychical researchers, and who were often sceptics, rule out conjuring tricks.

In some ways the record of the brothers Willy and Rudi Schneider in the 1920s was even more impressive. Their PK abilities were carefully documented, as Anita Gregory has shown in *The Strange Case of Rudi Schneider*. Some of the reports, notably that of Thomas Mann, show just how meticulous the precautions were and how impressive the phenomena. Yet already, psychical researchers were beginning to turn against physical mediumship. Some, notably the Sidgwicks, had always mistrusted it. Podmore had made no secret of his assumption that it could only be fraudulent. Ectoplasm repelled others, particularly when it emerged from mediums' orifices to take human shape.

This in turn has made the evidence from the era for straightforward psychokinesis seem less trustworthy. Some of the ablest members of the societies for psychical research in America, Britain and elsewhere have allowed themselves to be put in a false position by sceptics within the societies, even more than by outside critics. The impression has grown that on balance it is safer not to rely upon any of the evidence from the pre-Rhine era, as it was too tainted with fraud by the mediums to be trusted. This leaves Lodge, Richet and the others branded as dupes, which would be bad enough. Yet it needs to be emphasised that if the trials with Eusapia, 'Eva C.', the Schneider brothers and several more were fraudently conducted, their investigators must have been involved. There simply was no way in which the mediums themselves could have cheated. If proof were needed, it was given by the inability even of Houdini to provide any plausible explanation of how, say, 'Eva C.' produced the materialisations he witnessed.

The consequence has been that the societies have all but abandoned this line of research, which in some ways was the most productive of all. The materialising medium, Jule Eisenbud has remarked, is today regarded as the Whore of Babylon. The search for fresh evidence about the species 'is the last thing on the agenda of today's parapsychologist'.

Ectoplasm remains a mystery, and one which parapsychologists are unlikely to try to solve. Yet Gustave Geley, one of the ablest of the psychical researchers in Europe in the years following the First World War, offered a hypothesis which provides it with a possible evolutionary passport. At the chrysalis stage, he observed, certain insects undergo a curious change, hystolysis. The insect's body is dematerialised, melting into a kind of 'uniform pap, a simple amorphous substance in which the majority of organic and specific distinctions disappear'. Scientists had admitted themselves baffled by hystolysis; Geley thought it might be explained by 'supernatural physiology', partially disintegrating the organism before reconstituting it in a new form. That psi may account for the dematerialisation remains no more than a surmise; conventional science has yet to offer any plausible alternative.

J. B. Rhine

By the early 1930s it had become clear that no matter how convincing the proof of mental and physical mediumship might be to anybody who accepted communication and action at a distance, it was not making the slightest impression on those who did not accept this, and who were in effective control in the academic citadel. In 1934, however, they were confronted by an unexpected threat to their peace of mind in the form most feared by academics: a Trojan horse within the walls. Joseph Banks Rhine's monograph, *Extra-Sensory Perception*, presented results from hundreds of trials showing that a few individuals had the ability to guess what was displayed on concealed cards, and the successful guessers were neither mediums nor spiritualists but college students from Duke University.

Rhine and his assistants had begun to try to separate out ESP into its component parts: telepathy, precognition and retrocognition. The members of the Society for Psychical Research in its early years had been chiefly concerned with telepathy – psi communications between minds. Clairvoyance – psi perception of objects or events – was suspect, largely because of its fairground image. Frank Podmore, the Society's chief historian and publicist, reflected their feelings when he grudgingly admitted that clairvoyance might exist, but dismissed it as unimportant.

The research at Duke finally established clairvoyance in its own right with the help of simple tests using playing cards, or the specially designed Zener cards, twenty-five to a pack, with five different symbols. As the 'sender' or 'agent' turned the cards, the subjects would make their guesses as to which Zener symbols were being shown. Chance expectation was five 'hits' in each run through the pack. Some subjects scored consistently higher, averaging, say, seven hits. Anybody might do that by chance occasionally, but the odds against somebody doing it consistently mounted with each successive trial, suggesting that the guesswork was being reinforced by

ESP. If the sender was looking at each card as he turned it over, telepathy between sender and subject could be the explanation. Some subjects at Duke did just as well when the sender was *not* looking at the cards, and this ruled out telepathy, letting in clairvoyance.

Later, Rhine and his team at Duke were to embark on trials designed to test for precognition – to finding out whether subjects could guess what the next card to be turned up would be, at a rate higher than chance expectation – and for psychokinesis, the term Rhine preferred to telekinesis, and which, like 'ESP', soon caught on. These, too, were successful. It was the telepathy/clairvoyance testing, though, that took the fancy of the public. As trials were both easy and inexpensive to set up, psychologists in other universities were soon repeating the Duke experiments, some out of scepticism in the hope of being able to report negative findings.

Disappointment awaited them. In many parts of the world test subjects were found who scored significantly higher than chance expectation would explain. Sceptics began to insinuate that the statistical apparatus which was used must be faulty. The President of the American Institute of Mathematical Studies replied that if the experiments had been properly performed, the statistical analysis could not be faulted. Had the experiments been properly performed? Perhaps only the successful ones were being used to provide the data? That charge, too, was easily rebutted.

Another accusation sounded more damaging: that the symbols could be seen through the backs of the cards if the cards were held up to the light. This was true of some packs made commercially, when ESP guessing games became a popular pastime. It had not been true of the packs used in the initial trials, and even if it had been, many of the tests precluded peeking. In some, the subjects were not in the same room. In others, when they were asked to guess down through a pack the cards were not turned over until the run was finished.

Examining these and other criticisms, the psychologist Hans Eysenck, a hard-line behaviourist who had himself been sceptical about ESP, felt bound to admit in his *Sense and Nonsense in Psychology* that unless there was a gigantic conspiracy involving thirty university departments and hundreds of respected (and sceptical) scientists all over the world, 'the only conclusion an unbiassed observer can come to must be that there does exist a small number of people who obtain knowledge existing either in other people's minds, or in the outer world, by means as yet unknown to science'. Parapsychologists, as psychical researchers who concentrated on controlled experiments on the approved scientific model had now begun to call themselves, were understandably grateful for Eysenck's unsolicited testimonial. Behaviourism was then dominant in academic psychology, with B.F. Skinner as its prophet, and Skinner had been one of the most contemptuous critics of the research at Duke. That a leading behaviourist should have accepted the evidence for ESP was most welcome.

It was not simply the improbability of such a world-wide academic conspiracy that told against the theory that the results were being obtained by cheating. Cheating could also be ruled out, on so massive a scale, on the strength of a contention made a century earlier by Richard Whately. Whately had made a name for himself with a spoof, *Historical Doubts Relative to Napoleon Buonaparte*, in which he argued with disturbing cogency that Napoleon did not exist – though he was still alive, on St Helena, when the book appeared in 1819. Whately's real aim was to demonstrate how easy it was for a sceptic to demonstrate that Jesus never existed. (For this, and for his textbook on political economy eulogising *laissez-faire*, a grateful Whig government was later to make him Archbishop of Dublin.) Sceptical though Whately himself was about miracles, owing to the use the Vatican had made of them, he insisted upon one important reservation. 'When many coincide in their testimony, where no previous concert can have taken place, the probability resulting from this concurrence does not rest upon the supposed veracity of each, considered separately, but on the improbability of such agreement taking place by chance', he warned his fellow-sceptics. Even if each of the individuals was unworthy of credit, 'the chances would be infinite against their all agreeing in the same falsehood'.

If simple cheating was the reason why some subjects obtained positive results, many of them would surely have had a higher average of 'hits' – ten, fifteen, or even more. That so many, with very few exceptions, should have settled for comparatively low scores was inconceivable.

The few exceptions, too, tended to be in exceptional circumstances, as in the case of an experiment which John Langdon-Davis and Eric Dingwall made on the spur of the moment while they were staying in Spain. The cook and the maid, who were sisters in their employment, were under notice, as the cook had been found to be mentally unstable. Mrs Langdon-Davis suggested that before they left it might be worth seeing if they, and another servant, had any ESP ability, by giving them a Zener card test. The results were statistically staggering. The three of them made 1,900 guesses, of which 855 were correct, an average of over eleven per pack. Compared with the chance five 'hits' the odds against chance were astronomical.

Dingwall and Langdon-Davis were experienced investigators; the servants had never seen Zener cards before, and hardly knew what was expected of them. 'To suppose that these peasant girls were able to devise a system of elaborate fraud by which they were able to get these results', Dingwall felt able to claim, 'seems to me to be out of the question.' In the major trials with numbers of students, however, such massive deviations from chance were unusual, and it is to them that Whately's dictum applies.

Scientists had been demanding convincing proof of psi through results obtained in controlled, scientifically approved tests. They had been provided with those results in a form which, had they been presented in connection with any acceptable type of phenomenon, would have been accepted without question. It was convincing enough for the members of the American Association for the Advancement of Science to admit the Parapsychological Association, an international body of men and women acting in psi research, as an affiliate in 1969. It was not convincing enough to make any real impact on scientism.

The Rosenheim Poltergeist

From time to time the paranormal would excite controversy in the media, usually conducted on a frivolous level. One episode turned out to be an exception. The haunting of a lawyer's office in the Bavarian town of Rosenheim offered splendid opportunities for facetious coverage until gradually the facts beat the investigators, much as the facts of Palladino's physical mediumship had beaten Cesare Lombroso.

The anecdotal evidence for haunting is extensive – again, from all parts of the world, in every historical era. The experimental evidence is meagre, largely because ghosts tend to make infrequent appearances at irregular hours, and leave no trace. Poltergeists have been the exception. Often they are around for weeks, leaving in their wake a trail of broken cutlery, upset chairs, soaked carpets and so on, as if an invisible practical joker were at work. They have often been carefully investigated, and the reports have shown some significant resemblances. Some of them have been so well-attested that it has been difficult for all but the most die-hard sceptics, of whom there are always a vocal few, to attribute the manifestations to a human joker. Rosenheim was such a case.

During the summer of 1967 it was noticed that the tele-phone system in the lawyer's office was behaving oddly. The bells on all three of the office extensions would ring at the same time, though nobody was calling, and calls which were being made were constantly being cut off. The lawyer blamed the telephone company. The telephone company, having checked, insisted there was nothing the matter.

Soon, the vagaries of the telephone system constituted only one of the office's worries. Filing cabinet drawers would suddenly spring out, disgorging their contents. Lights would go out, to the accompaniment of loud 'bangs'. Electricians, when called in, thought that surges in the current might be responsible. The electrical system was put on a generator, so that it could be monitored. The lights continued to go out, still sometimes accompanied by the 'bangs'. Nothing could be found to account for either irregularity.

Assuming somebody must be victimising him, the lawyer filed a suit against a person or persons unknown. Detectives arrived and set traps, which were sometimes sprung – with nobody there to spring them. By this time the haunting was becoming a *cause célèbre*, featured on the German television network as well as in the press. To settle the issue, that winter two physicists were called in, Dr F. Karger of the Max Planck Institute and Dr G. Zicha of the Technical University in Munich. They introduced the latest refinements in monitoring equipment, including sound and video recorders to keep the office under constant surveillance. As if to mock them fresh phenomena developed. Light bulbs burst even when the current was not switched on, leaving the filaments unbroken, 'plaques were observed to jump off walls; pictures and calendars turned and twisted on the walls; and a heavy cupboard shifted 28cm.' On one occasion the tape in a video recorder which had been left running actually showed a picture turning on the wall through over ninety degrees.

The physicists had to confess themselves baffled. In their report they claimed that they had 'systematically eliminated or checked every physical cause'. Nothing had been found which could account for what had been witnessed.

They summed up their findings:

1. Although recorded with the facilities available to experimental physics, the phenomena defy explanation with the means available to theoretical physics.
2. The phenomena seem to be the result of non-periodic, short duration forces.
3. The phenomena (including the telephone incidents) do not seem to involve pure electrodynamic effects.
4. Not only do simple events of an explosive type take place, but also complicated motions (e.g. recorder curves, moving pictures).
5. These movements seem to be performed by intelligently controlled forces (e.g. the telephone incidents) that have a tendency to avoid investigation.

Another investigator who had been called in was more successful: Hans Bender, Professor of Psychology at the University of Freiburg, and the leading authority in Europe on poltergeists. When he ascertained that the disruption occurred only during office hours, he was able to concentrate upon the individuals on the small staff. The disruption, he found, ordinarily occurred only when one of the secretaries, Annemarie S., was in the office. She was highly strung, and once had been detected causing a hanging lamp to swing. As she had been an obvious suspect, however, she had been watched and on numerous occasions could not have been physically responsible for the effects.

In any case, by this time it had been discovered that nobody could have been responsible for one of the poltergeist's games. The telephone company had been persuaded to check incoming and outgoing calls. At times when the office telephones were not being used, it was found, calls were nevertheless being dialled. They were calls asking for the time of the day. Although a human joker might have thought of this, as a way to tease the employer, it was not a human joker. The telephone company had to admit that the calls were being dialled faster than they could possibly have been dialled in the ordinary way. They were the work of no human hand.

In many, though not all, poltergeist cases there has been a human 'focus'; a member of the household, usually a pubescent girl or boy, who appears to be linked to the manifestations, and is often blamed for them.

Annemarie, Bender now felt certain, must be the focus – though she was a little older than is usual in such cases. In her own, as well as in the office's interest, he suggested, she should leave. As soon as she did, the disturbances ceased. Had further proof been required of her role, it was soon to be provided. She became engaged to be married, and began accompanying her fiancé to the local bowling alley until he found that whenever she was present the automatic scoring system, operating electrically, was disrupted. He would prefer it, he told her, if she ceased to come with him. The engagement was broken off. When she married another man, and had children, the manifestations ceased.

Although the Rosenheim case made little immediate impact outside Germany, it encouraged psychical researchers to take on similar cases of haunting in America and Britain, and this has been leading to a greater public awareness of the ways in which they can upset what are usually regarded as commonsense attitudes about what can, and cannot, happen.

A recent case has been featured in Arthur C. Clarke's television documentary series 'World of Strange Powers', showing the plight of a group of householders in an ordinarily quiet Birmingham street. The problem has been stones, appearing from nowhere and smashing into houses, breaking windows, and necessitating the installation of protective wire meshing. When the police were called in they assumed they would soon find the culprits. They were wrong. 'We have probably wasted over 3,500 man hours,' the Chief Inspector in charge of the investigation admitted. Even when police officers had hidden themselves they had seen nothing, 'and the stones still come over'.

Poltergeist hauntings pose two problems for which psychical research has found no solutions. The first concerns the programme – the actual manifestations. The second concerns the programmer – the practical joker.

One feature of the programme in particular has excited attention. The action at a distance, the movements of objects when no physical force is being applied, has often been characterised according to witnesses as defying the normal effects of gravity. Fragile objects which fall do not necessarily break; sometimes they seem to be carefully placed on the floor. Sometimes objects float; sometimes they sail around corners. Other frequently encountered poltergeist effects have been showers of pebbles, or water, or excrement. Occasionally fires light up, and then extinguish themselves.

Unlike most hauntings of the traditional 'headless spectre' type, where the ghosts ignore any human who happens to see them, the poltergeist programmer seems to have a mission. In recent years it has usually been to disrupt the household, through activities ranging from one which delighted in taking off bottle-tops to massive destruction of a kind which can drive the family from their home.

This was not always the case. In folklore their record is far from being consistently anti-social. They kept the milk-jug full for Philemon and Baucis, and they would help families with their chores, as Milton showed in *L'Allegro*:

> And he, by Friar's Lantern led
> Tells how the drudging goblin sweat
> To earn his cream-bowl duly set,
> When in one night, ere glimpse of morn
> His shadow flail hath threshed the corn
> That ten day-labourers could not end.

Although obnoxious poltergeists have a long history, it is only in the past three centuries that they have acquired an almost totally unsavoury reputation.

It is as if the programmer, in this context, may itself be a medium, picking up unconscious human urges, beneficent or ugly, and translating them into actions of a kind which will demonstrate the reality of psi. Whatever the explanation, a look at the survey of about 500 cases which Alan Gauld and Tony Cornell have collected in their *Poltergeists*, coupled with a detailed examination of some of the individual case histories, should suffice to dispose of any lingering notion that they can all be explained away as the work of mischievous children, playing on the fears of credulous grown-ups.

Dowsing

Water divining – dowsing in Britain; water-witching in the United States – remains the form of divination which the public finds most acceptable. It might have established itself even more positively had it not been for a dispute about whether or not psi is responsible for the twitches that can be observed and felt on the traditional forked hazel twig, when diviners are over an underground stream. Some insist that this is a muscular reaction, analogous to cramp. Others believe that a psychokinetic force is acting on the twig.

Even the most hardened sceptics cannot dispute the existence of a force which operates on the twig, or whatever device is used. They have to explain it away as best they can; so Evon Z. Vogt and Ray Hyman describe it in their *Water-Witching USA* as 'entirely in accord with what we know of neuromuscular behaviour and ideomotor action'. Anybody who has felt it will testify that it does *not* resemble ordinary muscular behaviour. The twig twists and jerks as if being pulled or pushed by an invisible hand. In 1971 an American electronics engineer, Alvin S. Kaufman, employed strain-gauges to test whether the force worked directly on the muscles or on the twig. He found that it was on the twig. 'The amount of psychokinetic (if such it is) energy is great', he concluded, 'and dramatically evident.'

That dowsers who make a comfortable living out of their predictions, or who use their talents casually to help friends, should so often fail in tests has been seized upon by sceptics to cast doubts on the existence of any psi component. This is unwise of them: some subjective influences, in this as in other forms of test, can be a psi indicator. If the force which moves the twig (or the muscles) were electromagnetic in character, it would not be so perverse. As for the suggestion that the hundreds of diviners all over the world who make their living by showing where to site wells are using guesswork, it stretches incredulity too far. The evidence for the dowsing sense, as surveyed by Christopher Bird in *The Divining Hand*, is far too convincing to be brushed aside.

Opinion polls have shown that the British public is prepared to accept dowsing as readily as it accepts ESP. The likelihood is that it would have fully established itself, in spite of scientism's objections, if more dowsers had followed the course taken by Major-General J. Scott Elliot, described in 1977 in his *Dowsing: One Man's Way*. Following his retirement from the army Scott Elliot became interested in archaeology and began to use dowsing to detect and map underground sites, enabling the 'dig' to be less haphazard. Eventually he found he could use the twig or the pendulum for more homely purposes, such as helping friends to find lost objects.

The procedure is simple. He uses a pendulum, asking it questions to which it replies, by its rotation, 'yes' or 'no'. He cites the case of a brooch lost many miles from where the questions were being put. The owner had told him a number of places where it might have been lost. The pendulum rejected all of them except the car. Used over a rough sketch of the car, it indicated that the brooch would be found tucked away in a crevice at the back. There it was.

The results, Scott Elliot is careful to warn, are not always so correct. Nevertheless they are right often enough to be a distinct asset. Although not everybody enjoys the dowsing faculty, most people who become interested can develop it. Considering the time spent looking for missing keys, and the irritation it generates, this alone should prompt many of us to investigate the possibilities.

Uri Geller

'The contention, now frequently and plausibly made, that no observation is worth anything except under the most stringent conditions, is neither practicable nor wise in all cases,' Oliver Lodge warned in *My Philosophy*. 'Nothing is likely to carry real conviction except the cumulative effect of first-hand experience, of various kinds, under a great variety of circumstances.'

His warning was not heeded by parapsychologists. In Britain, particularly, the interest aroused by the work of Rhine and others in America gradually waned. Reviewing Professor Hansel's attack on psychical research in the *New Scientist* in 1966, Christopher Evans could claim that the book dealt parapsychology a blow from which it was unlikely to recover. An opinion poll taken two years later revealed that less than half the adult population of Britain believed in ESP.

In 1973 a young Israeli, Uri Geller, appeared in a late-night BBC television show, hosted by David Dimbleby. With them was Lyall Watson, whose *Supernature* had just become a best-seller, and Professor John Taylor, whom the BBC used as one of their reliable sceptics (a sceptic was still regarded as obligatory on such programmes). Few of the group of spectators in the studio, and of the TV audience – swollen, as it happened, by the fact that it came after that year's Miss World had been crowned – had ever heard of Geller, let alone knew what to expect.

What Geller did made him a national celebrity overnight. He was given a simple clairvoyance test, which he passed, before displaying the powers for which he was to become famous, bending cutlery by stroking it, starting up watches which had long ceased to tick. Taylor was so impressed that he admitted Geller had converted him to acceptance of psychokinesis.

During the rest of his short stay in Britain Geller bent cutlery and latchkeys with fine abandon, as accounts of reporters and science correspondents, most of them formerly sceptics, confirmed. Rosemary Collins of the *Guardian* wrote a mildly satirical piece; Geller invited her round to his hotel where he bent a fork for her. 'In case the fork should have been a stage prop', she reported in the *Guardian* the next day, 'I then produced my own key.' Geller did not even touch it, as it lay in her hand, 'but it was possible to feel the movement of the key as it bent upwards through 45° in the course of two or three minutes'.

The *Sunday Times* science correspondent Brian Silcock, also sceptical, arranged to accompany Geller to the airport the next day, bringing with him the key to his office desk, which he could not bend by main force. Geller bent it, without touching it, while it was lying in full view, in the palm of the

Sunday Times photographer's hand. At the airport the photographer bought a paper-knife shaped like a sword, which Geller stroked until it began to bend before giving it to one of the staff at the KLM desk to hold. It continued to bend. Geller thereupon caught the flight to Paris, 'leaving this initially highly sceptical science correspondent with his mind totally blown'.

Could it have been a conjuring trick? There were two possibilities, Silcock noted the following Sunday. Either Geller must have managed to get hold of the key in advance and put it into the photographer's hand already bent, or he must have had a duplicate key and substituted it. Both these explanations, Silcock had to admit, stretched credibility. How could Geller have known what kind of key to have for the purpose of substitution? Surely they would have noticed if the key had already been bent when it was placed in the photographer's hand? Either way, Geller would have run 'the most appalling risk of being exposed every time' – just as he would if he had tried to give the impression that the paper-knife was bending gradually on its own, when he was in fact distracting onlookers and bending it physically himself. It would have needed only one of them *not* to be distracted to catch him out.

Scores of accounts of this kind were to appear about Geller's prowess from all over the world. What has tended to be forgotten since is not merely that a great many sceptical individuals, then and later, reported keys bending or watches starting up in circumstances which, so far as they were concerned, precluded trickery, but also that a far greater number of people, everywhere Geller appeared on television, found that cutlery had bent, or long out-of-order clocks had started up in their homes. Following a radio programme he did earlier in the day before the Dimbleby show, baffled or irate listeners had written to the BBC to say that, while Geller was talking, strange things had happened in their kitchens or living rooms. Then and later the producers of TV shows on which he appeared learned to expect a flood of correspondence about its effects in scores of households.

The press was divided. Cynically, the *Sunday People* challenged Geller to a test: wherever he would find himself on Sunday morning at 12.30 p.m., he was to put his mind to the task of mental metal-bending, and to shout 'BEND'. He happened to have just arrived at Orly airport, where he duly shouted. 'Letters poured in to our offices by the hundred all last week', the next issue of the *People* reported. 'The experiment had worked on an astonishing scale.' Not only had scores of forks and spoons been found bent, but the most remarkable results 'involved your old time-pieces. An incredible 856 watches and clocks written off as useless were reported to have started ticking again.'

The *News of the World*, irritated at being upstaged by its old rival, sent a reporter and a photographer after Geller to expose him. 'We challenge the mind-bender', it told its readers; they would learn the following week how he did his tricks. While the two men were with Geller, a steel plate which the reporter had brought with him, too tough for him to bend by hand, began to curl up on its own, lying on a table, as they watched, 'until it formed an exact "V" shape'. Their hotel-room key suddenly snapped in two when nobody was near it. To add to their discomfiture, Geller took a picture of himself while the camera's lens cap was still on. He could not have had access to the film either beforehand or afterwards, yet when it was developed in London two clear pictures appeared of Geller's head and shoulders.

By this time the professional conjurors in Britain were alarmed. A few weeks later one of them showed the *Daily Express* how the tricks were done. In a front page splash – 'I have a mind-blowing message to transmit to Israeli showman, Uri Geller' – the reporter, Don Coolican, disclosed Geller's secret, 'straight out of a school chemistry book'. Coolican had been given it by a conjuror in breach of the stage magician's code; like many professionals, the conjuror 'is angry with Uri because of his claim to supernatural powers'. The cutlery-bending and the clocks starting up in people's homes, Coolican had to admit, presented difficulties, as the *Express* had also had its share of correspondence on the subject. But Geller's ability to bend forks by stroking them was easily explained. He was applying a chemical. Let him then, try to bend one in conditions where no chemical could be applied!

Contemptuously, Geller invited Coolican to pay him a visit. Submitting to the test which the conjuror had told Coolican to make, Geller bent the metal. Crestfallen, Coolican returned to London. He had been misled, he admitted. Geller was indeed a metal-bender – and, he now apologetically conceded, a mind-bender.

Geller subsequently submitted to a succession of tests by scientists in the United States, Britain and other countries, the results of which were published in *The Geller Papers* in 1976. They left no doubt in the minds of those who conducted them that he was not just a psychic metal-bender, but had other powers, from clairvoyance to what some of his investigators described as poltergeist effect; objects would move in his vicinity, sometimes after he had left. The phenomena would have been accepted as genuine had they been explicable in terms which orthodox scientists could accept. As they were not, Geller had to be exposed as a fraud.

In certain ways he made things easy for his sceptics. In his youth in Israel he had gone into show business to exploit his talent and he remained a showman, ambitious to become a film star – as well he might, as he had the looks and the personality. Scientific testing was something he put up with; he was not an easy subject. He owed much to Andrija Puharich, who had arranged for him to come to America to be tested at the Stanford Research Institute and who for a while remained his guru; but Puharich's biography, with its thesis that he and Uri had been chosen by extra-terrestrials as their earthly emissaries, did Geller a disservice, as did Geller's own description of his translocation, in a split second, from New York city to Puharich's home in Ossining. The fact that this was attested by friends made no difference. The tale confirmed doubters in the suspicion that he must be a charlatan.

A campaign of denigration followed from sceptics, appalled at the impression Geller was making on the public, and from conjurors, fearful for their future prospects. Geller, claimed the then editor of the *New Scientist*, Bernard Dixon, had been 'allowed private access to the cutlery provided for him on the Dimbleby Talk-In'. This was simply untrue. Martin Gardner asserted that Geller could not bend a key 'until he obtains strong enough misdirection to bend it instantly' – in other words, he must distract the witnesses' attention sufficiently to get the key into his own hands. Dozens of people have described how they have seen Geller bend a key which has never left the palm of the person presenting it.

The most damaging allegation came three years later. The

New Scientist, still pursuing its vendetta, carried an article by the American conjuror, the Amazing Randi, giving details of a confession by Geller's former manager, Yasha Katz, that he and Geller had faked the performances together, and adding that he knew Geller had committed theft. Katz was eventually to confess that all the information he had given to Randi had been false. People who had wanted to harm Geller, including Randi, had used him for that purpose.

Not surprisingly, the impression grew that Geller had been exposed. It was even widely believed that he had confessed. Geller, Randi claimed, had fled to Mexico with his brother-in-law Shipi Shtrang, as both were wanted for questioning in Israel, and they knew Israel had no extradition treaty with Mexico. This story, too, was false in every detail.

Quite apart from anything Geller himself did to prove that his abilities were genuine, there was good reason to accept that they were because, wherever he had performed, he had left a legacy – two, in fact. One of them took the form of 'mini-Gellers' – children (and a few adults) who came forward to say that they, too, could bend metal with the help of psi. Some were carefully investigated, notably by John Hasted, Professor of Experimental Physics at Birkbeck College at London University. A few showed that they were able to exert psychokinetic powers in conditions which precluded the possibility that they were using physical force.

If Geller was not the only metal-bender, the presumption that his powers were genuine was obviously strengthened, and some of the results with mini-Gellers were impressive. One of Geller's feats had been to deform wire made from the metal nitinol, which has the unusual feature of a 'memory'; when bent it returns to its original shape. Geller gently stroked a piece of wire until it formed a 'kink' which refused to straighten out. Sceptics argued that either he must have known that he was to be tested with nitinol and brought with him a piece already kinked, or that he had managed to distract witnesses so that he could use physical force on the wire. Although neither solution sounded plausible, Geller was so widely assumed to have been exposed that they were accepted.

In 1982 John L. Randall, an experienced parapsychologist and the author of a carefully researched book on psychokinesis, was testing a schoolboy who claimed to have PK powers. Why not try him on nitinol? Randall thought. After taping one end of the wire to the desk to prevent substitution, Randall asked the boy to stroke it. As he was doing so, the loose end, which he was not touching, reared up like a snake about to strike. Although Randall was able to straighten the wire by physical force, and also by heating it, it then returned to the shape into which it had bent while it was being stroked, showing that the boy 'had somehow succeeded in altering the memory of the wire'.

Geller's other legacy is less easy to evaluate with any certainty. It seems likely that he has been largely responsible in Britain, and some other countries – less in the United States, where his critics have been more vocal – for a resurgence of interest in the pàranormal. Television brought psi into people's homes, not just on the screen but in the kitchen, where spoons and forks were found bent, or in the loft, where old clocks started to chime again. Opinion polls in the 1980s have shown a marked increase in willingness to accept psi compared with those of twenty years ago.

Why, it has often been asked, if Geller's powers were genuine, did he not refute sceptics by doing fresh tests? To this he has a simple answer: sceptics would not believe in the results if he did. Conjurors were again saying what they had said a century before about Crookes and Richet, that scientists lack the qualifications to detect sleight-of-hand, a task which should be given to professionals. Geller submitted to investigation by two experienced conjurors. They reported that they could find no way in which his feats could be accomplished by sleight-of-hand. They were promptly repudiated by the executive of the Society of Magicians of which they were members.

Geller went for a while into the secular equivalent of a retreat. In the course of it he met Sir Val Duncan, Chairman of Rio Tinto Zinc. Duncan was an amateur water diviner, successful enough to make him suggest to his Board that they might use diviners to find seams of ore. They were appalled at the notion. Geller had clairvoyant, as well as psychokinetic abilities; why should he not use them, Duncan suggested, to find gold, ore, oil? Geller began to use them. In a very short time he was a millionaire, several times over. He may turn out to have found a much more effective way to demonstrate the reality of psychokinesis than by succeeding in any number of laboratory trials.

'Ruth'

In 1980 a book was published which, though not directly concerned with the paranormal, went some way to answering questions that had long perplexed psychical researchers. In *The Story of Ruth* Morton Schatzman, an American psychiatrist practising in London, described how an American woman had come to him as a patient because she was being harassed by the apparition of her father, who had raped her when she was ten years old and who still, in his apparitional form, clearly had designs on her. Her father was in fact still alive, but living in the United States. For Schatzman the most interesting feature of the case was that, to 'Ruth', the apparition was as real as if it *was* her father. It looked like him, it behaved as he had behaved, it even smelled like him.

Eventually Schatzman had an idea. Why shouldn't Ruth conjure up the apparition, instead of waiting for it to intrude? Understandably reluctant at first, she allowed herself to be persuaded by Schatzman's argument that if she could learn to materialise her 'father', she would be better placed to learn how to dematerialise him. So it turned out. When she summoned her 'father', he appeared. When she told him to leave, he left.

Apparitions had been one of the subjects selected initially for investigation by the Society for Psychical Research at its foundation. Two reports, 'Phantasms of the Living' and the 'Census of Hallucinations', were the immediate outcome. They did a great deal to clear up the confusion that prevailed at the time. Until Edmund Gurney had begun in 1882 to collect and sieve the case histories, the general assumption had been that hallucinations simply meant 'seeing things' that were not there. They were regarded and treated as a form of incipient insanity. Anyone who was unwise enough to insist that the apparition was real was considered to be either a liar or a lunatic.

To Andrew Lang this was absurd. Instances of hallucinations appearing or being conjured up had been reported countless times in history. Could it seriously be alleged, he asked, that the hallucinatory experiences of 'people like Iamblichus, Mr Crookes, Lord Crawford, Jesuits in Canada, professional conjurors in Zululand, Spaniards in early Peru, Australian blacks, Maoris, Eskimo, cardinals, ambassadors' were always the result of imposture, conscious or unconscious? Gurney was able to show that it was indeed nonsense. He found that most of the people who reported that they had encountered a phantasm – a hallucination of somebody who was still living – were eminently sane.

Not all hallucinations could be classified as psychic. They might occur as the result of illness or of drugs. But occasionally they constituted an indication of 'a fresh faculty rather than a degeneration', Myers believed. Although delusive if they did not correspond with anything that was actually happening, they could be regarded as veridical 'if corresponding to some actual event elsewhere' – picked up, he surmised, by telepathy.

Samuel Johnson, more open-minded on the subject than many of his contemporaries, had made a similar distinction 'between what a man may experience by the mere strength of his imagination, and what imagination cannot possibly produce'. If he heard a voice telling him 'Johnson, you are a very wicked fellow, and unless you repent you will certainly be punished', he would know that it had been produced by his imagination. 'But if a form should appear and a voice should tell me that a particular man had died at a particular place, and a particular hour, a fact which I had no apprehension of, nor any means of knowing, and this fact, with all the circumstances, should afterwards be unquestionably proved, I should, in that case, be persuaded that I had supernatural intelligence imparted to me.'

A good example of a veridical hallucination, one which strains 'coincidence' beyond tolerable limits, is the account of the apparition seen in 1928 by Colonel G.L.P. Henderson on voyage back to Britain from South Africa. One night, clearly in a panic, he woke his colleague Squadron Leader Rivers Oldmeadow to tell him that something terrible must have happened: 'Hinch' had just been in his cabin, 'eye-patch and all'. The apparition had kept repeating, again and again, 'Hendy, what am I going to do? I've got this woman with me, and I'm lost.' Then, in front of Henderson's eyes, he had disappeared.

'Hinch' – Raymond Hinchliffe – had been one of the most celebrated of First World War pilots, losing an eye in combat. In 1928 he had allowed himself to be persuaded to fly the Atlantic from east to west with Elsie Mackay, the daughter of Lord Inchcape, as his passenger, so that she would be the first woman to fly the Atlantic. Her presence on the aircraft was not to be disclosed until it landed. Henderson could not have known about the proposed flight, nor could he have known that it had come to grief, as the news was not put up on the ship's bulletin board until three days later. No trace of the missing aircraft has ever been found.

Unlike the traditional ghost, an apparition seems real. Nevertheless it is a hallucination. Hallucinations must be distinguished from illusions, William James commented. They are perceptions providing 'as good and true a sensation as if there were a real object there. The object happens not to be there, after all.' The 'good and true sensation' may come through any of the five senses. 'Hearing voices' means literally that: often individuals have reacted by turning around to find where the voice has appeared to be coming from, only to find nobody there.

To Lang, there was nothing surprising in this, or in the fact that some hallucinations are veridical. If action and communication at a distance had helped in the evolutionary process, and had been eased out in the course of time by development of the five senses of hearing, sight, touch, taste and smell, what could be more probable than that the sixth sense, when it is needed to force its way into consciousness, should use one or other of the five by projecting a hallucination, usually a vision? The German physiologist and psychologist Max Dessoir concurred. The conscious life of humans, he thought, 'seems to rest upon a substratum of reflex action of a hallucinatory type', the hallucinatory aspect providing 'the main trunk of our psychical existence'.

Some uncertainty remained. An apparition which produced actual changes in the visible world, Lang asserted, could not be a hallucination. Why not? If it is real to the touch, as some of the reported apparitions have been, why should it not be able to turn the handle of a door, make banging noises and

cause objects to float, poltergeist-fashion? The fact that poltergeists have rarely been visible is not a problem, as hallucinations have so often been reported as entering only one of
the senses.

Nevertheless Lang's view was sufficiently widely held to
deter psychical researchers from exploring the possibility of a
link between spontaneous veridical hallucinations and the
ectoplasmic materialisations reported in research with
mediums. Some of Eusapia's materialised forms appeared to
sitters as if they were deceased friends or relations come back
to life. Similar apparitions were frequently reported by the
investigators of the Brazilian medium Carlos Mirabelli in the
1920s (one of them, a poet who had died not long before, was
photographed sitting between Mirabelli and an investigator,
who is looking understandably alarmed). A materialised form
could have been held to fall within William James's specifications, in a sense – the person appeared to be there, and yet was
not there. Yet the force of colloquial habit intervened, making
it difficult to think of apparitions as 'real'.

The Story of Ruth has reopened the issue. As she proved to be
capable of conjuring up the apparition of her father at will,
Schatzman decided it would be interesting to find out just how
real the apparition was to her. In collaboration with Dr Peter
Fenwick of the Institute of Psychiatry, he gave Ruth tests
designed to check whether the hallucination *was* real. They
confirmed that it was. Her reactions were of the kind which
she would have made had somebody actually been sitting
where the apparition was sitting. They were quite distinct
from the reactions which would have been expected if the
figure had been an illusion, rather than a hallucination.

Can apparitions now be tentatively linked with ectoplasmic
materialisations? Ectoplasm, after all, has sometimes been
reported as visible and tangible. Sometimes, as in psychokinesis, only its effects can be seen or felt. Geley made the
daring suggestion that ectoplasm may turn out to be the basic
stuff from which animal matter is constructed. If so, the
evolutionary programme may have endowed humanity with
the potential ability to create entities and give them a
semblance of life.

It seems likely that there is also a link with exteriorisations
of the kind so often reported in poltergeist cases. The human

focus – foci, in situations where there are family tensions – may be projecting the forces which create the hallucinated entity. The story of Aladdin may in fact turn out to have an unexpected significance. Some eastern mediums could have had the same ability as Eusapia and Mirabelli to conjure up living forms – though not necessarily useful ones.

The issue is not simply academic. Apparitions have continued to be reported since Gurney's time. Flammarion provided a collection of them in *The Unknown*, and a more extensive one in the three-volume *Death and its Mystery*. Surveys since in Britain and America have confirmed that they are more commonly experienced than is generally realised. It is useful to have found that where they become nuisances, as in Ruth's case, ways can be found to bring them under control. This applies also to poltergeist-type infestations. Matthew Manning tamed his poltergeist exteriorisations, first through the practice of automatic writing and drawing, and later through healing. Annemarie of Rosenheim's exteriorisations ceased when she married.

Remote Viewing

When, in 1972, Harold Puthoff and Russell Targ began to investigate Uri Geller's psychokinetic powers, they were left in no doubt that the powers existed, but found it impossible to pin them down in controlled trials at the Stanford Research Institute. In trials for clairvoyance, on the other hand, Geller was remarkably successful, even to the point of drawing a bunch of grapes with the same number of grapes as the bunch they were using as the target.

Intrigued, they decided to investigate more systematically 'remote viewing', as they called it to get away from the associations of clairvoyance. In 1973 a New York artist, Ingo Swann, showed that he was able to 'see' places if he was given only the precise latitude and longitude, often with such accuracy that it left no doubt that he was using second sight. Hearing what was going on at SRI, Pat Price, a former police commissioner at Burbank, offered to help. Episodes while he was involved in tracking down suspects, he said, which originally he had attributed to intuition, had eventually made it clear that he had psychic powers, which could be tested.

Other volunteers arrived, and a protocol was designed to try to make the trials fraudproof.

Basically the procedure involved one of the investigators setting out in a car with sealed instructions about where to go. At a given time, he would stop at the target site they indicated and take a photograph of what he saw. Back at SRI, the volunteer would draw, or describe, what he or she 'saw' at the time. After an interval the investigator would open the next sealed envelope, which would direct him to the next target. There was no way, in other words, in which anybody could know in advance the order of the targets. The investigator's photographs and the subjects' descriptions and drawings would then be sent to an independent judge, who would match any which obviously resembled each other. The significantly positive results encouraged the investigators to present them in 1976 in the *Journal of the Institute of Electrical and Electronic Engineers*, doubtless to the irritation of some of its readers, and to the public in *Mind-Reach* the following year.

The inclusion of a section on Uri Geller roused sceptics. Without bothering to check, Martin Gardner claimed in the *Scientific American* that only the positive results had been kept and published. When Puthoff and Targ explained that this was incorrect, he could only reply lamely that 'someone had told him'. 'So we have a major US scientific publication exposing the inadequacies of a major research effort', they commented, 'on the basis of erroneous hearsay.' The Amazing Randi devoted a chapter of his book on Geller to the SRI investigations. Puthoff and Targ were able to show that it contained numerous factual errors; some of them complete inventions, such as his allegation that they had allowed Geller to have an accomplice with him during tests.

A more serious allegation, at first glance, appeared in *Nature* in 1978. In a few cases during the tests with Pat Price, argued David Marks and Richard Kammann of the University of Otago in New Zealand, the judge might have picked up clues about which pairs to match. They had also failed to replicate the SRI results in tests of their own in New Zealand. Charles Tart of the University of California, Davis, thereupon did a fresh run-through of the material with a different judge, cutting out any possibility of clues being given. The results were still strongly positive.

More to the point, Tart reminded *Nature* that Marks and Kammann had ignored the *quality* of some of Price's descriptions. Price had even on occasions actually named the target correctly. That Marks and Kammann had failed to replicate the results, too, was not surprising. All it showed was that the results were to be attributed 'to the quality of the subjects' descriptions themselves'. Marks and Kammann could not claim to have replicated the experiments, in other words, unless they had the benefit of Pat Price as the subject – and perhaps not even if they had, as they might not have established rapport with him.

In the course of the trials Puthoff and Targ found that some of their subjects could 'see' precognitively. Hella Hamid, a professional photographer who had been one of the finds of the remote viewing trials, was asked to try to 'see' what one of her investigators would be seeing when he arrived at the *next* target. In each of four tests her descriptions were so accurate that independent judges had no difficulty in matching them, the quality being such that they would have been matched even if the judges had been cued in a wrong direction. In one, she described a large, black iron triangle, saying that she had also heard a sound of 'squeak, squeak about once a second'. When, a few minutes later, Puthoff stopped at the selected target to take a photograph of it, it turned out to be a child's swing supported by a triangular black structure. The swing, in use, went squeak, squeak.

The Stanford Research Institute was a goverment-funded institution, relinquished by the university because of uneasiness about the nature of some of the work being undertaken on the government's behalf. Inevitably there were rumours that a Federal Agency or the Pentagon or both were funding psychical research. They were denied until, in 1981, the Congressional Committee on Science and Technology disclosed that they had been well-founded. 'Recent experiments in remote viewing and other studies in parapsychology suggest that there is "interconnectedness" of the human mind with other minds and with matter', it reported. The experiments had yielded 'some encouraging results'. Given the far-reaching implications, 'and given that the Soviet Union is widely acknowledged to be supporting such research at a far higher and more official level, Congress may wish to under-

11 Ted Serios would occasionally be able to materialise on
camera film, without the normal exposure, a 'mental' copy of
a photograph, such as this one of an aeroplane.

12 One of Hella Hamid's successful run of precognitive 'hits' in
remote viewing trials at the Stanford Research Institute. She
'saw' a black iron triangle and 'heard' a 'squeak, squeak'.

13 *Left*, Matthew Manning in his capacity as healer.

14 *Below*, Uri Geller consistently confounds conjurors' claims that he uses sleight-of-hand to produce already bent latchkeys or spoons. No conjuror can start thousands of broken watches and clocks from television studios or substitute objects such as this bracelet handed to him at Stonehenge.

take a serious reassessment of research in this country'.

The first clear intimation of what was happening behind the Iron Curtain had been the contents of Professor L.L. Vasiliev's *Experiments in Mental Suggestion*, translated into English in 1963. Unless it was a monumental hoax, it revealed the results of a series of carefully conducted trials along the lines that the Janet brothers, Ochorowicz and Myers, had taken in the 1880s, using hypnosis. Vasiliev had actually replicated their results, showing that he had found it was possible to hypnotise subjects through communication at a distance.

How could research of this kind have been conducted in Russia, where it had been regarded as counter-revolutionary? In a new edition in 1976 Anita Gregory, who together with her husband had brought out the earlier volume, explained that when Vladimir Bekhterev's research with dogs in the early years of the communist regime had convinced him of the need to study the subject of 'mental suggestion', he had been influential enough to establish it at the impeccably orthodox Institute of Brain Research in Leningrad. Had it been set up to study telepathy, it could not have survived under Stalin. Telepathy, according to the 1956 edition of the *Soviet Encyclopaedia*, was 'an anti-social, idealist fiction'. Experiments in mental suggestion, though, were considered to be ideologically reputable. It was not too difficult for Vasiliev to stretch this to cover mental suggestion at a distance.

Even so, Vasiliev could hardly have published his results in Stalin's lifetime. Under Khrushchev there was a thaw. When Gaither Pratt went to Russia in 1963 he was able to attend a conference in which psychical research was openly and seriously discussed. When Khrushchev was deposed, *Pravda* again denounced parapsychology. For a time it was once again dangerous to publish material about it; but so much had appeared in the period of the thaw that the imposed silence proved hard to maintain. In particular, the research with Nina Kulagina, who displayed psychokinetic abilities, and Rosa Kuleshova, a clairvoyant, had been too well documented by too many respected scientists to be ignored.

In the circumstances it was not surprising that US intelligence agencies had decided, albeit nervously, to fund research at the SRI and elsewhere. The work with Geller was disturbing, not so much for what he actually accomplished as for the

'almost limitless list of equipment failures' which accompanied his visits, including the wiping of computer programmes.
Ingo Swann managed to influence a magnetometer buried in a
vault and protected by elaborate shields from electromagnetic
or other known influences. When he concentrated, the range
of the oscillations on a chart recorder attached to it doubled.

The official in charge of the magnetometer did his best to
make light of the episode. He would be more impressed, he
said, if Swann actually stopped the oscillations altogether.
Concentrating hard, Swann stopped them for forty-five
seconds. As Targ admitted, this did not necessarily prove that
Swann was interfering with the magnetometer. He might
simply be interfering with the recorder. Either way, as
coincidence was wildly improbable, it was good evidence for
PK.

For nearly ten years, it was possible to keep the news of the
US government's role in psychical research under wraps, until
in 1980 an article in the *Military Review*, the army's professional journal, revealed that some of the Top Brass had been
taking it very seriously. Since then Martin Ebon's *Psychic
Warfare: Threat or Illusion?* and Ronald McRae's *Mind Wars*
have told what has been happening in considerable, even if
necessarily incomplete, detail, leaving no doubt that the CIA
and the Pentagon are satisfied that action and communication
at a distance are an established fact and, from the point of
view of defence, an embarrassing one.

According to a member of the House of Representatives
Committee on Intelligence – Charlie Rose, congressman for
North Carolina – some individuals in the Pentagon and the
CIA did their best to block psi research, and others, though
convinced by what they saw and read of psi's existence,
claimed that it would never be practical to exploit it. In his
own experience, he told McRae – 'I've seen some incredible
examples' – he was worried that the Soviets might be getting
similar results; 'if they develop a capacity to have people
mentally view secret centers within this country, we could
reach the point where we didn't have any secrets'.

In the meantime, though both sides still do their best to
keep those secrets intact, the results of research not immediately connected with strategic aims continue to be reported. A typical recent example described in *Psi Research*, a

journal which taps sources in Russia and her satellite countries, is the work of G.N. Dulnov *et al.* with Kulagina in 1978.
They describe how in carefully controlled conditions she was
able to move objects without using physical force, influence
objects in a cage shielded from electromagnetic effects, deflect
compass needles and disturb a laser beam.

There has even been a successful inter-continental trial. On
October 10, 1984 the *San Francisco Examiner* described a new
experiment in remote viewing. 'A Soviet scientist who has
never left his country will close his eyes today, clear his mind,
and attempt to use his psychic power to "see" – from 10,000
miles away – an undisclosed site in San Francisco where an
American researcher stands.' The researcher acting as
'beacon' in San Francisco was Keith Harary. The Russian
scientist was the healer Djuna Davitashvili. What she 'saw'
and described to the attendant group of witnesses, including
members of the Soviet Academy of the Sciences, contained
'many unique and striking correspondences with the target
location' – the merry-go-round on Pier 39.

The clearest indication that psychical research is being
taken seriously in Russia has been provided by Dubrov and
Pushkin in their *Parapsychology and Contemporary Science*, published in an English translation in 1982. Both have established
reputations in their own disciplines, Dubrov as a psychologist,
Pushkin as a physicist and metallurgist. They are well aware
of the resistance to accepting ESP and PK, and have a nice
sense of the way to trip up critics by citing Lenin – and even
Engels: 'with every breakthrough discovery, even in the field
of science or history, materialism should duly change its
form'.

They examine the evidence dispassionately, accepting it
when they regard it as satisfactory, as in the case of Kulagina.
The impression left is that a great deal of careful research is
being done in such areas as dowsing, psychic healing, and
exteriorisation (as in the influence that hypnotised subjects
exert on plants). Manifestly the book is no propaganda
exercise on behalf of Soviet science. They excoriate those of
their colleagues who refuse even to examine the findings for
'acting like people who have evidence of a crime and hide it in
order to avoid the inconvenience of coming forth with it'.
Extra-sensory perception and psychokinesis, they conclude,

are so important 'that neither science nor mankind have the right to ignore them'.

2

THE SCEPTICS' CASE

That some scientists have been using ill-conceived and sometimes dishonest arguments to discredit psychical research suggests that they lack better ones. Nevertheless there are certain arguments which need to be scrutinised, as they have sounded more reasonable. Four of them have many times been used: that there is no theoretical basis for psi; that psi phenomena cannot exist, because they are contrary to accepted scientific laws; that the experimental evidence produced by psychical researchers is fatally flawed; and that the historical and anecdotal evidence, where it cannot be attributed to illusion, can reasonably be accounted for by fraud.

The Four Counts

The Lack of a Theory?

'The chief obstacle to a more widespread scientific acceptance of the findings of parapsychology, as some of the fairest and most competent of sceptics have pointed out', the 1961 edition of the *Encyclopaedia Britannica* commented, 'is the almost complete lack of any plausible theoretical account as to the underlying causal processes.' It ought not to be an obstacle. No plausible theoretical account has yet been put forward for gravity or magnetism. It is only because of their consistency that they have achieved scientific recognition, in spite of their inexplicable action at a distance. As Charles Richet put it, 'we have no warrant to deny a phenomenon because we do not know its laws'.

Breaking the Laws?

Nor have we any warrant to deny that a phenomenon exists on the ground that it is contrary to the laws of nature. This assumption derives from David Hume's contention in his essay on miracles that there are certain immutable laws – men must die; fire consumes wood; lead cannot float. The choice of lead was unfortunate. It cannot float, but iron can, if lifted by a magnet. Had magnetism not been discovered, floating iron would have been in the miracle category.

As if uneasily aware that laws on the abstract might be regarded as too metaphysical a concept, Hume hastened to lend them backing – as he supposed – by defining a miracle such as a dead man coming to life as something which 'had never been observed, in any age or country'. There must consequently be a uniform experience against every miraculous event, 'and as a uniform experience amounts to a proof, there is here a direct and full *proof*, from the nature of the fact, against the existence of any miracle'.

It remains extraordinary that so shrewd a philosopher as Hume should not have realised the weakness of his argument. What has seemed to be the uniform experience of mankind has many times been overturned. Hume's argument against miracles was 'a tissue of fallacies which might be given for exposure to beginners in logic, as an elementary exercise', Andrew Lang complained. Hume had displayed 'the self-complacency and the want of humour with which we Scots are commonly charged by our critics'.

Ordinarily such sloppy reasoning would be the target of rationalist derision. Hume, as rationalism's secular equivalent of a patron saint, has had to be spared. True, of his biographers T.H. Huxley was clearly a little unhappy about it. Perhaps Sir Freddy Ayer is, too, as he has skimmed over it. Yet Anthony Flew, Professor of Philosophy at Reading University, has recently used Hume's theory as an excuse to devalue historical accounts. If the accounts describe anything happening which is inconsistent with the laws of nature, Flew argues, 'one cannot possibly know on historical evidence that it did so happen', because to the extent that we have good reasons for believing there are laws of nature, historians have to admit 'that one thing we cannot know on historical grounds is that a miracle occurred'. Professor C.E.M. Hansel, whose *ESP: A Scientific Evaluation* won him the reputation on both sides of the Atlantic of being the foremost critic of psychical research, has been even more explicit: 'the whole body of scientific knowledge compels us to assume that such things as telepathy and clairvoyance are impossible'.

Academic psychologists are not obliged to keep up with what is happening in other disciplines, or Hansel might have heard of Costa de Beauregard's contention that in quantum mechanics, phenomena such as telepathy, far from being impossible, are predictable. As for the 'firm and unalterable experience' of mankind, what has been taken to be firm and unalterable has time and again been found to be a misguided rationalisation of preconceived beliefs, as in the case of the eighteenth-century scientists' rejection of accounts of meteorites as a superstition, and the refusal of the medical profession to accept the reality of the mesmeric trance.

The early experiments in broadcasting provoked the same reaction. Stories of the ability of yogis to lower their respiration rate and their blood pressure at will, enabling them to rest for days in a state of suspended animation, used to be dismissed as occultist rubbish. When, early in this century, Johannes Schultz tried to demonstrate that ordinary men and women, too, could learn to control their autonomic nervous systems, he was mocked. Only when the results of experiments with bio-feedback began to appear in the 1960s were the yogis – and Schultz – vindicated. 'A few years ago it would have been considered "paranormal" to claim control over the blood pressure,' Robert Ornstein, Professor of Psychology at the University of California Medical Center, San Francisco, observed in *The Psychology of Consciousness* in 1972; 'now a freshman in a psychological experiment can expect to learn some measure of blood pressure control in half an hour'.

The Experiments Flawed?

The firm and unalterable experience of mankind, then, is not to be trusted; and no physicist would any longer rely upon the laws of nature. The notion of 'laws' has had to be replaced by the more flexible 'models'. It remains possible, though, to argue that the experimental evidence for psi is inadequate and untrustworthy, failing to provide the proofs which conventional science requires.

One of the proofs most often called for must first be dismissed as irrelevant. When the Society for Psychical Research was founded, Myers and Gurney worked on the principle that if enough evidence for, say, telepathy was to be collected, the range and similarities of the accounts would give them 'the strength of a faggot', on the analogy that whereas single twigs are easily snapped, a faggot composed of them bound together is not. Sceptics have replied with the counter-analogy of 'leaking buckets'. No matter how many of them you have, if each of them has even a small leak you cannot expect to conserve any water. One of the buckets must be cast-iron, copper-bottomed.

The challenge to psychical researchers to produce a single unimpeachable case history was put forward by John Tyndall and his fellow-sceptic G.H. Lewes in the late 1860s. Wallace

replied that so long as sceptics derived their assumption that
psychic phenomena did not exist from Hume, as they claimed
they did, they were contradicting themselves, as Hume's 'firm
and unalterable experience' argument manifestly ruled out
reliance upon 'any single case, considered alone, however well
authenticated'.

To place reliance on any single case was also contrary to
established scientific method, the philosopher F.C.S. Schiller
pointed out. Science relies on cumulative evidence. Sceptics,
he complained, 'will insist on taking the evidence in bits, and
rejecting it item by item'. Anybody who claims to be 'waiting
until a single absolutely conclusive bit of evidence turns up is
in reality a man who is not open to conviction, as he would
realise if he were a logician, because in logic single facts can
never be proved except as part of a system. Facts came singly,
but anyone who dismisses them one by one is destroying the
conditions under which the conviction of a new truth could
ever arise in his mind.'

Sceptics are not necessarily logicians. They have continued
to demand their leak-proof bucket. 'What is needed is one
completely convincing experiment – just one experiment that
does not have to be accepted simply on a basis of faith in
human nature,' George R. Price insisted in *Science* in 1955,
sweeping aside all the accumulated evidence on the ground
that no single experiment had fulfilled all the necessary
criteria. Yet as Schiller had pointed out, so long as there are
sceptics who deny the possibility of psi, there never *can* be a
single completely convincing experiment. They can always
allege that everybody concerned, subjects, experimenters and
witnesses, had been the victims of illusion or involved in
deception. Sidgwick had warned in his first Presidential
Address to the SPR that if the critics of psychical research
could find no other way to fault evidence, they would not
hesitate to accuse the researchers of fraud. This is precisely
what they have done. In experiments using statistics, Hansel
has laid down, where the data rule out explanations in terms
of chance, 'then the results can only be accounted for by some
kind of fraud'.

Interviewed by *Omni* in 1979, Carl Sargent, the first postgraduate student to be awarded a Doctorate of Philosophy in
Parapsychology at Cambridge, described how he had come up

against this objection. He decided to eliminate any possible type of deception, in a trial he was conducting, with the assistance of 'sealed envelopes, deposited suitcases, witnesses, Xerox copies', to the point of 'a panorama of paranoia'. Having obtained positive results, he proudly presented them at a conference where, to his amazement, 'the whole rigmarole was rejected on the grounds that any experimenter who is smart enough to think up a foolproof procedure is surely smart enough to get round it'.

It is unreasonable, therefore, to call for a single perfectly controlled test result. Sceptics are on more secure ground when they claim that parapsychologists have failed to obtain consistently repeated results.

This is not disputed. There are two reasons, parapsychologists explain. Scientists have required a far higher measure of repeatability in psychical research than is expected in other disciplines, for example in psychology; and testing psi presents problems which are not encountered in other disciplines.

For all we know, the forces responsible for psychic action or communication at a distance are as consistent as they are for magnetism. The inconsistency, or one of them, lies in the medium through which they have to pass: the brain. The human brain, Henri Bergson argued, is primarily designed as a filter. It had to take on this role in order to cope with the increasing flow of information reaching species through the senses. Ants have no need for individual brains, as they are directed by the group soul. With the development of the senses, sight, in particular, and of the ability to make judgments based on the information received through the eyes, the promptings of instinct needed to be brought under control, or there would have been endless clashes. The brain must have been 'specially charged with the duty of throwing back into the unconscious the presentations so provoked, because they would be very embarrassing in everyday life'. Occasionally, however, the urges 'pass through as contraband' – one of them being prompted by communication at a distance.

Bergson's theory has been generally accepted by psychical researchers. It helps both to make sense of extra-sensory perception and to explain its erratic performance. Psi gets through to us in two ways, the psychiatrist Jan Ehrenwald has suggested. One is 'need-determined': it is as if the filter mechanism concedes the urgency of the message, and lets it through. The other is 'flaw-determined': card-guessing tests may be singling out individuals whose filter is flawed – a little less discriminating than it is for the rest of us – so that they score above chance. Not enough attention had been paid to this distinction, Ehrenwald felt, or to its implications for research.

Need-determined psi has, or at least can have, a positive function. A revealing description of how it can work for some people was given by Rosalind Heywood in *The Infinite Hive*. In her case it took the form of an 'inner prompting' to action on behalf of others, 'which seems either beyond my normal capacity, or absurd in the light of facts known to me at the time, but turns out to be relevant in the light of other facts learnt later on'. These 'Orders', as she came to think of them, consisted of a simple urge to take some course, often related to her husband, as on an occasion when, in the wartime blackout, she suddenly felt she must meet him at the station as he would have no torch. He did, in fact, have a torch, but the battery had given out on the way to catch his train.

For obvious reasons, need-determined psi of this kind, with its strong signals, is unlikely to be picked up in laboratory trials of the card-guessing type. Researchers have had to rely on detecting the weaker signals of flaw-determined psi, except when they have been lucky enough to find psychics who seem to be able to exploit the flaws. A few have had outstandingly consistent records, notably Stefan Ossowiecki.

As a child, Ossowiecki had been the focus of poltergeist-type effects. Between the wars, he channelled his exteriorisations into clairvoyance, mainly to help friends and acquaintances to find lost or stolen belongings. A successful engineer, well-off and well-liked in his native Poland, he refused payment for his psychic services when they were required, and was always ready to co-operate in tests with psychical researchers, including Richet and Geley from France and Dingwall from the SPR. His record, Richet thought, was the best in the history of research into the mental phenomena of psi.

Then there was the young Czech Pavel Stepanek, in the 1960s. Stepanek was one of the European psychics who have been able to score significantly above chance in card-guessing tests, with only rare failures: Gaither Pratt thought him 'perhaps the outstanding test subject in the history of para-psychology', both in terms of the total of trials performed and the number of investigators (including conjurors) who had satisfied themselves that his powers were genuine.

In both these cases, particularly in Stepanek's, the volumi-nous records of the experiments made, the precautions taken, the results achieved, tedious though they are to plough through, make the contention that psi results cannot be repeated look unfair. Coupled with the results of the thousands of card-guessing trials on the Duke pattern, they impressed James McClenon when he was surveying them for his *Deviant Science*. The replication level, he confirmed, had in some cases been considerably higher than would be required in conventional psychology.

Sceptics have in fact been demanding that higher level, on the sensible ground that to prove the existence of ESP it is necessary to produce much stronger evidence than it would be to clear up some issue where psi is not involved. More than that, they have wanted psychics to be able to get results at any time, in any place. This is wilfully to misunderstand the nature of psi-abilities, as Ehrenwald has pointed out. Akin to love and ecstasy, they 'cannot be "willed" or coaxed into action'. On the contrary, the more actively the conscious mind is involved, as it is apt to be in tests, the less the likelihood of the psi information getting through.

By the same reasoning, it is not to be expected that individuals who happen to show up well in laboratory trials can necessarily exploit their talents for their own financial advantage. As E.G. Boring, Professor of Psychology at Har-vard and far from sympathetic to psychical research – he wrote the preface to Hansel's *ESP* – has observed, a performer at Zener card-guessing who averages seven correct guesses out of the twenty-five, instead of the chance expectation of five, is considered 'brilliant'. When people ask 'why these able percipients do not get rich by telepathing directors' meetings and playing the stock market with their superior knowledge, they do not know how small an advantage the best available telepathy of the modern age provides'.

Fraud?

When confronted by reports of psi phenomena which are hard
to dismiss on any other count, the reaction of sceptics has been
to insinuate, sometimes to assert, that they must have been
obtained by deception. Eusebe Salverte set the precedent. As
he was convinced that supernatural events were impossible,
he considered it legitimate to speculate how they might have
been staged. Writers following in his path, from Sir David
Brewster on to the Hansels and the Gardners of today, have
not hesitated to take the same course even if it leaves the clear
implication that the psychic, or the investigator, or both in
collusion, were guilty of fraud.

This technique was perfected by Frank Podmore, the first
historian of psychical research. As he found it impossible to
accept physical, as distinct from mental, mediumship, he was
free with his allegations of fraud. Ordinarily his target was the
medium, but if the precautions taken made it difficult to see
how they could have done their tricks, he did not hesitate to
cast doubt on the researcher. Inevitably this encouraged the
belief, even among psychical researchers, that their work had
been riddled with deception. Orthodox science by contrast
was assumed to be clean. The subjects, unlike mediums,
rarely had any inducement to cheat; and what scientist would
be so foolish as to fake his test results, knowing that he would
be shown up by the first person to repeat his experiments?

This complacency held good for nearly a century. 'Science
is a self-correcting system', C.P. Snow assured the American
Association for the Advancement of Science in 1960. 'No fraud
(or honest mistake) is going to stay undetected for long. There
is no need for any extrinsic scientific criticism, because
criticism is inherent in the process itself.'

How long was 'for long'? Soon, the cruelly penetrating eye
of the computer began to be directed at source material from
the distant past. Along with closer critical scrutiny by science
historians and by journalists, this has led to the conviction as
guilty of fraudulent practices of some of the greatest names in
science: Ptolemy, Galileo, Newton, Dalton, Mendel.

Some of the cheating has been venial enough, such as the
'massaging' or fudging of data to make good results look even
more impressive. Other cases are more serious, the neo-

Darwinians' record being particularly bad. Ernst Haeckel, widely regarded around the turn of the century as the world's leading expert on evolution, faked the illustrations in his *Natural History of Creation* and other works to fit his thesis. Three drawings of what were supposed to be the embryos of a dog, a chicken and a tortoise, to show how similar they were at that stage, turned out to be one and the same dog embryo. Taxed with this and other deceptions, Haeckel blandly admitted them, explaining in 1908 that 'the great majority of all the diagrams in the best biological textbooks, treatises and journals would incur in the same degree the charge of "forgery", for all of them are inexact and are more or less "doctored" '. It was the measure of the longing of his contemporaries for support for the Darwinian theory that this 'contrite confession', as he described it, was acceptable.

As Francis Hitching showed in *The Neck of the Giraffe*, the presentation of evidence for the neo-Darwinian theory has been riddled with what can best be described as false pretences. Drawings of what early man looked like appeared in profusion, based on the discovery of single bones. In one case, in 1922, the elaborate reconstruction was derived from a single tooth. The tooth was subsequently discovered to have come from a type of pig that had become extinct.

Predictably, the need to secure or retain funding has led to a rash of cases of fraud in recent years. 'I suspect that unconscious or dimly perceived finagling, doctoring and massaging are rampant, endemic and unavoidable in a profession that rewards status and power for clean and unambiguous discovery', Professor Stephen Jay Gould of Harvard has admitted. The self-regulating mechanism has broken down, causing a worried Lewis Thomas to wonder if this reveals a 'pattern of habitual falsehood in the process of science'.

William Broad and Nicholas Wade have shown in their *Betrayers of the Truth* that not merely have there been many cases recently where researchers have managed for a time to get away with fraud where science's safety net of repeatability ought to have trapped them much sooner; when they have been trapped, they have not necessarily been treated as pariahs. When William T. Summerlin was detected using ink to make patches on white mice to simulate grafts, Thomas announced that as he must have been suffering from 'an emotional disturbance of such a nature that he has not been fully responsible for the actions he has taken', he would be given a year's sick leave on full salary. In other cases – nobody can know how many – fraud has simply been hushed up.

In medical research fraud has become widespread, thanks to the willingness of the pharmaceutical industry to pay doctors for undertaking trials of drugs without worrying whether they are honestly carried out, so long as the findings are favourable. The report of the Kefauver Committee in the United States cited numerous examples, and there have been several cases in Britain. Nevertheless the General Medical Council has been far more lenient to doctors caught cheating than to doctors caught making love to their patients. Since it was given statutory powers in the 1860s – David Cargill, an Essex GP, has worked out – eighty-six of the ninety-four doctors convicted of the sex offence have been struck off the Register. Of the 123 who have been convicted of fraud and other forms of dishonesty, only sixty-seven have been struck off.

By contrast the record of psychical research seems reasonably clean. A young researcher in Rhine's laboratories was caught faking results of tests with animals in 1974, and four years later, S.G. Soal was posthumously convicted of having fudged some data. In both these cases not merely was the evidence of the fraud published there and then, but all the earlier findings of the two men were in effect struck from the record – though paradoxically in Soal's case this suggests the possibility that in some of the earlier trials he conducted, in the 1930s, he might have cheated to get *negative* results. Certainly at the time he was insinuating that the positive results being obtained in the United States were not to be trusted. 'Such things simply do not happen in England', he wrote, referring to material which was appearing from Duke and elsewhere: 'or if occasionally they appear to happen, they are quickly exposed as frauds or conjuring tricks'.

Harry Price, the celebrated 'ghost hunter' of the years between the wars, has also been retrospectively caught cheating. In his case, though, it was to 'expose' mediums and psychics, either out of pique or to boost his reputation as a hard-headed investigator. Price, a publicity-seeker first and a psychical researcher second, is the only exception to the rule

15 A typical 'reconstruction' of what early man looked like,
derived in this case from the discovery of a single tooth, which
was later unmasked as coming from an extinct species of pig.

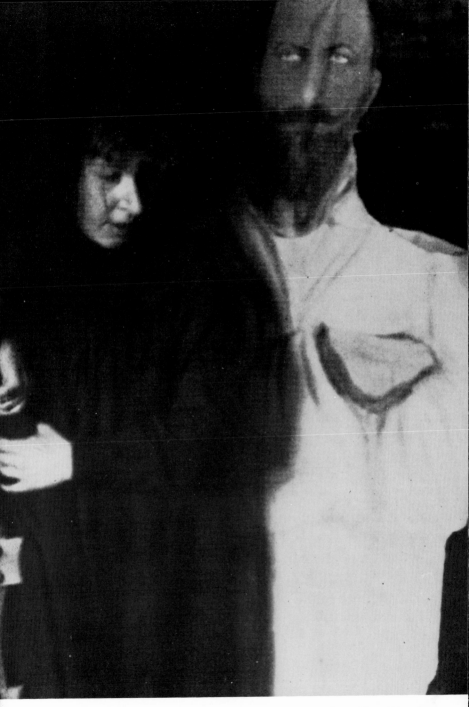

16 A manifestly bogus-looking materialisation from 'Eva C.'
Many critics resorted to the regurgitation hypothesis but, as
witness after witness testified, the figures could be seen
emerging from what started as a nebulous cloud of ectoplasm,
before vanishing.

that the three sirens, Fame, Advancement and Wealth, do not waste their time singing to psychical researchers. Funds have been hard to come by; an interest in such research is more likely to blight than improve the chances of academic promotion; and notoriety, rather than fame, has been the lot of those who have refused to be frightened off.

A lure of a different kind remains. Sceptics have come to rely on it as their main contention, providing a motive for fraud. Psychical researchers, they assert, have 'a longing to believe' in paranormal phenomena, which makes them an easy prey to crafty mediums and psychics.

This is a view which can only be put forward by somebody who either has no knowledge of the history of psychical research or is determined to ignore it. From the start it was dominated by men of sceptical temperament – Sidgwick, in particular, with what he himself admitted was his 'cold corrosive scepticism'. Signing a friend's application to join the Society, Alfred Russel Wallace told her she would not learn much, 'as the majority of the active members are so absurdly and illogically sceptical'.

Even when they were investigating a subject who they hoped might produce positive results in telepathy trials, those early psychical researchers took immense care to make them as foolproof and fraudproof as possible. The last thing they wanted was that anybody would be able to produce evidence that there had been flaws in the methodology, or that a subject had been boasting he had found a way to cheat. As William James put it, if he had to point to a scientific journal 'where hard-headedness and never-sleeping suspicion of sources of error might be seen in their full bloom', it would be the *Proceedings* of the SPR. That tradition has been preserved. It would be difficult to think of men with harder heads and more suspicious minds than most of the Society's Research Officers: Hodgson, Podmore, Dingwall, West.

Scepticism has remained one of the Society's hallmarks. It takes various forms. In extreme cases, by no means rare in psychical research societies, it manifests itself in an unwillingness, even a total inability, to credit any report of psi. The longer this habit of mind is cultivated, the more difficult it becomes to break, for a reason which Salverte, sceptical though he was, understood. 'When the improbability of a fact is the chief objection to the belief in its reality', he argued, 'the evidence which attests it regains all its value if the improbability is proved to be only apparent.' A present-day sceptic, suddenly confronted with some psi phenomenon which he knows must be genuine, would be put in a distinctly embarrassing position. Not merely would he need to look back over his past rejects to decide which of them should regain their value, he might also find that he imputed fraud where, in retrospect, psi becomes the more plausible explanation. Is he to indulge in an orgy of *mea culpa*? Not if he can help it!

A second category of sceptic allows himself to be convinced from time to time by what he has witnessed or heard, and later begins to suffer from 'cognitive dissonance', as Leon Festinger described it. In this context it takes the form of a chronic feeling of discomfort at having to hold two contradictory beliefs at the same time. Forks do not bend when stroked, yet they bend when Geller strokes them. A conjuror shows he can bend them by a trick; *ergo*, Geller is a conjuror too! The dissonance ceases.

The commonest of all forms of scepticism is produced by the fact that all of us have what Renée Haynes, a former editor of the SPR *Journal* and a perceptive writer on various historical and scientific aspects of psi, has called the boggle threshold: the point at which we feel compelled to say 'that's going too far!' A recent example has been the reaction to 'SORRAT', the Society for the Research on Rapport and Telekinesis, set up in the United States by Professor J.G. Neihardt. Its principal contribution has been the 'mini-lab', which anybody can set up at home by buying a glass tank of the kind normally used for tropical fish, inverting it, and then seeing if PK effects can be produced on the objects within, using a film camera to record any changes.

Unluckily for some of the experimenters, a few of the results they presented were too astonishing to be welcome. Not merely did objects move, but written messages appeared, along with apports and other manifestations of the kind that were once the commonplace of Victorian seances (though necessarily on a smaller scale). The reaction of some senior British and American parapsychologists was of scandalised revulsion. This was just the kind of nonsense, they feared, that would delight sceptics. A campaign arose to discredit SOR-

RAT, finding public expression in a deplorably vulgar film designed to discredit the enterprise by poking fun at it, which was actually shown at the SPR's centenary conference. Sceptics could not have behaved more vindictively than 'believers' in psi did on that occasion. Still, at least their conduct effectively disposes of the 'longing to believe' myth.

The myth disposed of, there remains another which has long accompanied it: that scientists, whatever their beliefs, are not qualified to detect conjuring tricks. Leaving aside the fact that on several occasions conjurors were invited to test mediums, Home and Eusapia among them, and admitted themselves unable to detect any trickery, it is only necessary to examine the precautions taken by psychical researchers in many of the series of experiments – attested by a range of witnesses who were invited to check for themselves – to realise that the phenomena which the mediums produced could not have been accomplished by trickery on the part of the medium, however brilliant a conjuror.

Take the case of 'Eva C.' – Marthe Béraud. Witnesses were invited to see for themselves that she did not bring anything with her into sessions, and during them they could sit beside her, in light good enough to watch what she was doing, as she produced her ectoplasmic materialisations. Even those sceptics who could not bring themselves to accept that the materialisations were genuine could and did satisfy themselves, as they admitted, that there was only one way in which she could have produced them. She must be swallowing a substance before the session, they claimed, and regurgitating it.

This was the verdict of the leading German critics of psychical research, and of Houdini, after they had witnessed the phenomena. Yet it requires only a brief look at the reports of scores of sessions, coupled with the photographs taken during them, to realise that the regurgitation hypothesis cannot be taken seriously.

For a start, simply because it was the sceptics' main, and almost only, line of attack, elaborate precautions were taken. As Richet recalled: 'her hair, armpits, nose, mouth and knees were examined; in some cases even examination *per rectum et vaginam* was resorted to'. Because the materialisations were often seen to come from her mouth, she had to drink bilberry syrup or coffee before sessions. 'Experimental rigour was even pushed to the point of giving her an emetic before a seance.' Yet the materialisations showed no sign of colouring.

Even if no such precautions had been taken, the regurgitation hypothesis breaks down when the records and the accompanying photographs are examined. The full-form materialisations which the young Marthe Béraud produced now look in the photographs as if an accomplice must have been smuggled in – but how can this allegation, made at the time, square with Richet's account of watching the form materialise gradually? As for the two-dimensional forms she produced later, in her 'Eva C.' period, they too were often seen to form gradually out of ectoplasm. In any case, it is obvious looking at them that they could not conceivably have been regurgitated.

With some other physical mediums the precautions were as careful. In Germany during the 1920s Baron Schrenck-Notzing was able to exploit his social standing and his wife's wealth to entertain savants, scientists and sceptics, in order to demonstrate to them that there could be no deception. Accounts ranging from the reports of Dingwall, the SPR's Research Officer at the time, in the Society's *Journal*, to Thomas Mann's description, show the elaborate pains taken to enable witnesses to see for themselves not merely that there was no trickery, but that there could be no trickery unless with their connivance.

We are confronted with a stark choice. Either objects did move at a distance for Eusapia and the Schneider brothers – either ectoplasmic materialisations did manifest themselves from Eva C. – or some of the best-known and most respected men and women of the period were liars, claiming to have taken precautions that had not been taken or to have witnessed phenomena that had not happened, or were cheats, conspiring with mediums to produce spurious accounts of sessions, week after week, to be illustrated with rigged photographs.

This is an aspect of the evidence that few psychical researchers appreciate. They have allowed themselves to be persuaded that the earlier researchers, although with rare exceptions honourable men and women, could have been duped by the mediums they were investigating. It is only necessary to consider Richet's case to realise that he could not have been duped when, after watching ectoplasm gradually forming itself into a figure, he proceeded to investigate it. 'I have heard the sound of its footsteps, its breathing and its voice. I have touched its hand on several occasions,' he asserted. 'I have been enabled through the drapery with which it was covered to feel the wrist, the carpal and metacarpal bones, which bend under the pressure of my grasp.' He even got the figure to blow through a tube into a flask of water, which bubbled, 'proving that the respiration of this phantom produced carbonic acid, exactly like our own'. Sometimes the ectoplasm issued from Marthe, sometimes independently of her, in a small stream or cloud, gradually developing into a face or a full-form, and eventually dissipating like a cloud; sometimes gradually, 'sometimes almost in an instant'.

Richet was a leading physiologist. His early disbelief in the physical phenomena of mediumship had been slow to evaporate during investigations of Eusapia, and he had remained suspicious of spirit forms. 'Whoever has the privilege of knowing this admirable investigator', Theodore Flournoy observed, 'knows well enough his scientific caution, his exceptional perspicacity, and his unrivalled experience at mediumistic seances.' Hard though it is to believe that he could have been duped, it is surely harder to believe Richet was a liar. He knew his research into mediumship could have won him praise only if he exposed it as fraudulent. As for the possibility that he was in collusion with Marthe, she would only have had to betray him – for which she could have expected a tempting fee from some journal – to destroy the career in orthodox physiology which, a few years later, was to bring him a Nobel prize.

Richet was far from being the only researcher whose scientific and personal reputation would have been destroyed if he had been detected in collusion with a medium. Others, whose attestations of what they witnessed in tests, and the precautions taken, make it clear that either the phenomena were genuine or that they must have collaborated in deception, include such names as d'Arsonval, Crookes, Pierre Curie, de Morgan, Fechner, Flammarion, Flournoy, de Gasparin, William James, Lodge, Lombroso, Morselli, Myers,

Ochorowicz, Wallace and Zöllner, all of whom enjoyed international reputations.

This list, too, leaves out many men and women of unblemished integrity who chose to give up their careers in orthodox science to undertake psychical research; as well as scientists, well-known in their day, whom they invited to participate in experiments and who testified to witnessing the phenomena. Eusapia, in particular, could only have done her 'tricks' if she was at the centre of a wide circle of conspirators. Surely, Flournoy mused, it could not have existed without a traitor who would have betrayed it? 'But I forget', he added characteristically, 'that I myself am part of this conspiracy, and that I have already said too much!'

The Significance of Psi Effects

The Variables

As the evidence against psi is so inadequate, how can the pretence be maintained that the evidence for psi does not fulfil science's requirements? The reason is that in one important respect it does not, and in the foreseeable future, cannot, fulfil them. Psi cannot be pinned down for research purposes in the ways that scientists have come to trust. Its route to acceptance is blocked by the idiosyncratic nature of its 'variables'. Although psychologists have to contend with variables, too, theirs are more easily pinned down, or at least allowed for, as in the case of expectancy-effect. It has come to be realised that an experimenter can transmit to his subjects, consciously or unconsciously, what he expects or hopes the result of a test will be, and that consciously or unconsciously they may help to obtain those results for him, so preventive measures have been devised.

From the start of the trials at Duke, the importance of eliminating this and other forms of experimenter-effect was recognised. Knowing that any slip-up in their precautions will be pounced upon, by other psychical researchers as well as by sceptics, parapsychologists have since taken great care to identify and control all known variables of this kind. Their precautions have in fact been considerably more stringent than those of orthodox psychologists, as Robert Rosenthal, Professor of Social Psychology at Harvard, realised when he was engaged on the research for his seminal *Experimenter-Effects in Behavioral Research*. The parapsychologists had been the pioneers in finding ways to bring experimenter-effects under control, he had found. So strict had their rules been that orthodox psychologists would be outraged if asked to introduce them in their own research.

A consequence of this experimental rigour has been the uncovering of a proliferation of variables. It has proved 'extraordinarily difficult', as Professor Jan Ludwig recognised in his balanced introduction to *Philosophy and Parapsychology*, a collection of papers putting the case for and against psi, 'especially without a highly developed theory, to control all the individual variables which might affect the performance of a subject at a particular time'.

The first to attract attention was decline-effect. A subject who had been scoring consistently and significantly above chance in card-guessing trials would lose the gift after a while. Richet had noticed this in some of his early experiments; fifty years later the team at Duke University came across it sufficiently often to realise that it was almost predictable.

Decline-effect brought about by fatigue or boredom has long been known to psychologists, and it was reasonable to surmise that some similar mechanism might be at work to account for it in card-guessing experiments. Still, it was annoying, the more so as sceptics could claim – falsely, as Rhine was able to show – that the decline was the result of stricter precautions being imposed upon successful subjects who were no longer able to cheat.

Not all the hidden variables that parapsychologists have uncovered have been unwelcome. Gertrude Schmeidler's tests, which showed that believers in ESP – 'sheep' – tended to score above chance, and sceptics – 'goats' – below chance, could be regarded as a confirmation of psi's existence. In some of its manifestations, so can displacement-effect, particularly when the displacement is in time – as when Whately Carington, testing subjects for ESP, found that some of them were displaying precognition. The tests consisted of putting up a drawing of some familiar object, selected by a randomising technique, on the wall of his study, leaving it overnight, changing it daily, and inviting volunteers to try to match it. The drawings and the guesses were sent to a scrutineer to be 'paired', whenever a guess hit the mark. Some volunteers, it was found, scored significantly above chance on the picture that was going to be put up the following evening.

Intrigued, Carington suggested to S.G. Soal that he should re-examine the results of ESP card-guessing tests he had conducted earlier with negative results. Accepting the challenge, Soal found that two of the subjects had scored significantly above chance expectation on the card *after* the one they were supposed to be guessing. Although none of Soal's results is now accepted, it seems reasonably certain that he did not cheat in this one, as he neither expected nor desired the result.

Precognition of this kind has been discovered in other trials, and can be added to the plus side as evidence for psi. Another type of displacement-effect, extremely common, has proved a nuisance. Clairvoyant perception, Wallace was one of the first to warn, is imprecise. An orange may be 'seen' as a ball, a poker as a walking stick. This, Eleanor Sidgwick suggested, is because psi communication comes through the subconscious mind, 'and therefore has to run the gauntlet of the passage from one stratum to another'. Not merely does this mean that the clairvoyant picture of the orange may emerge to consciousness as a ball: it may pick up associations on the way. One of the commonest forms of this type of distortion is the intrusion of the percipient's preconceptions, expectations or desires into the information as it is on the way through to consciousness – 'secondary elaboration', as René Warcollier, one of the ablest of French investigators between the wars, described it. As the psi-borne information came through, he found it tended to 'excite the imagination and the memories of the percipient' as a tune or a scent can do, and this made it harder to distinguish between the message and its associations. In particular, he observed, the use of language itself in connection with telepathy trials could cause problems because the messages can arrive as images, which have to be translated into words.

Sceptics have alleged that belief in displacement-effect exists merely to permit psychical researchers to classify 'ball' as a hit, when the ESP target has been an orange. If it was not found in other branches of psychology dealing with material coming through the subconscious, this would be easier to sustain. Freud's *Interpretation of Dreams* and some of his other works are full of examples of the way in which the promptings of the unconscious reach the surface in all manner of displacements, slips of the tongue, puns, gaffes and so on. They have since fascinated Jacques Lacan for whom, as a commentator has put it, 'the structure of the unconscious is knowable only by those who are prepared to admit and espouse its inexhaustible capacity for displacement'.

One of displacement-effect's implications, to which parapsychologists have paid insufficient attention in the past, is the extent to which allowance should be made for it in controlled trials. The way in which psi could be missed has been illustrated by the experience of a London journalist, Georgina Howell. She had gone to interview Doris Stokes, internationally the best-known medium in recent years, at the time of the publication of her autobiography, *Voices in My Ear*, in 1980. While they were having coffee Doris said that a message was coming through for her interviewer. It was from 'Clive', who had just 'passed on', requesting that his friend Tracy should be reassured; Clive was all right, in the spirit; Tracy must get on with her own life and not worry about him. Georgina Howell could not remember anybody she knew called Clive, or for that matter Tracy. At this point the photographer who had come with her said he felt that he must interrupt. His friend Clive, he said, had died – at three o'clock that morning. Tracy was the name of his girlfriend.

To spiritualists, this would count as excellent evidence of a communication from the spirit world. Most psychical researchers would attribute it to telepathic linkage between Doris Stokes and the photographer, coupled with displacement-effect. Both would agree that coincidence is highly improbable – as, in this case, was collusion. In short, it was good evidence for psi. Yet if the interview had been conducted in the controlled conditions which parapsychologists have so often felt obliged to adopt, the photographer would not have been present, and the message would have been put down as a 'miss' instead of a 'hit' displaced.

The most irritating, to psychical researchers, of the known variables have been labelled sceptic-effect and shyness-effect. When the anthropologist Francis Galton went to watch Crookes and Wallace testing mediums, he arrived in a sceptical frame of mind but prepared to watch. He had been 'utterly confounded by the results', he wrote to tell his cousin Charles Darwin, 'and very disinclined to discredit them'. Yet other scientists who had been invited, and who had made no attempt to disguise their contempt for the whole procedure, had been rewarded by witnessing nothing of any interest. Crookes was right, Galton feared: 'people who come as men of science are usually so disagreeable, opinionated and obstructive and have so little patience that seances rarely succeed with them'.

Even when no sceptic was present, it was often found that formal testing was enough to inhibit mediums, however scintillating their spontaneous performances might be. Daniel Home could produce only some feeble raps when he was asked to demonstrate by a committee of inquiry – though in later trials, in his case, shyness-effect was overcome.

Both effects are commonly enough encountered in everyday life – and in literature: the sight of Murdstone's cane sent the lessons which David Copperfield had learned 'slipping off, not one by one, or line by line, but by the entire page', as if on skates. A golfer who can sink putts of a yard forty-nine times out of fifty when there is no need to sink them will often miss if the putt is for the match, and still more often if there is a wager on the outcome.

Sceptic-effect and shyness-effect are embarrassing because sceptics can and often do claim that they are a cop-out. The medium is inhibited, they assert, because if he knows the test will be properly controlled, or that a sceptic will be present, he will be detected in trickery as soon as he goes into his usual repertoire. The problems they present, though, are real enough even without having to contend with sceptics' ribaldry. Sceptic-effect is not just a matter of waves of hostility, shyness-effect not just a matter of blocking the ability to do something automatically without thinking. In both psi may be involved.

De Morgan made this point in a letter to Wallace, recalling his early experiences with a medium. He had come to the conclusion that the state of mind of the investigator affected the phenomena, either because the medium was put off by the investigator's attitude or because the spirits were offended. De Morgan had been impressed by the medium's ability to bring him into communication with his dead father, who had told him things which he knew that the medium herself could not possibly have discovered; yet when George Henry Lewes

allowed himself to be persuaded to test her, the 'spirit' had
made an ass of itself.

It was not necessary to think in terms of offended spirits.
The phenomena may be blocked by unconscious psychic
processes – including unconscious scepticism. Henry Sidgwick's 'liberal heart', William James was to recall, had to
work with an intellect 'which acted destructively on almost
every particular object of belief that was offered for his
acceptance'. To Crookes, Sidgwick was one of those people
who 'are so constituted that nothing psychic will take place in
their presence'.

Sidgwick appears to have been what has since come to be
described as a psi-inhibitor, a species by no means uncommon
in societies for psychical research. They are not necessarily
sceptics, though often they become incapable of accepting
evidence for psi because they have been unable to obtain it
themselves. Psi-sceptic-effect, blocking communication or action at a distance, is now well established, and is only one of
many psi-effects which have been detected.

For many years psychical researchers admitted sceptic-
effect and shyness-effect, but attributed them to direct
Murdstone-effect. The belief in the existence of inhibiting
psychic forces was a relic of the superstitious doctrine of evil
spirits, Walter Prince assured the SPR in his 1930 Presidential
Address. It should be repudiated, 'especially as it has been
thoroughly disproved'. At Duke, where the emphasis was so
heavily on maintaining scientific controls, the possibility of
psi-experimenter-effect was for many years ignored.

The first warning note was sounded in 1949 by Gardner
Murphy, next to Rhine the most influential figure in parapsychology and, as a past president of the American Psychological Association, even more influential in academic circles.
Extra-sensory perception, Murphy had come to believe, does
not lie within the individual, in the sense that sight does. 'I
believe, on the contrary, that it is strictly interpersonal,' he
told the members of the SPR in his Presidential Address,
twenty years after Prince's. 'It relies on the relations between
persons and not *in* the persons as such.' Consequently it must
be in 'certain specific relations between the psychic structure
of one individual and the psychic structure of another that our
clue lies'.

The Fisk/West Experiments

If this was right, the importance of his hypothesis for para-psychology could hardly be overestimated. A member of the Council of the SPR, G.W. Fisk, thought of a way to test it with the co-operation of Dr D. J. West, then the Society's Research Officer.

Fisk was one of the many hard-working, self-effacing SPR members whose careers and characters have belied the common impression of a psychical researcher as eccentric, deluded, or both. Before the First World War he had worked as a teacher in China, and after it, when he returned there, as a labour superintendent in a mining company. On coming back to England he went into partnership with a man who was an expert on spring balances; together they were responsible for the anglepoise lamp. He had been interested in the paranormal in China, in particular noting the ability of the Chinese to orientate themselves to the points of the compass even when deprived of any clues as to where north and south lay; but he remained sceptical, first making his mark in the SPR when he discovered how spurious above-chance scores might be produced in a new form of test which had been presented. In Rosalind Heywood's opinion he was 'sceptically scientific, yet open-minded and humorous, humble and kind'.

One of Fisk's innovations was to send out cards with clock faces on them in sealed envelopes to volunteers, inviting them to try to guess the time by clairvoyance. The method had the double advantage of simplicity and of enabling him to check whether any of the subjects were persistently guessing, say, an hour before the times (set by a randomising technique) on the clock faces – indicating displacement-effect. The subjects recorded their guesses, and returned them to Fisk. A few, he found, were scoring above chance expectation. With these he was soon achieving gratifyingly positive results.

Why should Fisk be getting them when other SPR members often could not? West, as it happened – later to be the Society's President – had won the reputation of a 'psi-inhibitor'. Positive results from the tests he was involved in were rare. The experiment tried was simple, but ingenious. Fisk sent out cards as usual, without telling the subjects that included among them were cards which West had been responsible for randomising, in an order which Fisk had not seen. When they were returned, the correct guesses on the cards which Fisk had randomised were, as before, significantly above chance. The correct guesses on the cards which West had randomised, with a single exception, were at the chance level.

'The fact, if fact it be', the investigators commented in their report, 'that the person who actually prepares the lists of random numbers, arranges the cards in packs and finally assesses and marks the score sheets, should have some influence over the result is very mysterious and surprising.' It would also have very serious implications for the whole future of parapsychology, as West intimated later at the symposium on the whole subject sponsored by CIBA in 1956. To ensure that the designer of trials did not wittingly or unwittingly influence the results, it had been suggested that he should absent himself entirely from the trials. Now, West pointed out, it had been demonstrated that experimenter-effect could not necessarily be banished simply by quarantining the experimenter. Fisk had had some contact with the subjects of the trials, usually by correspondence. West had had none. He did not even know who they were. Nor, of course, did they know of his role. Yet it appeared to have had a significant effect.

In a second test, in 1958, working with a single woman subject, Fisk did not send out the clock faces. He selected them at home, leaving her to try to guess them by ESP and to post him her results. Again, unknown to her, West set half the clock faces, neither Fisk nor West knowing the times the other had set. Again, the subject scored significantly higher than chance on the cards set by Fisk, only at chance level on those set by West.

In an article 'Psi and the Nature of Things' in 1963 Jule Eisenbud rammed the implications home. Parapsychologists had been desperately trying to fit the investigation of psi processes into a science-as-usual framework, conducting experiments 'on the curious assumption that the subjects in them will not use the very faculties they are being tested for', and that while being tested, 'they will use those faculties only within the confines of their designated roles in the particular design employed'. The possibility had been ignored that subjects might not keep within such confines. Everybody,

Eisenbud complained, had behaved as if there were some sort of gentleman's agreement committing subjects, experimenters, judges and other participating personnel 'to stick faithfully to their designated roles in the experiment as scripted'.

Yet still, for a time, the implications of the research continued to be ignored. Although Fisk and West received the McDougall Award for distinguished work in parapsychology, researchers in general behaved as if their findings had never been made known. The 'controls' became if anything even more rigorous. Asked some years later why so little attention was paid to the findings, Rosalind Heywood – shrewdest and kindliest of the members of the SPR Council, in those days: 'catalyst in chief', as Arthur Koestler described her in his dedication to her in *The Roots of Coincidence* – replied 'everyone has been too embarrassed'. To have to admit that all the effort which had been spent on making trials both objective and rigorously controlled had been wasted was too painful to face.

This was understandable in the light of a report in the *Journal of Parapsychology* in 1973. A girl who had volunteered to prepare symbols for a clairvoyant test happened to be keeping notes of how she was feeling. At one stage of the work she had just received a note turning down her application for a job; at the same time she was suffering from a cold, and associated aches, so that she found it difficult to concentrate on what she was doing. When the trial was completed, although the overall results were negative there was a strong correlation between her moods and her subjects' scoring rates.

Eventually, however, the 'gentleman's agreement' Eisenbud had referred to was broken by Rhea White in two lengthy articles in the *Journal* of the American SPR in 1976. 'Although traditionally it has been assumed that it is the subject's ESP or PK that is being measured', she recalled, 'there are some indications that various other persons taking part in an experiment on the experimenter's side of the fence, as it were, are influencing the subject's scores. These persons may determine whether the subject will score positively, negatively, or at chance.'

'Some' indications, Rhea White went on to show, was a massive understatement. The evidence was overwhelming. 'The potential influence of persons other than the subject should be taken into account in designing ESP and PK tests', she concluded, 'to see if we can catch them red-handed, as it were, instead of merely noting their tracks after the fact, when little can be done to increase our understanding of how they came to be there.'

The same problem has arisen in connection with trials of psychics who, like Uri Geller, produce psychokinetic phenomena. In the period during which the psychic Matthew Manning was tested in many different countries, from 1977 to 1979, he was involved in thirty-two separate trials, of which seventeen produced positive results. He was interested to note, he has since recalled, that there were some investigators with whom he consistently produced them, others with whom he as consistently failed to produce anything at all. 'The researcher plays a vital role in the ultimate result of the experiment,' Manning concluded. 'He is a part of it, just as much as the subject, which is obviously why hostile researchers and scientists fail to produce results.'

Quite often, too, there were results – but not of a kind which could be registered. PK effects would be seen or heard in some other part of the laboratory. Perhaps, Manning surmised, this might be because the investigators had been unconsciously frightened of witnessing a PK event, or of being involved in a successful test, though not strongly enough 'to prevent *some* effect occurring'.

From his experience with physical mediumship, Oliver Lodge had foreseen that problems would arise if attempts were made to impose controls on PK: 'we cannot always tell beforehand what precise phenomena are going to be present'. Objects which the medium might be trying to move would remain fixed, while others in a different part of the room would fall, or float. In any case, precautions taken in experiments would obviously be 'ineffective against an "apport", or vice versa'.

Apports were frequently encountered in spiritualist seances, in poltergeist hauntings and in tests of some mediums, such as Palladino. After the 1930s, when physical mediumship ceased to interest parapsychologists, they were put out of mind as a source of potential embarrassment. Orthodox scientists, hard enough to convince of straightforward ESP or PK, could not be expected to take them seriously. With Uri Geller, they came back into the reckoning, as his investigator, Professor

17 Houdini demonstrating the 'box' he designed to test the medium 'Margery' – only to be humiliated in the attempt.

18 *Top left*, Alfred Russel Wallace   19 *Top right*, Daniel Dunglas Home
20 *Bottom left*, Camille Flammarion 21 *Bottom right*, Sir Oliver Lodge

John Hasted, found; and even more with Matthew Manning.

As a schoolboy, Manning had been the focus of the poltergeist happenings which he described in *The Link*, and which were well-attested by, among others, the headmaster of his school, who might earlier have expelled him on the strength of the crazy manifestations that his schoolfellows had to put up with. Eventually Manning learned how to sublimate and subjugate such psychic forces by taking up automatic writing and drawing, but when he went on radio and TV programmes, as the first of the mini-Gellers to attract attention, the studios were plagued with electrical faults in the lights and the cameras. Later, in his home, fresh poltergeist-type events occurred.

The 'Jester'

They foreshadowed a fresh source of embarrassment for parapsychologists: jester-effect. As in poltergeist hauntings, the form they took often suggested a practical joker, determined to plague his investigators. A precaution parapsychologists have felt compelled to take, to satisfy the demand for controls, is to ensure that test runs are randomised, so that it cannot be alleged that the subject has managed to get hold of a proposed sequence in advance. On one occasion when Manning was being tested to find whether he could influence a subject's heart rate paranormally from another room, the investigator decided to make it a properly controlled experiment by arranging some periods in which Manning would try to exert his powers, others when he would not. To randomise the sequence a coin was spun. Tails came up thirty-two times running, before it was decided that a different method would have to be used. Twenty cards were shuffled, half of them blanks. The first ten to be turned over were all blanks. Eventually they settled for random number tables. No sooner had the experiment begun than the monitoring equipment broke down. There was nothing the matter with it: it started up again with no difficulty as soon as the experiment had been abandoned.

This could be explained as psi-effect by Manning or his investigator, or both together, but there have been many occasions when the disruption has appeared to be caused by a 'discarnate entity', as researchers who shy away from the term 'spirit' have described it. One form it has taken was described by Mrs de Morgan, wife of the celebrated mathematician, in her *From Matter to Spirit* in 1863. In table-turning sessions, which she liked to study with detachment, she found that the table often behaved as if in the course of a sitting it was developing a personality of its own, reacting to the personalities of sitters – sceptics in particular. With some it seemed to go into a sulk; nothing would happen and the session would have to be abandoned. With others it would be galvanised into action. On one occasion, when a suitor of the daughter of the householder said he preferred to watch and settled down comfortably to enjoy himself, the heavy boarding-house-type table instructed the sitters by the rapping code to get out of its way. Although they were not touching it, it moved towards him and pinned him down to the back of the sofa.

Poltergeists have become notorious for their ability to produce manifestations which have every appearance of being the work of an intelligence, and frequently one which takes a malicious pleasure in making things difficult for investigators. The physicists who investigated the Rosenheim outbreak described the effects as having a tendency to evade investigation. Trying to obtain photographic evidence of the depredations of a poltergeist in a London suburb in 1977, Guy Playfair found that expensive sophisticated equipment, installed and worked by experts, malfunctioned as if somebody even more expert was playing tricks with it. To rely on conventional physical controls in such circumstances becomes futile.

The evidence pointing to the existence in such cases of an intelligence which appears to have a life of its own is now overwhelming. What remains in dispute is whether it indicates the existence of entities in, as it were, their own right, or of exteriorised forces from a split-off personality, or – as the lawyer and physician Joseph Maxwell, one of the psychical researchers in France in the early 1900s, suggested – 'a compound of the elementary consciousness of the sitters'. In his experiments things seemed to happen 'as though the nervous influx of the sitters creates a field of force around the experimenters'.

Recently a group in Toronto has provided remarkable confirmation of Maxwell's theory, in experiments to see if an entity could be 'conjured up', in the original sense of that term. They invented a historical personage, providing him with a fictitious personality, and began to invoke him in table-turning sessions. Soon 'Philip' was responding to their questions with raps and movements of the table. Eventually he took on a character of his own, as if he had been endowed with an existence independent of the group – even contradicting their version of his life story. The outcome of the 'Philip' experiment was significant not simply because it repeated the lesson often learned from a study of mediums, that information which purports to come from a deceased person is coming from another source, but also because it showed that a group can literally conjure up a personality of the kind commonly encountered in poltergeist hauntings, capable of producing psi effects as if it were independent of investigators, subjects and witnesses and others concerned in experiments.

Synchronicity

Jester-effect, and psi-experiment-effect of the kind revealed by the Fisk/West trials, add to the other problems parapsychologists face in their efforts to produce evidence of the kind that conventional science demands. Recently yet another hidden variable has surfaced, still further to confuse the issue: synchronicity, which Jung defined as 'a coincidence in time of two or more causally unrelated events which have the same or similar meaning'.

There are problems here. An implication of Jung's theory was that synchronous coincidences are meaningful. But many coincidences, though so striking that it is hard to attribute them to sheer chance, do not appear to have any message unless, as in one of the most celebrated of them – the story related to Camille Flammarion by the poet Émile Deschamps – jester-effect is at work.

While at school, Deschamps was given some plum pudding to taste by M. de Fortgibu, an émigré who had just returned from England. Ten years later, seeing a plum pudding in the window of a Paris restaurant, he asked if he could have a slice. It had been reserved, he was told, for M. de Fortgibu, who was there taking dinner. Thus far, simple coincidence would be easy to sustain. Years later, invited out to dinner, Deschamps heard that he was to have plum pudding. He related the story to his hostess, joking that M. de Fortgibu might be expected to join them. M. de Fortgibu, by now an old man, tottered in. He, too, had come to dinner with some friends and had rung the wrong doorbell.

Sceptics have tended to take the line that however weird the coincidence, chance is the most reasonable explanation. A ship called the *Caroline* was wrecked, the sole survivor being a man called Golding, a few days after Arthur Law had written a play about a man called Golding who was the sole survivor of the wreck of a ship called the *Caroline*. Ivor Tuckett actually used the tale in his *Evidence for the Supernatural*, a book published in 1911 with the aim of demolishing that evidence, as 'a case of pure coincidence', rather than of precognition; 'of that there can be no doubt'. Presumably he would have been equally dogmatic about another case had he been writing a year later.

In 1898 the then well-known American novelist Morgan Robertson had published a story, *Futility*, describing how the largest liner in the world – 'unsinkable' because of its water-tight compartments, and therefore not needing to carry a full set of lifeboats – had been so designed that even if it hit an iceberg at speed, it would still float. On a transatlantic voyage it did hit an iceberg, and sank with the loss of most of those on board. The liner's name was *Titan*. Fourteen years later the *Titanic* – which in such matters as tonnage, the number of passengers, the number of lifeboats and the construction of the water-tight doors, might have been modelled on the *Titan* – met the same fate.

As Robertson could not have known about the *Titanic*, which was not even on the drawing board at the time he was writing *Futility*, the odds against coincidence are long. Investigating the whole affair, Eisenbud found evidence which makes precognition even more plausible. Not merely was Robertson fascinated by the occult, and by Fate, he believed he was a medium. As a journalist wrote in *Morgan Robertson the Man*, to which friends contributed their recollections of him, Robertson thought that 'some spirit entity with literary ability, denied physical expression, had commandeered his body and brain for the purpose of giving to the world the literary gems which had made him famous'. Robertson himself could not write stories, as he admitted. He always had to wait for them to come through to him from this discarnate writer who used him as a physical channel.

The case for accepting psi as a possible component in coincidences was put forcibly by Richet, who recalled an occasion when the arrival of a postman coincided with an accident in a dream he was having. He was being driven in a car with the wife of the explorer Jean Charcot, whom he did not know. They were travelling so fast that he feared an accident: 'the accident happened and I awoke' – the 'accident' being the postman's interruption to deliver a registered letter. Taking the letter, Richet fancied (he did not know why) that there was some link with his dream. It came from a friend who lived in the Azores, 'asking for an introduction to Jean Charcot, whom I did not know, who was due to reach the Azores a few weeks later in his yacht'.

It had not been simply this, or similar experiences which had happened to him, Richet insisted, which made him believe that coincidences could be a product of psi. 'In themselves these cases prove nothing, but they reinforce the large number of proofs collected by more favoured observers.' In *The Invisible Writing* Koestler described how in 1937, while under sentence of death in a Seville gaol, the recollection of a passage from Thomas Mann's *Buddenbrooks* gave him 'great spiritual comfort'. In it, Mann described how Consul Thomas Buddenbrooks, knowing he was shortly to die, had fallen under the spell of a book which for years had lain unread in his library – Schopenhauer's *On Death*, in which death was explained not as a final extinction, but as a transition. The day after he was freed, Koestler wrote to Mann to thank him. In his reply, Mann told him that on an impulse he had gone to his library and picked up the book, which he was actually re-reading when the postman arrived with Koestler's letter.

Knowing how sceptics would seize upon the lack of any attestation, Koestler regretted that in the course of his vicissitudes over the next three years, before he found sanctuary in England, he had lost the letter. When Mann's diaries were published, shortly after Koestler's death, the entry for May 22, 1937 described his having received a 'stirring letter from the journalist Koestler' at the moment that he was reading that very chapter, which he had not looked at for thirty-five years.

Granted that psi may be in operation, some of these cases can be accounted for by straightforward telepathy or pre-cognition. With others, the meaningful component appears to point to intervention of the kind that Socrates attributed to his daemon. Camille Flammarion recalled how, while he was writing his *magnum opus* on the atmosphere, a wind suddenly blew through his study and whisked pages out of the window. As it was raining, he did not think it worth pursuing them. To his astonishment, when he next went to the printers they had set the entire chapter. What had happened, he found, was that the porter at the printers on his way to work, seeing the rain-sodden sheets of paper had picked them up, put them in order (none were missing) and delivered them without ex-plaining what had happened. The printer had gone ahead and set them, assuming they had come as usual from Flammarion.

Albert Paine – amanuensis, biographer and literary execu-tor of Samuel Clemens (Mark Twain) – described a similar episode in Clemens's life. One morning he had been dictating something about an article he had published earlier, and they were lamenting that they could not lay their hands on a copy. Later, as Clemens was walking down Fifth Avenue, thinking about it, a total stranger came across to him through the traffic and thrust some clippings into his hand. It had occurred to him that morning, the stranger told Clemens, to send them and he had intended to post them. Seeing Clemens, he had taken the opportunity to hand them to him; 'and with a word or two he disappeared'. Among them was the article.

More remarkable examples of providential coincidences were included in Koestler's collection, *The Challenge of Chance*. Sir Alec Guinness described how ordinarily he would wake up on Sunday mornings even before his alarm clocks (he used two) rang, in time for him to go to Mass before catching the train to the country. On July 3, 1971 he slept through both, and had to take a later train. The one he would have caught was involved in an accident, and the front coach, in which he always sat, had toppled on its side, several passengers having to be taken to hospital.

The most remarkable case of all in *The Challenge of Chance* concerned an episode where a man had thrown himself in front of a tube train in London. The train had pulled up just in time; it was on him but had not run over him, so that although seriously injured he was not killed. An inquiry revealed that it was not prompt action by the driver which had saved him, as was at first assumed. A passenger in the train had pulled on the emergency brake handle. Although Koestler's attempt to find out more was blocked, the fact that a passenger had been responsible was not disputed; London Transport even admitted they had contemplated prosecuting him. As the passenger could not conceivably have seen what was happening in front of the train, either chance coincidence or psi must have been involved. As Koestler observed, if it was ESP 'we must also assume that it was a precognitive impulse, anticipating the event by a couple of seconds'.

Was it precognition? May it not have been 'need-determined' psi coming through in the form of psychokinesis? Eisenbud has surmised that what we take to be coincidence or, if we accept psi, assume to be precognition, may often be psychokinetic guidance. His experience as a psychoanalyst has suggested to him that the experience of encountering somebody we particularly do not want to meet may be the consequence of self-punishment unconsciously guiding us into the situation, much as Freud thought it prompted gaffes.

The Unknown Guest

Psychical researchers, it seems, are now being compelled to realise how perceptive Gardner Murphy was to warn that psi is an interpersonal affair. More than that, they have to take into account the existence of a form of programming, manifesting itself through the intervention of entities, variously thought of as gods, spirits, 'controls', ghosts, poltergeists, demons, fairies and so on – discarnate intelligences with psi powers which can behave as if they represent a third force impinging on interpersonal relationships.

Maurice Maeterlinck recognised their existence, and vividly described them in 1914 in his portrait of 'The Unknown Guest'. The 'guest' was commonly regarded, he had found, as a deceiver, playing 'mischievous and puerile pranks'. Not so: the 'guest' 'does not deceive itself any more than it deceives us; it is we who deceive ourselves'. Immured as we are in our bodies, we cannot tune in properly to its instructions, so 'it roams around the walls, it utters warning cries, it knocks at every door, but all that reaches us is a vague disquiet that is sometimes translated to us by a half-awakened gaoler who, like ourselves, is a lifelong captive'.

The 'half-awakened gaoler' is the medium. As part of him is earthbound, he puts his earthbound interpretations on what he hears. If he believes the dead survive, he assumes his information comes from them. The 'guest' 'seems to care but little as to the garments in which it is rigged out, having indeed no choice in the matter'. Maeterlinck declined to join in the dispute between spiritualists who assumed that the 'guest' was a spirit, and psychical researchers who preferred to believe that everything could be accounted for in terms of the subconscious mind – for might not the subconscious, too, have a claim to immortality?

Rhine had begun to realise before he died that his early belief that psi could be satisfactorily demonstrated in controlled trials had been an illusion. His methodology, he recalled, had been based on the assumption that the standard physical controls could be used in experiments. 'Now, however, I recognise that all the reliance on physical conditions for the containment of psi have been futile, based as they have been on a now discredited assumption – discredited by psi research itself,' he wrote in 1977. 'All the relevant research of the past has shown that psi cannot be screened out by physical barriers, whether space, or time, or any other known physical condition.' At the Parapsychology Foundation's 1983 conference, which had 'The Repeatability Problem' as its theme, one of the leading British psychical researchers, John Beloff, sadly admitted that when dealing with such unstable phenomena, replication might not be possible. It could 'cynically be argued', one of the younger British members, Susan Blackmore, remarked, 'that parapsychology's only repeatable finding is the unrepeatability of psi'.

What, then, can parapsychologists do? For some, psi effects remain a challenge to be met and overcome. To detect the influence of psi is of paramount importance for certain research projects, Rex Stanford of St John's University, Jamaica, has asserted. 'We may, at least for the present, be forced to play the role of both scientist and shaman,' he admits, but everything possible must be done to eliminate the possibilities of 'psi-related ambiguities'. To do otherwise would be 'to place the role of the magic-maker above the role of the scientist'.

The role of the magic-maker has little appeal for many of the younger generation of parapsychologists who have come up through postgraduate courses in universities in Britain and the United States, and have been hoping to preserve their scientific credentials. Parapsychologists – one of them, Richard Broughton, has lamented – are experiencing a crisis of confidence, because they are 'no longer very sure where the psi in their experiments is coming from'. Another – Brian Miller – echoing Stanford's worry about how to determine whether psi effect is influencing results, has expressed his fears that if its source cannot be identified, parapsychology is doomed to be 'a pretty toy we cannot do anything with'.

Parapsychology may be doomed to failure in its efforts to impress orthodox scientists by using their research procedures, yet there is another way of looking at it. If psi effects occur, they presumably can occur in conventional research, influencing subjects' minds through experimenter-effect, or even promoting poltergeist phenomena in the laboratory. Wolfgang Pauli's work as a theoretical physicist won immense respect internationally, but his colleagues became wary of his presence: 'something usually broke in the lab', his friend George Gamow recalled, 'whenever he merely stepped across the threshold'. Incidents of the kind were so common that they were actually given a name: the 'Pauli Effect'.

The evidence that psi is in operation – or, to put it more cautiously, that forces are at work within conventional scientific research which resemble psi in the way that they operate – has been mounting in recent years. Startling differences between the results obtained by teams of experimenters are common, according to Harry Collins and Tom Pinch, sociologists at the University of Bath. They have to be explained away as the product of undetected errors or, when that might create resentment, by joky references to 'gremlins' or 'the fifth law of thermodynamics'.

The most striking example has been the results of repetition of a series of experiments which had been made by two postgraduate students at the University of Texas, R. Thomp-

son and J.V. McConnell. After 'training' planarium flat-
worms to contract when a light was switched on, they found
that if the worms were cut in half, and each end allowed to
regenerate, both halves retained the lesson they had been
taught. Even more remarkable, when the worms were chop-
ped up and fed to other planariums, 'memory transfer-effect'
was found. The cannibals retained the learned-behaviour
pattern.

Naturally these results excited great interest, and as the
experiment was relatively easy to perform, many teams
repeated it. Positive results were published in *Nature* and in
Science. One research group even claimed to have tracked
down a chemical linked to avoidance of the dark. Then,
gradually, doubts surfaced. By 1971, a survey revealed the
trials had yielded 133 positive findings; almost exactly the
same number were either negative or equivocal. *Nature* and
Science ceased to accept contributions on the subject. The
replication studies, critics claimed, must have been inadequately controlled. Covert accusations of fraud, as well as
incompetence, began to circulate.

Recalling the controversy, McClenon describes it as an
example of the process 'by which labelling a research field as
deviant can terminate progress'. So long as the results
appeared consistent, they could be presented to and published
in the scientific journals as fascinating anomalies which the
next advance in microbiology or biochemistry would surely
explain. As soon as it was found that replication was giving
contradictory results, critics were able to make the point that
Thompson and McConnell's 'discovery' did not accord with
the prevailing dogmas on the transmission of behaviour. On
the contrary, it was too close to the Lamarckian heresy for
comfort. Once in the 'deviant' category, the subject became
virtually taboo.

The question that ought to have been asked – why, if the
cannibals did not retain the behaviour pattern, did so many
teams report that they did? – has also been tabooed, except
when it is unkindly resurrected as a curiosity by sociologists.
The scientific establishment does not care to contemplate
what amounts to a stark choice. Assuming the positive
findings were wrong, was it incompetence, in the form of a
disturbing level of experimenter-effect promoting grossly in-

accurate interpretations of the results? Or was it a fraud? Or both? Some disorder must be endemic in laboratories to breed such errors. Could it be psi-experimenter-effect? Perish the thought!

The same possibility arises in relation to Rosenthal's 'experiments with the experimenters'. In 1963 he invited twelve students to run laboratory rats through a maze. Half of the experimenters were told they had Maze-Bright animals bred from stock which had shown itself better than average in such tests; the other half were told they were getting Maze-Dull rats. The rats were in fact from the same stock, yet not merely did the Maze-Bright animals perform significantly better than the others, they actually improved their performance in the way which could be expected through normal learning, whereas the Maze-Dull rats did not. Unless the Maze-Bright rats did better because they were handled more gently, Rosenthal could think of no explanation except that they were being influenced by the experimenters' expectations.

An even more remarkable example has been related by Neal Miller, Professor of Psychology at the Rockefeller University, New York. Miller, a hard-line behaviourist, got it into his head in the early 1960s that if behaviourist principles were sound, it should be possible for laboratory rats to learn how to exercise some control over their autonomic nervous systems. For a century medical students had been taught that the autonomic nervous system operates automatically. It cannot be brought under the mind's control by humans, let alone by animals. Any idea that it could be was dismissed as an old wives' tale spread by travellers and colonial officials who had been duped by yogi and fakirs. So far-fetched was Miller's notion, in fact, that for a time he could find no assistant prepared to work for him. When eventually he did, his expectations were fulfilled. The rats were able to acquire a significant degree of control over their temperature, their heart beat, their blood pressure, and certain visceral responses. Other researchers, persuaded to carry out the same experiments, obtained similar results; and in 1969 he published his findings.

As it happened, 1969 was the year in which the results of a number of experiments were published which showed that human subjects, using bio-feedback, had learned to control their temperature and their blood pressure. Miller's findings did not cause quite so much of a sensation as they would ordinarily have been expected to do. The twist to the story, from his point of view, was that when his experiments were repeated *after* 1969 they ceased to give the same results. Five years later he had to admit that while the early results had 'appeared to be robust', and had been replicated by six different experimenters, 'it had been impossible to repeat the experiments on heart rate or intestinal contraction'. The only explanation he could think of was even less plausible than Rosenthal's 'gentle handling'. The drug curare, Miller surmised, which had been used in the experiments to eliminate unwanted muscular reactions, might have declined in quality. Miller himself thought this unlikely. 'The unexplained difference between earlier repeated success and present repeated failure', he lamented, 'is an extraordinary perplexing dilemma.'

Had such a failure of replication occurred in parapsychology, sceptics would certainly have diagnosed fraud. Perhaps they did, covertly, in Miller's case. It was his good fortune that the parallel experiments with humans confirmed his hypothesis. Again, psi-experimenter-effect can only be advanced tentatively as the explanation. Yet it is more plausible than the alternatives so far put forward; and the possibility of psi-experimenter-effect is now taken seriously by some leading physicists. To a question as to whether the observer's intentions can influence the outcome of an experiment Brian Josephson, Professor of Physics at Cambridge and a Nobel Laureate, has replied that it might 'if the observer was emotionally involved in the outcome of the experiment and particularly wanted one result to come out rather than another'. Perhaps 'some kinds of psychic phenomena can be considered as establishing a coupling energy between oneself and the thing one wants to influence'.

Recently there have been a few encouraging signs that scientists other than physicists, however uneasy they may be at the notion of psi as a coupling energy intervening in research, are aware that something is intervening to upset preconceived theories, and that the anomalies it produces ought to be brought out into the open and studied, rather than furtively brushed under the academic carpet. A Society for

Scientific Exploration, its membership drawn from full-time workers in universities or research institutes who have made 'a substantial contribution to a recognised field of knowledge', has been set up in the United States to investigate and report on them. A feeling remains, however, that the 'substantial contribution' needs to be in some conventional field. Psychical research is not yet 'recognised' in that sense. Calling themselves parapsychologists and aping conventional scientific procedures has not worked.

Although experiments of various kinds derived from the Duke era must continue, and will be useful if they uncover more evidence for psi-effects, they will not carry conviction to outsiders. No matter how impressive the results of impeccably controlled trials, the great majority of scientists and of the general public are never going to see them – and in all probability would not understand them, so abstruse and jargon-ridden have the reports become.

What can psychical researchers do, to put their message across? First, as many of them now realise, they will have to give up the quest for repeatability on the scientific model. Admittedly some psychic may come along who can, say, levitate at will in controlled conditions. The greater likelihood is that, as Gaither Pratt suggested, absence of repeatability is a fundamental feature of psi. 'We may, I think, move closer to the heart of our phenomena if we take as fundamental what we may call the law of *recurrence*,' he suggested. 'The genuine psi phenomenon is, along with its other defining characteristic, one that happens intermittently and unpredictably, again and again.'

Unluckily many leading psychical researchers have become conditioned to ignore, and even sometimes flatly to reject, evidence for psi that does not fit orthodoxy's specifications, in spite of the warning Lodge gave in 1933: 'my view is that no record of any experiment can be made watertight and free from suspicion, if lurking grounds for suspicion exist in a critic's mind'. Elaborate controls would not suffice. If he wanted to cheat scientists, Lodge claimed, he would give them as much apparatus to attend to as possible, guaranteeing the maximum distraction. In any case, he argued, 'the real strength of our position lies in the phenomena themselves, namely that they can be experienced by a number of people,

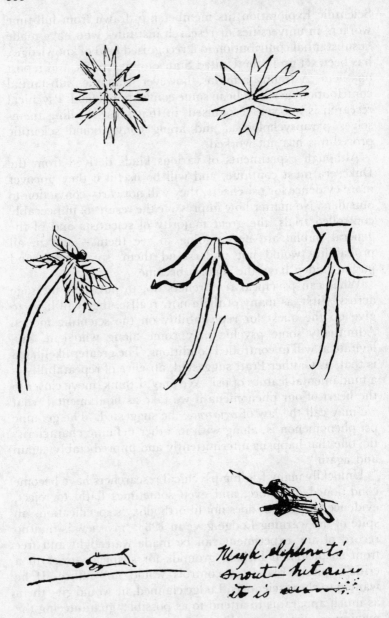

Figure 6 Some of Mrs Sinclair's clairvoyant 'hits' and 'near-misses',
illustrated in Upton Sinclair's *Mental Radio*.

and by one person after another, as time goes on, until the cumulative evidence becomes overwhelming'. Uncontrolled experiments, he urged, should not be despised because sometimes 'phenomena occur of such vigour, and of so simple and striking a character, that they overcome suspicion and constitute their own demonstration'.

How right Lodge was has recently been shown in the results of a poll in which one of the questions scientists were asked was what had led them to accept psi. Almost without exception those who accepted psi replied that it was some personal experience. The experimental evidence must often have reassured them, but its influence – compared to, for example, the influence of J.W. Dunne's *An Experiment with Time*, containing an account of his precognitive dreams and encouraging readers to look out for their own dream glimpses – has been negligible.

Scientists may believe that they are impressed only by the weight of hard scientific evidence. In practice, like the rest of us, they are more impressed by what they encounter, or what is reported by individuals whom they know and trust. Einstein illustrated this when he explained why, although he could not accept telepathy, he had agreed in 1930 to contribute a preface to the German edition of Upton Sinclair's *Mental Radio*, in which Sinclair described tests he had made of his wife's clairvoyance, illustrating it with drawings she had made of concealed target pictures. Any dispassionate study of the book shows that it would be absurd to invoke coincidence. Either Sinclair's wife was clairvoyant, or the two of them must have perpetrated an elaborate fraud, or at best, hoax. To Einstein, as he recalled to Jan Ehrenwald, it was 'out of the question in the case of so conscientious an observer and writer as Upton Sinclair that he is carrying on a conscious deception of the reading world: his good faith and dependability are not to be questioned'. Sinclair's experiments were 'of greater weight than the large-scale statistical tests in which the discovery of a minute statistical error may upset everything'.

C.J. Ducasse, Professor of Philosophy at Brown University, Rhode Island, made a similar point after he examined the laboratory results which Rhine had produced in tests for psychokinesis, and their possible relevance to reports of levitation. Ducasse's 'habit-begotten and habit-bound, adversely prejudiced, practical self', as he described it, made it very hard for him to believe that levitation was possible. His 'rational, philosophically open-minded, scientifically inquisitive self' had to concede that some carefully controlled and recorded PK tests with dice at Duke and elsewhere increased that possibility. Nevertheless, if he were to be told by somebody he regarded as reliable 'that in his own dining room, and in good light, he had seen Professor Rhine rise 18 inches in the air, and that, as Crookes did with Home, he passed his hand under, above and around Rhine and found nothing, then such a report would be even more convincing both psychologically and rationally than are the reports of dice-casting experiments'.

In the long run, and indeed in the short run, psychical research can recover only by going back on its tracks and relying, as Richet, Geley, Schrenck-Notzing and others did, on persuasion by demonstration. They were unlucky in that they were rowing against the materialist floodtide. With materialism all but defunct, the task should now become less difficult.

3

THE CASE AGAINST SCIENTISM

The arguments used by sceptics to discredit psi are so manifestly inadequate that suspicion is aroused. Why are scientists worried? If all is well in their territory, they surely do not need to worry about psi. It is not as if parapsychologists are picking up university posts or obtaining research funding at orthodoxy's expense. If psi has no basis in reality, as sceptics maintain, why not leave the research to collapse from its own inadequacy? That they are so anxious to ridicule this research suggests that psi must frighten them.

Dogmas in Decline

It is easy to understand why. A century ago scientists elevated what had been a workmanlike theory into a dogma. The physicist John Tyndall preached rationalist materialism as a faith. 'Every meal we eat, and every cup we drink', he told the British Association for the Advancement of Science, 'illustrates the mysterious control of mind by matter.' That fellow-scientists of the calibre of Wallace and Crookes should accept the existence of psychic phenomena appeared to him to be rank treachery.

In Germany Wilhelm Wundt held the same view. When a professor of philosophy claimed that the phenomena of physical mediumship could no longer be doubted, Wundt asked him how scientists would get the courage and perseverance to continue their work if the laws of nature, on which their work depended, were 'done away with'.

So it was not entirely surprising that when they *were* done away with – by the quantum physicists in the 1920s – the scientists' immediate reaction was to behave as if the laws were still in existence. Although every feature of materialist physics had been dethroned, Alfred North Whitehead observed in 1934, it still reigned supreme in 'the market-place, the playgrounds, the law courts, and in fact the whole sociological intercourse of mankind' – even among scientists: 'a touching example of baseless faith'.

Whitehead would not have needed to revise that view had he been around to do so half a century later. Hard though it may be to understand why scientists can continue to accept a discredited, baseless faith for half a century, rationalist materialism has had a couple of advantages which have enabled it to survive. Quantum theory is not merely incomprehensible to anybody except physicists; in the form in which it filters down to other disciplines, and to the public, it remains theory, without any obvious day-to-day practical application. Teachers at schools and universities find it convenient to assume that the old laws hold good for all practical purposes.

This would not have been unreasonable if it had been recognised that materialism was being retained simply out of pragmatism. Scientists have found it humiliating to accept this. As Heisenberg noted, they had originally been aware of science's limitations; 'this modesty was largely lost during the 19th century', because they had begun to believe they would soon have all the answers (Haeckel could seriously claim in 1899 that of the seven great riddles of the universe, six had been solved, and the seventh – whether or not there is freedom of will – was an illusion). Science, Heisenberg believed, was at last learning its lesson: that it needed to be conscious of its limits. Physicists might be learning the lesson. Scientists in general were not.

In 1950 the President of Harvard, J.B. Conant, neatly illustrated scientism's hold over science when he remarked that established habits of thought are never overturned simply by the accumulation of facts which refute them, 'only by the substitution of a different system into which they can be fitted, and which is sufficiently plausible to supplant its predecessor'. The notion was taken up and expanded by Thomas Kuhn, of Harvard's History of Science Faculty, in *The Structure of Scientific Revolutions*, introducing his concept of the paradigm – the set of guidelines within which scientists function. Normal science, he asserted, is chiefly concerned 'to force nature into the preformed and relatively inflexible box that the paradigm supplies'. Contrary to the general view, scientists are not concerned to investigate new kinds of phenomena. 'Indeed, those that will not fit the box are often not seen at all.' (Much as in Soviet street maps, as E.F. Schumacher was to recall in this context, churches are shown only if they have been converted to museums. His own education had 'failed to show large "unorthodox" sections of both history and practice in medicine, agriculture, psychology and the social and political sciences, not to mention art and so-called occult and paranormal phenomena, the mere mention of which was considered to be a sign of mental deficiency'.)

Confronted with psi, scientists did not merely have to ditch the old paradigm without having a new one to replace it. They were faced with the disturbing realisation that if it had to be ditched, an embarrassing amount of what they had believed in and taught would have to go, too, for a reason which Arthur Koestler indicated in his autobiography. He was an old friend of the philosopher of science Hans Reichenbach, and when they met again at Princeton in 1952, Koestler mentioned Rhine's work on ESP at Duke. It was all hokum, Reichenbach thought, based on faulty statistics. When Koestler assured him that the statistics had been vetted by internationally recognised experts in the field, he went pale: 'if that is true, it is terrible, terrible. It would mean that I would have to scrap everything and start again from the beginning.'

As a mathematician Reichenbach would have been less affected than most scientists by the need to incorporate telepathy into his structure. Other disciplines are faced with much more serious problems. Biologists, psychologists and anthropologists will have to go back to the beginning, to find which of their research results need to be amended or scrapped, because the possibility that ESP or PK might influence the results was not allowed for. No wonder, then, that scientists have been fighting this rearguard action to keep their territory free from so unwelcome an intruder.

When new phenomena begin to alter thought-patterns, Heisenberg observed in 1974, scientists feel the ground is being pulled from under their feet. 'The difficulties at this point can hardly be overestimated. Once one has experienced the desperation with which clever and conciliatory men of science react to the demand for a change in the thought pattern, one can only be amazed that such revolutions in science have actually been possible at all.' Science can be 'a security system, a complicated way of avoiding anxiety', Abraham Maslow has commented. 'It can be a way of avoiding life.'

Absorbed in their specialist pursuits, scientists have adopted a variety of methods to keep psi out of sight, even if it cannot be kept out of mind. Often they have been unscientific; sometimes unscrupulous. The period when an accepted paradigm is breaking down, Kuhn noted, increasing as it does scientists' problems, 'is usually preceded by a period of pronounced professional insecurity'. The greater the feeling of insecurity, the greater the readiness of the beleaguered garrison to use or approve of tactics which its members would ordinarily consider deplorable.

Some eminent scientists who have watched demonstrations of psychic phenomena have lied about what they have seen, or found excuses to claim later they were duped. Some in private accept psi but, being embarrassed by it, prefer to behave as if it does not exist ('to live with a paradox is like being married to a shrew', as Arthur Koestler put it. 'After a while you no longer hear her nagging, and settle down in comfortable resignation.'). Some have twisted what they have seen to fit the prevailing orthodoxy with the help of ingenious distortions. Some have turned a blind eye to the evidence, yet have had no hesitation in denigrating it. Some have set up tests in the hope of discrediting psi, backing out when they have obtained unwelcome results. And scientists in general have permitted the smearing of psychical researchers past and present by camp followers whose behaviour has been reminiscent of the unscrupulous hack John Giffard, denounced by the Irish patriot leader Henry Grattan as so obnoxious to the Unionists that he was 'only supportable by those dirty acts the less vile refuse to execute'.

Goethe lamented this when he watched it happening in his own time, with belief in the laws of nature becoming as ingrained as faith in God had been earlier. 'If anyone advances anything which contradicts, perhaps threatens to overturn, the creed which we have for years repeated, and have handed down to others', he lamented, 'all passions are ranged against him, and every effort is made to crush him.' In its 1980s form it has shocked Dean Robert G. Jahn of Princeton. Too often established science has resisted possible threats to its established paradigm, 'and let's be frank, possible threats to personal belief', by erecting dubious defences. 'In some cases it has resorted to uninformed criticism and allowed personal biases to replace legitimate intuitive insight. Worst of all, on occasion it has invoked categorical rejection and guilt by association to justify dismissal of all efforts, to address this topic' – the topic being psi.

A medical scientist who is shrewd enough to realise that a constellation of assorted symptoms constitutes an identifiable disease is commonly rewarded by having his name attached to it for posterity, as in Parkinson's disease. Similar awards may reasonably be offered to the men who have recognised and identified certain disorders to which sceptics and scientists are particularly prone, leading them to evade their responsibilities or, in some cases, to betray their principles. Of these, one of the most commonly encountered in the history of psychical research has been cognitive dissonance, as L. Festinger described it. One of its symptoms is the tension engendered when facts or experiences threaten a cherished assumption. It can lead us to accept any evidence, however implausible and however dubious its source, which helps to restore our old faith.

Festinger's Syndrome

The earliest and most blatant example of the destructive effects of Festinger's 'cognitive dissonance' was Sir David Brewster's when he realised that his reputation was in jeopardy through the accounts of his sessions with Daniel Home. His pretence a few weeks later that he had realised Home was cheating was only to be exposed by the publication after his death of the description of what he had witnessed, written at the time. The pattern has been repeated several times since.

When Robert Browning went with his wife to a seance with Home he came away baffled. A table had levitated, though he could see for himself that Home was not touching it. When one side of it had reared up, the lamp and ornaments on it had not fallen off. Hands had appeared, one of which had taken a wreath off the table and placed it on Elizabeth's head. An accordion played, though nobody was touching it. Although he could not accept that spirits were responsible, Browning admitted he could not account for the levitation or the other phenomena.

In a letter written at the time, he speculated on the ruses a conjuror might employ at seances. A month later, these had been converted into tricks which, Browning claimed, Home *had* employed. It had all been 'a cheat and an imposture' – to him; much to his wrath, Elizabeth continued to insist that Home was genuine, until Robert's loathing of him had become so paranoid that she decided it was best to avoid the subject. For his part, he did not publish 'Mr Sludge the Medium', the nastiest of his poems, until after her death.

In the 1870s Wilhelm Wundt was striving to bring Fechner's rather mystical psychophysiology into line with the prevailing materialism. He was consequently appalled by what he, Fechner and others witnessed when they attended a

session with the American medium Henry Slade: gusts of
wind through the room; the attentions of an invisible hand,
pushing and pulling at the sitters; the levitation of a table.
Wundt could conceive of no way, he admitted, in which Slade
could have been physically responsible for the effects. Eight
years later he was claiming that conditions for observation
had been inadequate, that he had not been allowed to make a
proper investigation of the table, and that he had witnessed
nothing which could not be accomplished by sleight-of-hand.

Wallace related another example in his autobiography. In a
letter to *Nature* in 1880 the biologist G.J. Romanes had
suggested that psychic phenomena should be investigated by
some of the leading scientific men of the day. Wallace wrote
mildly to inform him that it had been, and was being,
investigated by well-known scientists. When the two men met,
Romanes explained that he had been impressed by the
mediumistic powers of a member of his family. He had
satisfied himself that they could not have been faked. He had
also, though for some reason he did not disclose this to
Wallace, held seances in his own house with a professional
medium, Charles Williams, and had described them in letters
to Darwin. While Williams was securely held, a disembodied
'face' and 'hands' had appeared. One of the hands had taken
up a bell and rung it. Again, Romanes had felt there could not
be trickery. His brother had walked around the table to satisfy
himself there were no wires or other gadgets.

To Wallace's astonishment, a few years later he read
articles in which Romanes implied that all psychic phenomena were produced by trickery, and contrasted the Wallace of science with the Wallace of spiritualism and astrology –
'the Wallace of absurdity and incapacity'. Wallace, who in the
meantime had seen Romanes's letters about the Williams
seances, asked him what had happened to change his mind.
Could it be that there were two Romaneses, as well as two
Wallaces, one being a Romanes 'of incapacity and absurdity'?

Romanes replied apologetically: 'it certainly did not occur
to me that I was hitting below the belt'. Since writing the
letters to Darwin, he explained, further work with Williams
had shown him to be an impostor. 'Have you found out *how*
the things you saw in your own room and in the presence of
your own friends were done?' Wallace asked. All mediums, he

reminded Romanes, were accused of imposture. He would be interested to know how the fraud was detected.

It was detected, Romanes explained, by a test in which he had asked Williams to sit in a cage of perforated zinc. While Williams was in it, nothing happened, proving that Williams must have been using trickery, as if his powers were super-natural they should not have been affected. With remarkable patience, Wallace pointed out the illogicality of Romanes's attitude, to no avail.

Many more instances of this kind have occurred over the past few years. When conjurors claimed that they could put pictures on film in cameras without using the lens, as Ted Serios was doing in Chicago, Jule Eisenbud invited them and some scientists to come and see for themselves that Serios was not using tricks. The conjurors backed down, but ten 'presti-gious observers' from the university community in Denver, Colorado, accepted the invitation. They were shown how conjurors claimed the 'trick' was done and invited to see for themselves that Serios was not using sleight-of-hand. If they were satisfied they were to allow Eisenbud to name them in his book on the subject. They were satisfied, and he did name them. Some time later, a sceptic took the trouble to telephone the 'prestigious observers' to ask whether they still stood by their signatures. Some of them hedged, saying they no longer felt confident that Serios had not deceived them. Some actually cited features of the test which, they now claimed, were unsatisfactory – to Ian Stevenson, 'a particularly glaring example of such backsliding'.

The claim that information has come to light since a test is often used as an excuse, as it was by the physicist Jack Sarfatti. After witnessing trials held with Uri Geller at Birkbeck College, Sarfatti enthusiastically endorsed Geller's powers in *Science News*: 'my personal professional judgment as a Ph.D. physicist is that Geller demonstrated genuine psycho-energetic ability at Birkbeck, which is beyond the doubt of any reasonable man'. Two years later, after he had seen the conjuror the Amazing Randi do his imitations, Sarfatti re-tracted, in spite of the fact that Randi was not performing in the same controlled conditions.

In 1977 some tests were held in Grenoble of the PK powers of Jean-Pierre Girard. The protocol had been worked out in

advance between the then editor of *Nature*, David Davies; the
psychologist and sceptic Chris Evans; and James Randi. In
the course of one of the tests, Girard succeeded in bending a
metal bar. Among those present was Bernard Dreyfus, research director of the Nuclear Study Centre in Grenoble and
Chairman of the French physics society. Dreyfus observed the
phenomenon, which was also filmed. Could he hope to
extricate himself from the possibly damaging consequences of
an admission of what he had seen?

He could, and did. The metal bar, he pointed out, had bent
only slightly – an excuse reminiscent of the Victorian parlour
maid's, when taxed with having given birth to an illegitimate
baby: 'it was only a little one'. He added that it had bent only
at the end of a long session – a dubious excuse, since it was
natural for the session to end as soon as its objective had been
accomplished. Dreyfus later felt justified in writing to *Nature*
that he had not seen anything paranormal that night. The
videotape of the metal-bending, however, is in the possession
of Professor John Hasted. As Hasted has put it, 'posterity will
be able to judge'.

Perhaps the most striking case of Festinger's syndrome has
been the re-conversion of Professor John Taylor. Impressed
by Uri Geller's performance on television, Taylor not merely
abandoned his role as one of the media sceptics, but wrote a
book, *Superminds*, presenting the case 'that for one modern
"miracle", the Geller effect, there *is* a rational, scientific
explanation'. It appeared in 1975. Five years later, in his
Science and the Supernatural, Taylor went into contortions to try
to explain why he could not have witnessed what in *Superminds*
he claimed he *had* witnessed, because he had been unable to
find the (for him) 'rational, scientific explanation'.

Taylor's excuse was that PK cannot exist because he had
found that none of the known physical forces (gravity,
radioactivity, electromagnetism and the force which holds the
nuclear constituents together) could account for it. It might be
claimed, he admitted, that there is a fifth force; as there has
been absolutely no scientific trace of it we must discard the
notion 'if we wish to preserve the scientific viewpoint'. That
viewpoint, he explained, is that all reality can be explained,
'by one aspect of it – the physical'.

'You wonder', Larry LeShan, author of several books on

related subjects, observed in a lecture he gave in London in 1984, 'how his wife would feel about that?' Would he tell her, 'Dear heart, the reasons we stay together are simply a function of certain atomic laws and physical activities'?

The frequency with which scientists who have accepted psi on the strength of a demonstration have later backed down suggests that the emotional conflict caused by the departure from what has been a lifetime assumption, and the relief at being able to return to it, has been powerfully reinforced by the realisation that to break ranks is to court ridicule. What would happen, the shrewd Scotsman of letters Patrick Procter Alexander asked after his own scepticism had been sent spinning by an evening with Daniel Home, if T.H. Huxley were induced to investigate, and came to the conclusion that Home's feats were genuine? His fellow-scientists would simply tell each other that Huxley had gone off his head, or even hint at collusion between him and Home.

A few months later, this was to happen to William Crookes. His announcement that he proposed to conduct a scientific investigation of physical phenomena had been hailed as an advance; his report that they were genuine damaged his reputation. 'The first thing I ever heard about Sir William Crookes was that he *had* been a brilliant scientist', the philosopher F.C.S. Schiller recalled, 'but that recently he had unfortunately gone off his head.' He was also charged with collusion.

Even when they escape such smears, scientists who accept psi are automatically labelled 'believers' who can no longer be trusted to investigate psychic phenomena impartially. Sceptics whose minds remain firmly closed to the evidence contrive to delude themselves that as they alone are impartial, only tests which they conduct can be regarded as scientific. The pressure on conventionally orientated scientists such as Taylor to return to the fold is consequently strong. 'You know that very influential people in the physics community are *a priori* strongly prejudiced against parapsychology, so it has been dangerous to speak of it for sociological reasons', one of them is quoted as saying by Harry Collins and Tom Pinch in their *Frames of Meaning*. 'Right or wrong, my feeling is that Taylor is very aware of this and is trying to be as conservative as he can.'

Polanyi's Syndrome

During the seventeenth century sceptics who were busy taming the supernatural, bringing everything within the laws of nature, often explained away remaining mysteries, Keith Thomas noted in his *Religion and the Decline of Magic*, 'by proffering hypotheses about natural events which we would regard as entirely spurious'. The tradition has been maintained to this day. 'Any contradictions between a popular scientific notion and the facts of experience will be explained by other scientific notions: there is a ready reserve of possible scientific hypotheses available to explain any conceivable event,' Michael Polanyi, chemist and philosopher of science, noted in *Personal Knowledge*. This had enabled scientists to dismiss 'whole ranges of experience which to the unscientific mind appear both massive and vital' as of no scientific interest; among them, extra-sensory perception.

Hyperesthesia

Because psychologists have so often encountered what appear to be indications of psi in their work, particularly in connection with altered states of consciousness, they have been particularly in need of plausible 'scientific' explanations. A typical example has been their reliance, when hard-pressed, on 'hyperesthesia'.

That some people's senses appear to sharpen in certain circumstances has long been common knowledge. The hypothesis that they can become superhumanly (as distinct from supernaturally) acute was originally put forward by James Braid in the 1840s when he was investigating subjects in the mesmeric trance state, and found that some could tell him what he was doing behind their backs. When he pointed a finger at them, they reacted as if they could sense what he was doing. Anxious to avoid attributing this to clairvoyance, Braid surmised that under hypnosis (as he called it to get away from the occult associations of mesmerism and animal magnetism) their five senses were sharpened into a condition of hyperesthesia, so that they could actually feel the tiny movements of air which his pointing finger would transmit.

Hyperacuity of the senses was taken up by W.B. Carpenter in the 1850s to account for table-turning. Under hypnosis, he claimed, people became capable of feats of strength beyond their normal capacity (a view since confirmed by tests). Without being aware of it, sitters were moving and lifting heavy tables by 'quasi-involuntary muscular pressure'. He avoided the term *unconscious* muscular pressure: the existence of a subconscious mind was still rejected, as too closely identified with the idea of a soul for scientists' comfort. Quasi-autonomous movements ranging from tics to falling about with laughter were recognised. This, combined with the fact that the great Faraday had lent the theory the seal of his approval, established hyperesthesia as a stock explanation whenever cases which might otherwise be regarded as manifestations of psi were reported.

Among those who welcomed it was Alfred Lehmann, Director of the Psychological Laboratory at Copenhagen. 'The subconscious mind is a ridiculous chimera', he asserted; 'there is not the slightest proof of its existence'. He regarded the idea of telepathic communication as even more absurd. Such was Sidgwick's reputation for integrity, however, that Lehmann felt compelled to take seriously the results of the SPR findings in telepathy experiments. Conducting similar trials in his own laboratory, he was able to satisfy himself that although positive results were obtained, the explanation was hyperesthesia. The proof, he claimed, lay in the fact that the subjects often guessed the number 'seven' when the 'agent' was looking at a card with 'zero' on it, and vice versa. The agent must have been whispering the number, though unaware he was doing so. The subjects would have picked them up by hyperacuity of hearing, confusing 'seven' and 'zero' because in English they sounded similar.

This was all very well in Lehmann's trials, Sidgwick tartly replied; it would not explain what had happened in the SPR's, where the agent whispered not 'zero' but 'nought' – if, indeed, he whispered anything. Nevertheless hyperesthesia continued to be offered as the explanation for successful findings in telepathy tests, unless fraud could be alleged.

It surfaced again with the remarkable results obtained by Gilbert Murray, Regius Professor of Greek at Oxford, in the guessing game he used to play with his family and friends at his home outside the city. Murray would leave the drawing room and take himself out of earshot while one of the company thought of a past event, say, or a scene from literature; they would then recall him, and he would tell them what the chosen event or scene was.

After a time his daughter had begun to take a record of his guesses: and the first two, from 1910, are fairly typical.

Agent: 'Dad's little German hairdresser cutting Dennis's hair.'

Murray: 'A funny little man walking down the street knocking on doors – he looks foreign – he's just like my little German hairdresser.'

Agent: 'At Amalfi, the Marchese recognising grandfather in the summer-house on the terrace – us there.'

Murray: 'It's you at Amalfi, I think in the dining room, or it might be the terrace, and your Marchese is there.'

Five years later a member of the SPR went through the guesses, 500 or so, which had been made in the course of this and subsequent games, and reported that one in three, on average, had been 'hits', two out of five 'misses' and the rest 'near-misses'.

The First World War was at its height when this report of Murray's prowess appeared in the Society's *Proceedings*, and it attracted little attention. A second, along the same lines – and showing much the same proportion of 'hits' – which Eleanor Sidgwick prepared in 1924, started up a controversy. In a letter to *The Times*, the eminent physiologist John Scott Haldane explained that the results were achieved by hyper-acuity of hearing – the explanation which, he claimed, Murray himself accepted.

Murray had for a time thought that hyperesthesia might be

the explanation. The chosen words were usually read out loud before he returned to the room; and occasionally his guesses were of a kind which suggested that he might have misinterpreted something he had heard without being conscious of having heard it – 'Masefield', where the word used had been 'Mansfield', for example. There had been other occasions, however, when he had picked up not merely the target when it had not been spoken out loud, but also ideas which were only in the mind of the agent at the time. In any case, the way in which the information reached Murray's conscious mind did not suggest that he was hearing it. As he explained, it came to him first as a general impression – say, of a country – and then gradually formulated itself into the specific target, sometimes with the help of other senses. Even smell occasionally provided him with clues, helping him to guess a fantasy target correctly: an opium den off Piccadilly Circus. Hyperesthesia would not do: telepathy, he decided, must be the answer.

There was to be further evidence to discredit the hyperacuity theory after Murray's death. Going through his papers E.R. Dodds, his successor at Oxford, found the record of nineteen sessions of the guessing game played during Murray's later years, when his record of 'hits' was actually slightly better than before. 'Can his hearing really have remained hyperacute at 80?' Dodds asked. Nevertheless Dingwall, anxious as always not to admit psi unless every other possibility had been eliminated, argued in reply, 'the weight of the evidence tends towards hyperesthesia rather than telepathy'.

This prompts a question: what evidence is there for the existence of hyperesthesia, in this form of hyperacute hearing? Although Dingwall cited a number of possible examples, as with Murray's they can more plausibly be accounted for by ESP. Although in his paper on the subject Dingwall suggested that hyperacuity of hearing was 'a very curious phenomenon which it would be most desirable to study very closely', he omitted to mention that the fourth Baron Rayleigh, a scientist with a reputation almost as high as his illustrious father's, *had* studied it closely, concluding that hyperacuity of hearing is a myth. If it exists, he pointed out, it would have been detected in routine tests.

That there are people with unusually acute hearing, and also altered states of consciousness in which the hearing of

some individuals markedly improves, is not in dispute. Yet as
Robert Thouless pointed out, except in this context pyscho-
logists ordinarily assume that the limits of sensory perception
are well-established. As there is no good evidence for
hyperesthesia, and as many well-attested facts of extra-
sensory perception cannot be explained by hyperesthesia, it
need no longer be regarded as 'a serious obstacle to the
acceptance of evidence for extra-sensory perception'.

Realising the frailty of the case for hyperesthesia, the editor
of *Psyche*, a behaviourist journal, accused Murray in 1924 of
using 'conscious hearing plus successful guessing plus similar
associations', a charge repeated many years later by a col-
umnist in the *Spectator*. The notion that Murray should have
found amusement in putting his ear to the keyhole, throughout his long and distinguished life, is the measure both of the
alarm sceptics feel when confronted with good evidence for
psi, and their lack of scruple in finding excuses to reject it.

Cryptomnesia

'Speaking in tongues' has frequently been reported since the
best-known account appeared: the description in Acts of
Pentecost, when the disciples 'were all filled with the Holy
Ghost, and began to speak with other tongues, as the Spirit
gave them utterance'. The onlookers were astonished, 'because that every man heard them speak in his own language';
here were these men, all Galileans, speaking Persian, Arabic
and many more.

Usually 'xenoglossy', the term Richet provided for it, has
been attributed to spirits possessing individuals and speaking
through them. To rationalists this was not a welcome explanation. It is with relief that they have been able to suggest an
alternative, cryptomnesia: the ability some people have shown
to keep a memory in their subconscious minds without
realising it is there, so that if it surfaces they are not aware
that it is a memory.

The first description of cryptomnesia is usually credited to
Samuel Taylor Coleridge. In his *Biographia Literaria* he described how an illiterate Göttingen woman in her twenties had
become possessed, 'as it appeared by a very learned devil. She
continued incessantly talking Latin, Greek and Hebrew, in

very pompous tones and with most distinct enunciation', the sentences, though disconnected, being intelligible. A young doctor who decided to look into her background eventually found that, as a 9-year-old, she had worked for a Protestant minister; 'and the solution of the phenomenon was soon obtained. For it appeared that it had been the old man's custom for years to walk up and down a passage of his house into which the kitchen door opened, and read to himself with a loud voice out of his favourite books.'

To Coleridge, 'this authenticated case furnishes both proof and instance that reliques of sensation may exist for an indefinite time in a latent state, in the very same order as they were originally impressed'. Coleridge, however, neglected to say where it was authenticated; nor did he attempt to explain how, as Andrew Lang curtly commented, an ignorant girl could have 'consciously acquired and afterward subconsciously reproduced huge cantles of dead languages, by virtue of having casually heard a former master recite or read aloud from Hebrew and Greek books'.

Why, then, should psychologists swallow a story which had reached Coleridge on the testimony of rumour? In *The Enchanted Boundary* in 1930 Walter Franklin Prince delivered an even harsher judgment. An opium addict and a drinker, Coleridge had begun to show, in the words of one of his biographers, 'diminished power to distinguish fact from fiction'. The incident described had taken place sixteen years earlier; neither the girl, the master nor the physician were identified; and Coleridge did not even claim to have seen or talked to anybody concerned in the case.

For Prince, xenoglossy was one of the symptoms of multiple personality, which his namesake Morton Prince had managed to extricate from the occult category and re-establish as a psychiatric disorder. Possession by spirits could be left as a superstition: the emergence of a split-off personality or personalities would account for the symptoms. Walter Prince was ready to accept a psychic component in xenoglossy; Morton Prince regarded it as a symptom, to be treated rather than investigated.

In spite of a few cases which attracted publicity, in particular the 'three faces of Eve' which gave birth to a number of books and a Hollywood film, most cases continued to be diagnosed as schizophrenia until the gradual realisation that the diagnosis was being discredited by tests. They showed humiliating differences among the psychiatrists over which patients were, and which were not, schizophrenics; and this led to research designed to try to find more specific diagnoses. Eventually tests at the National Institute of Mental Health in Bethesda have found ways which, it is believed, can be used positively to identify multiple personality disorder: MPD.

This had a curious outcome. Predictably, battle has been joined between psychologists who believe in the genetic model of intelligence, arguing that heredity is of fundamental importance in the creation of personality (and presumably of multiple personalities), and those who believe that MPD represents a way which has been learned of escaping from intolerable situations, as in the notorious case of Billy Milligan.

Billy has won forensic fame as the first criminal in the United States, according to his biographer Daniel Keyes, to be found guilty but insane on the ground that he suffers from multiple personality. He had several recognisably distinct personalities. One of them, 'Arthur', spoke with a British accent, and read and wrote fluent Arabic. Another, Ragen, spoke English with a noticeable Slavic accent and read, wrote and spoke Serbo-Croat. In general, the behaviour of the personalities could not be accounted for by Billy's having learned how to mimic all their characteristics and their accents, let alone having learned the languages on the sly.

Now that MPD is a fully-fledged psychiatric syndrome it is more difficult for psychologists to avoid discussing its symptoms. Billy's ability to speak in accents and in languages he had never learned has been described in scientific journals. The term xenoglossy has been avoided because it has been too closely identified with psychical research; but it has been possible for, say, Hilary Roberts, a Manchester psychologist, to refer to Billy's linguistic capabilities in the *New Scientist* without showing any nervousness about the implications, or hastening to attribute them to cryptomnesia.

If past experience is a guide, it will not be long before Billy's different languages *are* attributed to cryptomnesia – either that, or it will be denied that he really could speak fluently in them. Admittedly the evidence for a psi component in xenoglossy is not strong enough to impress some orthodox para-psychologists, such as Ian Stevenson; but it is extensive and, in many cases, decidedly more plausible than cryptomnesia.

Incombustibility

The way in which queasy 'scientific' explanations for phe-nomena are replaced, when they become untenable, by other and sometimes queasier notions has been abundantly illus-trated in connection with incombustibility – the ability of the human body, in certain circumstances, to withstand heat of a kind which would ordinarily be expected to have destructive consequences. It has been reported in three main contexts: ceremonial fire-walks, in which the participants step barefoot over white-hot coals, ash or stones; trials by ordeal, in which suspects hold a heated iron bar or plunge a hand into boiling water; and trances, spontaneous or induced, in which indi-viduals or groups allow fire to play around them.

Fire-walks have been reported by travellers and missionar-ies from tribal communities the world over. They were known in classical antiquity through performances by members of religious cults – as they still are, in some eastern countries. Trials by ordeal also have a long history, and a wide geographical distribution. Although they are now rarely en-countered, the presumption that some people really do prove their innocence by emerging from them unscathed remains strong because, as the eminent historian of medicine Henry Sigerist remarked, the method would have been pointless if it had inevitably pointed to guilt.

That feet and hands should become temporarily incom-bustible is easier to swallow than that whole bodies should enjoy protection of the kind which according to the Old Testament, saved Shadrach, Mesach and Abed Nego in Nebuchadnezzar's burning fiery furnace. Yet there is evidence for this, too, which is not easy to dismiss. Even David Hume had to admit that the ability of the *convulsionnaire*, Marie Souet, *La Salamandre*, to remain unharmed when suspended for half an hour just above a raging fire had been attested by 'witnesses of credit and distinction' (he might have added that they were hostile witnesses). In light good enough for equally credible witnesses to see his every move, Daniel Home used literally to play with fire, even bathing his face in the coals. Recently in the United States Jack Schwartz has given laboratory demonstrations of his ability to resist extreme heat without pain or scarring.

The usual explanation has been that as incombustibility is impossible, there must always be some protective device. Fire-walkers, Marcus Terentius Varro asserted in the second century BC, use a liniment to protect their feet. 'A saturated solution of alum preserves any part strongly impregnated with it from the action of fire', Salverte noted in his *Occult Sciences* in 1829, adding that the protection afforded was even better if the soles were then soaped.

For Sir James Frazer the solution was even simpler. Without troubling to investigate, he pointed out that as savages were inured to walking barefoot from infancy, their soles were so hardened that 'the skin is converted to a sort of leathery or horny substance which is almost callous to heat'.

Unluckily for such confident pronouncements, investigators who have taken the trouble actually to attend fire-walks have realised that some other explanation must be looked for. In 1898 Dr T.M. Hocken, thinking that perhaps the temperature of the 'oven' might be low enough for walkers to come through unscathed without artificial assistance, brought a thermometer with him, and a contraption to suspend it over the heated stones. The mercury promptly soared to 270° F. and would, he estimated, have gone considerably higher if the solder he had used had not melted, terminating this part of the test.

Before the walk began, Hocken examined the soles of the participants. They were soft and flexible, 'by no means leathery'. He satisfied himself that nothing had been applied to them, using touch and smell to do so, and 'not hesitating to use my tongue as a corroborative'. After the walk, which was taken slowly – the leader took nearly half a minute to cross about ten yards – he examined their soles again. He could detect no signs of burning.

For the most part, evidence of this nature, though abundantly confirmed since, has simply been ignored. As recently as 1961 two American psychologists claimed that as fire-walkers have seldom worn shoes, 'the epidermis of the soles of their feet is reported to us as being 1/8 to 1/4 inches in thickness' – their readiness to accept such 'reports' without checking being characteristic of the way in which sceptics brush aside unpalatable findings.

Physiologists, however, have been uneasy about the 'leather soles' notion. At the best of times very inadequate protection would be given to the feet, nor could it account for success in trials by ordeal, or the way in which some individuals have been able to plunge their hands into molten metal. Beads of sweat, W.B. Carpenter suggested in 1877, must be responsible for the protection by forming a film on hands or on feet. He cited the way drops of water perform on a heated iron, 'in the application of the familiar test by which the laundress judges the suitability of its temperature'.

This was eventually to become the most favoured explanation. In 1958 Dr Mayne Reid Coe claimed that he had been able to demonstrate its validity in trials in Florida. He used the analogy of the way globules of water slip around in a frying pan for a while, before vaporising. Ingenious though the idea was, anybody who inadvertently puts a hand on a hot frying pan is likely also to skip around, for a different reason. Sweat may in certain circumstances give momentary protection; it cannot account for the protracted protection enjoyed by fire-walkers.

Recently, in the 1980s, the issue has been further confused by the realisation that the fire-walk need not be regarded as an esoteric pursuit. 'Fire-walking is all the rage in California', the *New Scientist* reported in the summer of 1985. Soon, it became popular in England, too.

The California-type 'coal stroll' is ordinarily preceded by a period of indoctrination, derived from the belief that the mind, through suggestion and auto-suggestion, has as yet barely tapped its powers over the body. Certain altered states of consciousness, the theory is, provided by religious fervour, by hypnotism, by hysteria, or by some technique to promote auto-suggestion, promote incombustibility.

Nevertheless problems remain. Although the *Skeptical Inquirer*, self-appointed guardian of traditional rationalism, can no longer safely use the traditional rationalisations – alum, horny soles or sweat globules – it has felt bound to continue to reject what it regards as the mumbo-jumbo of the preparatory indoctrination. Dr Bernard Leikind, a plasma physicist, has

described how he had the courage to dispense with the
preliminaries. He feared the worst, but found that it was like
walking over warm moss. At fire-walks in London, too, some
of the participants have claimed that they were unaware of
any altered state of consciousness, yet did not suffer.

This presents a fresh problem. How is it that often on these
fire-walks some people get burned? The only plausible explanation to present itself is not one that sceptics relish: that
the protection is provided by some kind of group coverage, of
the kind so often observed in outbreaks of mass hysteria. It
has long been recognised that such outbreaks are selective.
Since the last war, for example, there have been several in
hospitals; many of them have affected only staff, not patients.
Can it be that the protection in fire-walks is afforded to people
who are unaware of its source, and not extended to others,
perhaps because they are not tuned in to the group mind?

Some support is given to this hypothesis by accounts which
have indicated that the protection only lasts so long as the
ceremonies are in full swing. Ordinarily they are conducted by
a leader, or guru. In one of the accounts Sir Oliver Lodge
collected between the wars, V.E. Stowell of the Imperial Bank
of India, Bombay, recalled that when he and other Europeans
joined in the walk, one of them was still on it when a halt was
called to the proceedings; 'before he could hop off his feet were
slightly scorched. We roared with laughter.' According to
Monsignor Despatures, Bishop of Mysore, three men who
ignored their leader's announcement that a ceremonial fire-
walk was over were so badly burned that they had to be taken
to hospital.

Yet even if the group protection hypothesis were to be
accepted, for want of a tolerable alternative, sceptics would
still be faced with a frequently reported, and in conventional
terms totally inexplicable, side-effect of incombustibility. Protection can also be given to whatever the walkers are wearing,
or carrying.

In the Old Testament story Shadrach, Mesach and Abed
Nego were bound in their coats, their stockings and their hats
before being consigned to the burning fiery furnace, yet not a
hair of their heads was singed, 'neither were their coats
changed' by the fire. The sheet in which Marie Souet, *La
Salamandre*, was suspended over the blaze was not harmed.

Daniel Home was able to confer protection from burning coal on handkerchiefs. Basil Thomson – at the time a colonial officer, later to become head of the Criminal Investigation Department at Scotland Yard – watched Fijian fire-walkers attach highly combustible fronds of tree-fern to their ankles which did not burn, though 'there were flames shooting out among the stones'.

Flames came up to the level of Stowell's ankles on his Bombay fire-walk. Not merely did he feel nothing; to his astonishment his white trousers showed no signs of being scorched. At the Mysore ceremony Mgr Despatures watched in amazement the Maharajah's bandsmen parading and playing through flames which were as high as their heads, 'flickering round the sheets of music without setting them on fire'.

'How can we account for it?' Despatures asked. Unable to think of any material cause, he was reluctantly compelled 'to believe in the influence of some spiritual agency which is not God'. Even if a spiritual, or psychic, agency is in operation there is presumably some yet to be discovered mechanism by which the insulation is provided. As it is unlikely to suit materialist preconceptions, doubtless the *Skeptical Inquirer* will in the meanwhile be seeking some new rationalisation.

Medawar's Syndrome

Sir Peter Medawar's dictum that scientists tend not to ask themselves questions until they can see the rudiments of an answer, helps to explain their reluctance to take psi seriously. The feeling that the answers cannot be found within orthodox science's structure is a powerful inducement to ignore the subject, as Eduard von Hartmann pointed out in 1869: 'the prevailing rationalist and materialist tendency of our time finds it convenient to deny or to ignore all facts of this class, because they cannot be understood from a materialist point of view'. From the point of view of any impartial judge 'the absolute denial of all such phenomena is consistent only with ignorance of the accounts; which, again, arises from not wishing to be acquainted with them'.

Sometimes scientists are confronted with questions that cannot easily be avoided, as in the case of the termitaries. 'We do not like the notion that there can be collective societies with the capacity to behave like organisms', as Lewis Thomas has put it; and although for a few years Henry Morton Wheeler's concept of 'superorganisms' did duty, as less embarrassing than Marais's 'soul', it clearly explained nothing. Great was the relief when the discovery of pheromones helped to provide part of the answer; but as the main question has remained unanswerable in conventional materialist terms, and could be explained in terms of psi programming, it is not asked.

Animal Psi
An even more striking illustration of Medawar's point is the way in which scientists have ducked an issue which arose early this century, when numerous stories were circulating of the apparent ability of some animals, particularly horses

and dogs, to pick up the thoughts of their owners. Some appeared to do even better, answering questions put to them when the questioners themselves did not know the answers.

The most celebrated of these performers was a horse, 'Clever Hans'. His owner, Wilhelm von Osten, found that the horse could answer questions by tapping with his hoof, one tap for 'A', two for 'B' and so on; not just this, but he could solve abstruse mathematical problems – abilities which created a sensation in Germany. Sceptics who came to expose the horse and its owner as frauds found themselves baffled. In 1904 a panel of scientists, convened to investigate Hans, testified that his abilities were genuine.

One of the investigating team, Professor Carl Stumpf, was not quite satisfied. Soon afterwards he reported that a graduate student, Oskar Pfungst, had discovered that Hans could only answer questions whose solution was known to someone present. No charge of dishonesty was levelled against von Osten or anybody else. Hans, Pfungst claimed, was able to pick up the information visually through, presumably, his owner's unconscious signals, trivial enough to have escaped the notice of other investigators, but observed by Pfungst. He had himself been able to get the horse to answer correctly simply by concentrating his attention on the number, though he was not aware of making any movement which would give the number away. Public opinion promptly 'underwent a complete and sudden about-face', Maeterlinck was to recall. 'A kind of cowardly relief was felt at the extinguishing of a miracle.'

Was Pfungst telling the whole truth? It tended to be forgotten that following the reports about 'Clever Hans' there were reports of 'mini-clever-Hanses', such as those owned by Karl Krall of Elberfeld, which Maeterlinck himself investigated. Although, like human mediums, they were fickle, sensitive, easily put off, he thought he had been fortunate with them – and with their owner, who was sufficiently sure of their abilities to agree to the tests Maeterlinck proposed to ensure that they were not responding to sensory clues. Left alone with one of the horses, Muhamed, Maeterlinck experimented with words which came into his mind, such as WEIDERHOF – the name of the hotel in which he was staying. Muhamed tapped out WEIDERHOZ. When Krall returned and chided him, Muhamed altered the 'Z' to an 'F'.

When Maeterlinck gave Muhamed and another of Krall's horses more stringent tests, they gave correct answers in nearly every case. Finally he thought of one which 'by virtue of its very simplicity, could not be exposed to any elaborate and far-fetched suspicions'. He took three cards, each bearing numerals, shuffled them without looking at them and put them on a board where Muhamed could see them. 'There was therefore, at that moment, not a human soul on earth who knew the figures spread at the feet of my companion' – yet without hesitation, Muhamed rapped out the number that the three cards formed, an experiment which succeeded with the other horses, 'as often as I cared to try it'.

The horses, therefore, could not have been picking up clues unwittingly given to them by Maeterlinck, and there were many other examples from this period which suggested that Pfungst's explanation was inadequate. In 1914 William Mackenzie published the results of experiments with dogs which, he argued, disproved the theory of human indications because the dog, Rolf, answered mathematical posers faster than his investigators were able to do. In Russia a few years later Vladimir Bekhterev was able to satisfy himself that a pair of circus dogs which had been displayed as mind-readers really could read minds.

Bekhterev, President of the Psychoneurological Academy and Director of the Institute for Brain Research in St Petersburg, was fully aware that the dogs might be picking up minute sensory clues if he gave them simple problems to solve. Such clues would hardly account for their ability to carry them out, when he silently 'willed' them to perform certain actions. To be on the safe side he put screens between himself and the dogs while 'willing' them. They continued to do his bidding. Just in case their circus training might have given them some faculty of which he was ignorant, Bekhterev repeated the experiments with his own dog, with the same results. Yet when his report appeared in 1924, so firm was the conviction in orthodox circles that animal mind-reading had been accounted for by Pfungst that it was ignored.

Again and again, the story of Clever Hans has been related as if it had been a triumph for Pfungst. Even so open-minded an ethologist as Professor Thorpe cited the case in 1962 as an example of 'the pitfalls to which a worker in this field is exposed'. Five years later, however, a former director of the Zürich zoo, Professor R. Hediger, drew his colleagues' attention to an aspect of the Clever Hans affair, the significance of which, he feared, they had not grasped. They had dismissed the whole episode as of no significance to them because Pfungst had shown that the horse had simply been picking up visual clues given by its owner or investigator. Was not this ability to pick up visual clues itself of profound significance? Why had it been ignored, rather than made the starting point of research into communication between humans and animals?

How much has been lost because of the failure to explore 'anpsi' – psi in animals – can be gauged in Henry Blake's *Talking with Horses*, an account of his forty years as a trainer, in which he established communication with his horses of various kinds, using it in the stables or on the hunting field. Not merely could they understand what he was trying to put across to them; they enjoyed some form of extra-sensory perception, which enabled them to communicate with each other at a distance. If something frightened one of them, others would show they had picked up the signal.

Recalling the story of 'Clever Hans' in his *How Real is Real?*, Paul Watzlawick complained that the baby had been thrown out with the bathwater. It was an illustration of the way in which scientists, in their fear of getting involved with psi, do not care to grapple with problems which are too near the boundary for comfort. It would be a rash young ethologist who ventured to suggest that the time has come to revive this line of research – unless, of course, he offered to provide an explanation not involving psi.

In this instance, the Society for Psychical Research bore some of the responsibility; in particular the Cambridge nucleus of Sidgwick, Myers and Gurney. Telepathy, they believed, would offer evidence of the evolution in humans of higher faculties. To Myers it constituted evidence for the soul, and for life after bodily death. Communication at a distance of the kind that intrigued Selous and Marais did not interest them; on the contrary, it was something of an embarrassment. Although Andrew Lang, with his assertion that what people called the sixth sense had been the first, did not agree, he was not influential in the Society. Nor was Sir William Barrett, although he had been chiefly responsible for setting it up. His surmise that psi might have an evolutionary role did not please the Sidgwicks, who tended to regard him as society hostesses traditionally regard gawky country cousins.

So powerful has the influence of the Cambridge nucleus remained that as recently as 1963 John Beloff, observing that paranormal phenomena almost invariably occur in connection with a human person, cited animal ESP as 'perhaps the marginal exception'. Marginal? That would have surprised hundreds of pet owners the world over, had they read it.

Anecdotal though most of the material is, there is plenty of it. In 1940 the Duke University team began to check the accounts which flowed in to them about pets who appeared to have displayed psychic abilities. The basis for acceptance of any case history was that the source seemed reliable, and that there was corroborative testimony. By 1960 some 50 accounts had passed the test, most of them concerning cats and dogs. Some of them defied explanation along conventional lines – notably the achievement of a Persian cat, Sugar, which jumped out of the car in which a family were leaving California for their new home in Oklahoma, stayed a few days with their former neighbours before disappearing, and then turned up, over a year later, at their new Oklahoma residence.

Occasionally it has been possible to trace the route taken by a lost pet 'homing' to its owners. In *Bobbie*, published in 1926, Charles Alexander described how a collie, lost in Indiana, turned up the following year in Oregon, 3,000 miles away. Detective work revealed that he had stayed for short periods in Iowa, Colorado, Wyoming and Idaho, before reaching his home. Still more remarkable was the feat of another pet dog, Tony, which the family had given away to friends in a town near Chicago, because they were moving to a new home in Michigan, over 200 miles away. He rejoined them six weeks later, having circled Lake Michigan – as they were able to check from a locality-tag he had acquired on the way. Tony, in other words, had not 'homed' in the usual sense of the term. He had found his way back to his owners, over territory he had not known before, to their new home.

As these accounts can be dismissed as anecdotal, there has

been no pressure on orthodox scientists to investigate. Yet one result of experiments, though not directly concerned with psi, may yet turn out to have provided significant evidence if a way can be found to repeat it.

The experiments were begun in 1920 by William McDougall, newly appointed to the Chair of Psychology at Harvard, his aim being to see if it would be possible to detect Lamarckian inheritance in rats. They had to learn to escape from a water tank by swimming to two exits, one illuminated, the other dark. If they tried to escape by the illuminated one, they received an electric shock. The number of times they went for it before they realised they must leave by the dark exit indicated how quick (or slow: some took over 300 journeys before they made the correct decision) they were at learning. Over a period of fifteen years, during which the learning speeds of thirty-two generations were tested, it was found that later generations were learning significantly faster.

The experiment was repeated in Melbourne by W.E. Agar and some colleagues over a period of twenty years, with fifty generations of rats. In 1954 they reported that they had obtained similar results to McDougall's. Yet there was one curiosity. They had a control group of rats who did not undergo the training, yet the progeny of the controls also 'learned' more quickly.

'These results seemed completely inexplicable; they made no sense in terms of any current ideas, and they were never followed up,' Rupert Sheldrake has recalled in *A New Science of Life*. 'But they make very good sense in the light of the hypothesis of formative causation.' Sheldrake's hypothesis is that growth is not simply a matter of following a genetic blueprint; it is shaped by a 'morphogenetic field', comparable to a magnetic field, connecting across space and time, so that embryos develop by 'tuning in' to the forms of past members of the species. Retrocognition of this kind, he believes, also accounts for instinctive behaviour. Where a species learns something new, as the rats did in Agar's experiment, the lesson may be transmitted by 'resonance' to other rats, altering their morphogenetic fields, and those of their progeny.

The hypothesis has obvious significance for psychical research. 'It is not inconceivable that some of the alleged

phenomena might turn out to be compatible with the hypothesis of formative causation,' as Sheldrake cautiously puts it.
'In particular, it might be possible to formulate an explanation of telepathy in terms of morphic resonance.' So it is not
surprising that the editor of *Nature* should have described the
book as 'the best candidate for burning for many years' –
thereby giving 'a tremendous boost for sales' for the delighted
author. Nor is it surprising that the McDougall and Agar tests
have not been repeated. The procedure would take too long
for anybody anxious merely to discredit the findings, and
would be beyond the resources available to psychical
researchers.

One experiment undertaken recently in Siberia, however,
has lent some confirmation to Sheldrake's hypothesis. Serguei
Speransky, investigating group behaviour in mice, separated a
group into two sections, deprived one of them of food, and
watched the other in a different part of the house, to see if they
showed any reaction. The group being fed ate more food, as if
they were picking up the hunger signals. A colleague at the
Leningrad Medical Institute who repeated the experiments
obtained similar results.

Spontaneous Combustion

The strangest example of the blindness of those who do not
want to see is the attitude of forensic scientists to the
phenomenon which has become known as spontaneous combustion. Although it is not a common occurrence, when it
happens it has often left traces of a kind which cannot be
accounted for in conventional scientific terms.

In 1966 a gas man, doing his meter-reading round in
Coudersport, Pennsylvania, entered the house of a retired
doctor, and was surprised to find a cone of ash on the floor,
and light blue smoke hanging over it. Looking for the doctor,
he eventually found what remained of him in the bathroom: a
foot, still in its shoe. When the coroner arrived, he realised
that the doctor's body (except for the foot) had turned to ash;
beneath it was a small hole in the floor, through which the ash
had dropped to form the cone seen by the gas man. Otherwise,
apart from some slight charring, no damage had been done by
the conflagration.

As Francis Hitching has commented in his *World Atlas of Mysteries*, this left the coroner, as it leaves us, with certain unanswerable questions. The first guess was that the doctor, having inadvertently set his bathrobe alight, had rushed to the bathroom to dowse it. But the robe, lying in the bath, was barely singed. Even if it had begun to burn, how could that have incinerated the doctor? Why did the gas man smell, not burning flesh, but an odour which, he said, put him in mind of a new central heating system at work? Why was there no sign of the fire in the living room – if that was where the robe had caught alight? 'And why was the paint on the bathtub, only inches away from the charred floor, blackened but not blistered?' Baffled, the coroner settled for a verdict of 'asphyxiation and 90 per cent burning of the body'. We shall never know how many cases of spontaneous combustion have been dealt with by such evasions.

In spontaneous combustion the fire seems to spread from the inside out. Extremities – the end of an arm or a foot – may be left untouched. Furniture beside what is left of the corpse often shows no sign of heat. Sometimes the clothes that were being worn have not burned. Photographs of the remains can provide incontestable proof that fire from some external source, such as a match struck in a gas-filled room, could not possibly have been responsible. The immense heat required to burn a human body would certainly have sent furniture and fittings, and probably the entire house, up in flames. Yet all that remains often resembles the best-known of all descriptions – Dickens's in *Bleak House*, based on an instance he had come across: a greasy coating on the walls, a burnt patch on the floor, and what Guppy and Jobling, investigating to find where the smell is coming from, take to be 'the cinder of a small charred and broken log of wood' – all that remained of Krook.

As Michael Harrison observed in *Fire from Heaven* some cases are well-attested – so well that occasionally a coroner has been honest enough to admit that something has occurred which cannot be accounted for by conventional physiology. In the *Medico-Legal Journal* in 1961 Dr Gavin Thurston, Coroner for Inner West London, relating a case of what he chose to describe as 'preternatural combustibility', observed that although such instances are rare, and lie near the borderland of myth, 'nevertheless there are undisputed instances, and this seems to be one, where the body was burned in its own substance, without external fuel, and in which there has been a remarkable absence of damage to surrounding inflammable objects'.

To a query from Harrison, however, Thurston replied, 'I can state without qualification that no such phenomenon as spontaneous combustion exists, or has ever occurred.' Preter-natural combustion, he insisted, 'has always been started by external fire' – a view echoed by Keith Simpson while he was Professor of Forensic Medicine at London University: 'though body fat when deteriorating and oily can burn, some other condition has to be present to start fire. About 250°C. is necessary, and the body itself will not do this.'

Harrison had no difficulty in demonstrating this was an evasion. Although preternatural combustions have often taken place close to some external source of heat, such as a fire in a grate, or a lamp, they cannot be explained away so easily. As if aware, in fact, that his explanation would not do, Simpson added, 'of course, as soon as ignition is effected, the fat will burn at a far lower temperature'. In some of the well-attested cases not only is there no evidence that any external source of heat was responsible, even where the 'other condition' has been present, it has not approached a temperature of 250°C. In any case, though fat may indeed burn at a lower temperature, bones, as Simpson well knew, do not.

An example of the continuing unwillingness even to con-template the possibility of spontaneous (or preternatural) combustion has been provided by a recent inquest. On January 28, 1985 a 17-year-old cookery student at a Technical College in Widnes, Cheshire, was walking down a corridor with some friends when 'there was a smell of smouldering and we saw her skirt burning', as one of them recalled. She was taken to hospital, where she died a few days later.

The initial assumption was that her clothes must have caught alight while she was beside a stove, but at the inquest it was disclosed that she had been wearing a protective apron, and that it was the clothes she had on underneath it which were on fire. In the absence of any other theory, the possibility was raised of spontaneous combustion – 'a theory most of us have treated highly sceptically', a Fire Prevention Officer noted, but 'it should be examined'.

This was not the view of the coroner when, four months later, the inquest was resumed. Although in the meantime experts had examined the evidence without being able to find any explanation, he told the jury to ignore speculation about spontaneous combustion. In this he was supported by the Home Office pathologist, on the ground that 'the necessary chemical reactions were not evident'. Apparently nobody thought to ask what the necessary chemical reactions are to identify spontaneous combustion, if spontaneous combustion does not exist.

The Black Box

Occasionally scientists have felt so confident they can demolish claims which appear to support psi, that they agree to take part in tests – only to find to their embarrassment that the results are positive. They then do their best to forget.

Early this century an American neurologist, Albert Abrams, experimenting with percussion as an instrument of diagnosis, made the bizarre discovery that if a healthy subject held some diseased tissue, the 'tapping' would produce a noise characteristic of the disease. There must be a 'bio-current', he decided, which varied according to people's state of health. Further experiments convinced him that there was no need for a human intermediary. He designed a diagnostic instrument, the 'Abrams Box', which would provide readings from a drop of a patient's blood, and began to manufacture and sell it.

Abrams believed his invention was scientific. To orthodox medical scientists it was barely disguised quackery, with an even less well disguised commercial motive. When in 1924 the news came that a British version was about to come on the market, Thomas Horder agreed to chair a Royal Society of Medicine committee with the equally barely disguised purpose of exposing the box as fraudulent.

The instrument chosen for the tests was an emanometer, adapted from the Abrams 'box' by a homeopathic physician practising in Glasgow, Dr W.E. Boyd. Using it, Boyd was required to identify substances (to have asked him to identify human disorders or symptoms would have put him and the committee at risk of a breach of regulations laid down by the General Medical Council). In the first test he scored twenty-five out of twenty-five. In five trials he made only two errors. Later, in a trial where the controls were even more rigorous, the success rate was maintained. The fundamental propositions underlying the assumption on which Abrams's machines were based, the committee felt bound to report, had been established 'to a very high degree of probability'.

Later experience with the 'Black Box', as it came to be called, showed that the boxes were not, as Abrams and some of his successors hoped, capable of supplying objective diagnostic information. It appears that somebody with psychic powers is required to operate them successfully, as they are subject to all manner of disconcerting psi effects. Horder did not know this. For all he knew, the principle upon which the box operated might have been one of the most important discoveries in the history of medicine. He could not help realising, however, that the principle, whatever it might be, broke the laws of nature as they then stood. To become involved in occultist research might have jeopardised the prospects of a career which was to culminate in his appointment as royal physician. He made no move to have the box investigated further.

He did not need to. After he had read the report to an audience at the Royal Society of Medicine, the Chairman inquired whether members who were present would like to discuss it there and then, or on some later occasion. The vote was in the negative to both propositions. Members did not want to put the questions that the report prompted, knowing as they did that there could be no answers of the kind they would wish to hear.

The Gregory/Mayo
Syndrome

When materialist rationalism established itself in the course of the eighteenth century, splitting phenomena into the two categories, natural and supernatural, scientists assumed the supernatural could not exist. Occasionally they have been compelled to realise they have been wrong. They do not care to admit they have been wrong, if they can help it. They prefer, if possible, to gloss over their mistakes.

At the beginning of the nineteenth century meteorites did not exist. A few years later they did. No inquest was held to apportion blame. Sackcloth was not worn. Instead, the impression was given that science had taken another forward step in its progress towards the goal of the unravelling of all mysteries.

The injustice of this rankled among the minority of scientists who were seeking to prove that certain phenomena which orthodoxy still rejected ought to be recognised: two, in particular. Dowsing – divining for underground water or for seams of ore – had long been practised, and a great deal of evidence had accumulated that it worked, even if its results were not consistent. The reality of the mesmeric trance state, and of some of its by-products, was even more extensively attested. Yet both were still kept in the supernatural category.

Herbert Mayo, a former Professor of Physiology at King's College, London, was convinced that dowsing would soon have to be allowed to occupy its rightful place. He was under no illusions that, when it was, people like himself who had championed the cause while it was still heretical would receive any credit. 'A new truth has to encounter three normal stages of opposition', he lamented in 1851 in his *Letters on the Truths Contained in the Popular Superstitions*. In the first, 'it is denounced as imposture'; in the second, 'cursorily examined, and plaus- ibly explained away'; in the third, 'decried as useless'. When eventually it is accepted 'it passes only under a protest that it has been perfectly known for ages – a proceeding intended to make the new truth ashamed of itself, and wish it had never been born'.

Mayo's words have often been echoed since, with varia- tions. Usually they are attributed to somebody more famous, much as a certain type of jest is commonly attributed to Winston Churchill. Its implication, that scientists are not the best judges of the truth, is rarely grasped, so accustomed are they to appropriating it when it eventually forces itself upon them.

The same year William Gregory published his *Letters on Animal Magnetism*. Professor of Chemistry at Edinburgh Uni- versity, Gregory enjoyed an international reputation in his own field. It had shocked him that fellow scientists should have been so obtuse as to refuse to face the facts which Franz Mesmer and his disciples had established. It also shocked him that when in the 1840s James Braid's findings at last per- suaded some scientists to accept the reality of the trance condition, they twisted the evidence to fit their preconcep- tions.

Hypnotism

The story of the transition from animal magnetism, or mesmerism, to hypnotism (Braid's term), of hypnotism's eventual transfer from the supernatural to the natural, and of what has happened since, adds up to what is perhaps the most serious of all the indictments of scientism in action, because of the cost in terms of unnecessary human suffering. Scientists cannot, in this case, claim that past mistakes are water under the bridge.

The initial objection to animal magnetism when Mesmer advanced the theory in the 1780s was based on the same assumption that had led to meteorites being rejected as a superstition. A belief in healing forces coming from space was too close to the old belief in divine intervention to be acceptable. Mesmer's theory that the force which he used for healing was a form of bio-magnetism might conceivably have won acceptance, or at least tolerance. It was the link with the planets that was unacceptable.

From the point of view of winning over orthodox science, the research carried out by Mesmer's followers, conscientious though much of it was, made animal magnetism even less welcome. They found that they could exercise control over the will and the imagination of subjects, instilling obedience in a way that was too close to discredited notions of witchcraft to be acceptable. They also often encountered the 'higher phenomena', as they were described, usually clairvoyance and 'community of sensation' – the ability of some subjects in their trances to 'taste' whatever the hypnotist was tasting, 'feel' what he was feeling. This seemed all too clearly to be a revival of occult superstition. So, to doctors, did the mesmerist's claim that, in the induced trance, patients could be operated on without feeling pain. The demonstrations, eminent members of the medical profession who could be persuaded to attend them explained, merely showed how well patients could endure pain without showing it if the incentive to do so – the bribe offered by the mesmerist – was sufficient.

For over half a century, at a period when there were still no anaesthetics, the profession refused to recognise mesmerism's pain-killing potential. Invited in 1842 to a demonstration in which a patient's leg was amputated, the physiologist Marshall Hall said afterwards he knew it had been rigged, as if the man had really been insensible to pain his other leg would have twitched in sympathy. Later, Hall told the Royal Medical and Chirurgical Society that the patient had confessed to the deception. When the patient wrote indignantly to the Society to say he had not confessed, and that he had not felt pain, Hall explained that he had heard about the confession from 'the most honourable and truthful of men', who assured him that he had heard it from somebody in whom he reposed full confidence. The Society supported Hall, a verdict the *Lancet* praised as 'impartial'.

By the 1840s James Braid had introduced his notion of hypnosis as a physiological process, and W.B. Carpenter explained that hyperacuity of the senses in the hypnotic trance state could account for some of the 'higher phenomena', such as freedom from pain and community of sensation, which had earlier been rejected. The rest of the higher phenomena, such as the accurate descriptions which Alexis Didier was giving in the 1840s of what was happening in people's homes, were left in the superstitions category.

Gregory knew this was fallacious. He had witnessed many tests in which clairvoyance had been exhibited of a kind that could not be achieved by hyperacuity of any or all of the five senses. Yet here was Carpenter, brushing the reports aside because they did not suit his purpose. Carpenter and others, he complained, now accepted certain phenomena observed in the hypnotic trance state which, when they had seen them earlier demonstrated by mesmerists, they had denounced as 'mere humbug and imposture'. Yet they did not think to apologise. When demonstrations showed that some of the phenomena could not be accounted for by hyperesthesia, humbug and imposture were alleged again. They continued to reject the evidence as 'deliberately and recklessly' as before.

That the pain-killing properties of the trance state had at least been confirmed was of little comfort to patients, as in the 1840s anaesthetics came into general use. A handful of doctors, however, experimenting with hypnosis along Braid's lines, found that it gave them the power to treat patients' symptoms by suggestion under hypnosis. A French country doctor, A.A. Liébeault, exploiting the cheapness of the method compared to treatment with drugs, made himself a local celebrity and in 1882, a century after Mesmer had tried in vain to persuade the members of the Academy of the Sciences to recognise animal magnetism, their successors formally accepted hypnosis.

They were induced to accept it by Jean-Martin Charcot's demonstrations of his control over the will and imagination of patients diagnosed as suffering from hysteria. Again, as Mayo and Gregory had foreshadowed, there were no apologies. The trance could still be regarded as physiological, the psychological element slipping in through pathology's side door. The trance, Charcot explained, was a mental symptom of organic hystero-epilepsy. Hysterics were notoriously suggestible. The hypnotist's control over will and imagination could at last be safely conceded.

As soon as research into hypnosis was acceptable, experiments were undertaken and reported from all over Europe. Two problems promptly surfaced. Charcot's hypothesis of hystero-epilepsy was quickly shown to be nonsense. The great majority of sane people, in fact, could be hypnotised. The hypothesis was quietly buried, without ceremony. The other problem was more difficult to handle. Scores of reports began to reappear of the 'higher phenomena' which could not be accounted for by hyperesthesia.

The most remarkable of them came from Pierre Janet. Along with his brother Jules, Frederic Myers and Julian Ochorowicz from the University of Lemberg in Poland, Janet investigated the case of 'Mme B.', diagnosed by a Le Havre doctor as a hystero-epileptic and thought a suitable subject for investigation. Not merely did 'Mme B.' display clairvoyance and 'community of sensation' – when Jules in another room burned himself on the arm, she squealed and rubbed her own arm, as if it had been burned – but they were able in a series of carefully controlled tests to show that she could be hypnotised from distances of up to half a mile. One or other of the investigators would watch her, taking the times when she went into her trance. These would then be compared with the times when the hypnotist in another house had gone through the motions of inducing the trance. Out of twenty-five tests of this kind, only three were failures.

This was far from being the result Janet had wanted. He was soon to move back into mainstream psychology, becoming France's leading theoretician. Still less was it what Ochorowicz had wanted. He had spent years trying to account for community of sensation without having to accept clairvoyance. He left Le Havre emotionally shaken, he was to recall. 'I had at last witnessed the extraordinary phenomenon of action at a distance, which upsets all currently received opinions.' Because it upset them, the report of the Le Havre experiments, along with all the other reports about clairvoyance and community of sensation in this period, were ignored. So was the report of a committee of the British Medical Association, confirming that hypnosis, far from being a disorder, was of value in the treatment of minor disorders. Enmeshed in rationalist materialism, scientists did not want to know.

Hypnotism fell into a kind of limbo. As trances were now recognised, they were no longer in the occult category. Yet the odour of occultism remained attached to hypnotism, fed by works such as du Maurier's *Trilby*, in which Svengali's powers over the unfortunate heroine were those of a sorcerer. It was not taught in medical schools, and only peripherally in academic psychology. In Britain it flourished chiefly in music halls, until banned from the theatre by an Act of Parliament.

Professional hypnotists have since moved over to the club circuit, to which the Act does not apply. Their stock procedure is to call for volunteers from the audience, find by simple tests which of them will make the best subjects, and put them through a routine designed to exploit the hypnotist's control over their minds and their imaginations in ways which will impress and amuse the audience. To amuse, subjects are told to behave like kittens; they go down on hands and knees and lap up imaginary milk from imaginary saucers. To impress – to prove the volunteers are not simply pretending to be hypnotised – the hypnotist commonly asks them to hold out their forefingers, under which he waves the flame from a lighter.

Not merely do the volunteers feel no pain, they show no sign of a burn afterwards, no reddening, no blisters. The implications for medical science ought to be obvious. In the trance state, the mind can switch off not merely the mechanism by which we feel pain, but also the process by which the body ordinarily reacts to a burn. Hypnotists, in other words, have been practising the same craft as the shamans and the gurus who lead fire-walks.

The ability to banish or relieve pain by inducing an altered state of consciousness has a renewed usefulness now that it has come to be realised how dangerous the use of drugs can be for that purpose, on account of their side-effects and of the risk of addiction – not to mention their expense. The provision of a measure of protection from the effects of burns is potentially of far greater value. Apart from fire-walks and club occasions, there is plenty of well-attested evidence from controlled trials to confirm that the protection exists.

A century ago Professor Joseph Delboeuf of the University of Liège 'branded' a hypnotised servant girl with a red-hot iron on both arms, and suggested to her that she would feel no pain in her right arm. Not merely did she feel no pain: when the bandages on both arms were removed, the right arm showed no sign of inflammation, though the left was blistered and painful, until he used suggestion under hypnosis to remove the pain.

Many trials since then have confirmed Delboeuf's results. Some also suggest that the earlier hypnosis is used, the more effective it can be in preventing the usual consequences of even the most serious burns. Experiments have convinced Dabney Ewin, an associate professor of surgery at Tulane University, that the time-lag between the damage done immediately by a burn and the response – inflammation, blisters and eventually scarring – can be most effectively employed by hypnotising the patient and suggesting that the response need not occur. Photographs show how effective the method can be even in cases where the individual could ordinarily expect to be badly scarred for life.

The present position is that although hypnosis is theoretically a recognised adjunct of medical treatment, periodically recommended by committees which investigate its uses, it is still not in the medical curriculum, and is employed by only a minority of doctors. Yet in connection with burns alone its value could be very great. Millions of people are accidentally burned every year, many of them needing to go to hospital. If tests confirm Ewin's findings, the benefit of immediate hypnotic treatment could be striking. It seems certain, too, that auto-suggestion can be learned and applied for the treatment of minor burns in the home.

As Guy Lyon Playfair points out in his *If This Be Magic*, the excuses which have been put up within the medical profession for declining to bring hypnosis into the mainstream of conventional medical treatment are legion – it takes too long, is too uncertain, and so on. They are based on ignorance. Only one of them is really valid. It is not possible to be a successful hypnotist without confidence in the ability to hypnotise, and to make effective use of the trance condition. Medical training being what it has become, few doctors can hope either to acquire the confidence or to know how best to treat patients with its help.

One other argument is often used to justify the failure to incorporate hypnosis into standard medical practice: that the ways in which altered states of consciousness influence neurophysiological processes are as yet imperfectly understood.

This is certainly true. It will remain true so long as little attempt is made to investigate. One area, in particular, has received little attention, except in the form of occasional attempts to explain it away in conventional terms: hysteria.

Hysteria

Charcot's instinct was correct, even if his interpretation was mistaken. Like hypnosis, hysteria is a condition in which the human body reacts to subconscious commands in abnormal ways – as in the case of the *convulsionnaires* of St Médard in the 1730s, who became resistant to fire and to savage blows. Had David Hume known about hypnotism, he would not have needed to cite the phenomena as his example of the best evidence (though not good enough for him) that he knew of miracles. He could have rationalised them by attributing them to auto-hypnosis.

Hysteria in its commonest form manifests itself in loss of control by the mind of the body. The limbs may flail around, in anguish or in laughter; or they may seize up, as in the case of the tube crash at Moorgate station in London in 1975. Witnesses on the platform described how the driver had looked as if he was transfixed, as the train accelerated through the station into the wall beyond. Half a century before, the coroner's verdict might well have been death from hysteria, as in the First World War the way in which Flying Corps pilots had killed themselves, by 'freezing on the joystick' when their aircraft went into a spin, was notorious. Subsequently hysteria, not being readily accountable for in materialist medical terms, has become an unfashionable diagnosis. It hardly featured in the batch of implausible explanations of the tube crash – such as that the small amount of drink the driver had consumed the night before might have been responsible.

In the same way, cases of mass hysteria are commonly attributed to food poisoning, or a gas, or an unknown virus. Hysteria is considered only when all other explanations have been ruled out, and often not even then. Yet some of its aspects deserve closer scrutiny, in particular the programming. Why, for example, in an outbreak at the Royal Free Hospital in London in 1955, was it only the nurses and a few other members of the medical staff who succumbed, while the patients remained unaffected? Why should this be a common feature of outbreaks in hospitals?

The most plausible explanation of mass hysteria is that it represents a regression to the termite stage of evolution. The psychic 'infection' is transmitted to particular groups, much as different messages are passed to different elements in the termitary.

The psychical researcher Whately Carington, observing the way the Nazis were stirring up mass hysteria, argued that the same forces were at work at, say, a Nuremberg rally as those which directed the movement of flocks of birds. Not that the Nazis had deliberately set out to exploit psi – ready though some of the leaders were to do so, when it suited them, by consulting clairvoyants. They had simply realised that blind devotion to the Führer could be generated on such occasions. 'In their own perverted way, they have builded better than they knew,' Carington observed. They had set in motion, 'below the surface, forces which their crude and materialistic barbarism is quite incapable of comprehending' – the forces of biological action and communication at a distance.

The Lid-sitters

Universities

The attitude of the academic world to psychical research has been generally unsympathetic, and often hostile. 'Why do so few scientists ever look at the evidence for telepathy?' William James asked in one of his lectures. 'Because they think, as a leading biologist, now dead, once said to me, that even if such a thing were true, scientists ought to band together to keep it suppressed and concealed.' The fear of the equivalent of a counter-reformation, with the risk that obscurantism might regain the upper hand, has continued to provide a ready excuse for the suppression.

'Men of science are afraid lest, if they give an inch in this matter, the public will take an ell and more,' William McDougall told the members of the SPR in his Presidential Address in 1920. 'They are afraid that the least display of interest or acquiescence on their part may promote a great outburst on the part of the public, a relapse into witchcraft, necromancy and the black arts.' Yet the best defence against a revival of discarded superstitions, he insisted, was psychical research. As the lid of Pandora's box had been lifted, there was nothing for it but to continue to explore the contents. 'It is the policy of sitting on the lid of the box that is risky.'

The lid-sitters have remained in charge. Examining the response to questionnaires in the United States, the sociologist James McClenon has found that the highest level of scepticism about ESP is today to be found among the élite scientists who control the scientific establishment, and it extends to rejecting the claim of parapsychology to be an academic discipline. The answers reveal that the rejection is rarely based on familiarity with psychical research. Within the élite, the tendency is for those who doubt the existence of ESP 'to cite *a priori* reasons for this opinion'. Because members of the élite feel that part of their role is to define what is, and what is not, science, they are inclined 'to stigmatize scientists who investigate anomalous experiences (or who attempt to induce such experiences under laboratory conditions) as silly, incompetent or fraudulent'.

'It is never written, and rarely stated', J. Richard Greenwell has observed, 'but individuals producing anomalous data, or proposing the study of anomalous events, will, in time, be gradually "punished".' In his *Parapsychology and Self-Deception in Science* R.A. McConnell has related and documented a case-history of the 'punishment' meted out to a graduate student at the University of Pittsburgh, whose crime it was to state that she was taking her higher degree in biophysics and sociobiology with a view later to undertaking psychical research – anathema to sociobiologists. Before she could even begin, she was required to do an extremely time-consuming experiment (900 hours, McConnell estimates) three times, because the results did not conform to her supervisor's expectations, which they showed to be false. In spite of the fact that her papers were accepted by the editors of *Science* and of a leading journal of sociobiology, it took her nine years before she was eventually granted a Ph.D. Although it is never easy to be certain how far an interest in psi can be held responsible for, say, the failure to obtain promotion in the academic hierarchy, the fact that only two universities in Britain applied for the Koestler Chair, well funded though it was, is a sufficient indication of the contempt in which parapsychology is held.

When universities have accepted bequests, they have not necessarily used them for the purpose for which the donors hoped they would be used. The assumption has been that it will be possible to divert the money to research of a kind of which the universities will approve. When the Philadelphia Spiritualist Henry Seybert left money in 1884 to the University of Pennsylvania to found a Chair of Philosophy, on condition a committee was appointed to investigate spiritualist phenomena, its members assumed that the phenomena were bogus, conducted a spurious investigation and had no difficulty in agreeing that there was no point in wasting the money on further psychical research. Other American universities have solved the problem of legacies of this kind by accepting them and appointing sceptics to be the beneficiaries, as both Harvard and Stanford did in the 1920s.

Recently the University of Colorado has engaged in a variation on this theme, caustically related in 1970 by Charles Gibbs-Smith.

For many years the American Air Force had clung to the belief that reports of unidentified flying objects could all be accounted for naturally. During the 1960s a few of them were so well-attested, often by pilots, and so hard to explain, that the decision was taken to ask the university to investigate, half a million dollars being offered for the purpose. A committee was duly set up under Dr Edward Condon. Its report in 1968 was dismissive.

Before the university had accepted the funding, when there was still uncertainty whether it *should* be accepted, the academic who had been named as project co-ordinator had prepared a memorandum giving his reasons why the offer should be taken up. 'Our study would be conducted almost exclusively by non-believers who, though they could not possibly *prove* a negative result, could and probably would add an impressive body of evidence that there is no reality to the findings,' he had explained. 'The trick would be, I think, to describe the project so that, to the public, it would appear to be a totally objective study; but to the scientific community would present the image of a group of non-believers trying their best to be objective, but having almost zero expectation of finding a saucer.' The best way to do this, he suggested, would be for the committee to concentrate not on the actual sightings, but 'on the psychology and sociology of persons and groups who report seeing UFOs'. Scientists would 'get the message'.

A researcher, finding a copy of this memorandum, leaked it to *Look* magazine. By this time the committee's deliberations were almost at an end. It was too late to disguise the fact that they had followed the course which the memorandum had outlined. What had happened could only be viewed 'as a deliberate act calculated to deceive; to deceive first the scientific community, and through them, the public at large', Gibbs-Smith pointed out. 'I know of no modern parallel to such a cynical act of duplicity on the part of a university official.' As the discovery of the document had at a stroke destroyed the whole value of the report, the university had simply squandered the funds with which it had been provided. What made matters worse was the fact that at no time had the memorandum 'been repudiated, or even deplored, by any of the parties to the deal. Neither the University of Colorado nor the Air Force has had a word of explanation to offer for behaviour which cuts at the very roots of scientific integrity.'

An internationally respected figure for his works on the history of aviation – he was soon to become the first Lindbergh Professor of Aerospace History at the Smithsonian Institute at Washington – Gibbs-Smith was understandably outraged. His view that scientific integrity had been damaged was not widely shared, in university circles. Is not one of science's functions to eradicate superstition? The way in which the University of Colorado had set about it was not considered to be duplicity, as the lack of any shocked reaction showed. Had an investigation of, say, meteorites been similarly rigged, the disclosure would have reverberated around the academic world. Those concerned would have been lucky not to lose their jobs. But UFOs? If the Colorado University authorities were blameworthy, surely it was for not having burned or shredded all copies of the memorandum . . .

Scientists

Scientists who have assumed that evidence for psi must have been obtained by delusion or deception have often felt justified in using deception themselves, much as threatened politicians resort to Watergate-style tricks. Faraday's fear and loathing of spiritualism led him to think of it as so great a menace to science that he was justified in setting up his bogus experiment 'to turn the tables on the table-turners'. John Tyndall boasted that he had cheated in an experimental session Wallace had arranged, by contributing his own 'raps'. T.H. Huxley pretended he had unmasked a medium, when from his own account it is clear that he was only speculating how the medium *might* have tricked the sitters.

W.B. Carpenter adopted a different course, easier to take at the time than it has since become. Having detected Sir David Brewster exploiting his anonymity in the *North British Review* to praise Sir David Brewster, Carpenter began to use the same technique himself in journals such as the influential *Quarterly Review*, in which he blatantly puffed his textbook on physiology.

When Crookes published the illustrated report of the tests which he had conducted on Daniel Home, assisted by the astronomer William Huggins and the lawyer Serjeant Cox, Carpenter realised that the only way in which Home could have cheated would have been by using some mechanical device. As the three investigators were standing beside Home, in good light, this was inconceivable unless they were hopelessly gullible. Crookes and Huggins were Fellows of the Royal Society, Cox a well-known barrister. Could they really have been so easily duped?

They could, Carpenter insinuated. Crookes, he claimed, had been made a Fellow of the Royal Society 'with considerable hesitation' as he was known to be a specialist, 'utterly untrustworthy as to any inquiry which requires more than technical knowledge for its successful conduct'. Huggins was a brewer by trade, only an amateur astronomer. As Cox was not a scientist his testimony was worthless.

This was egregious fabrication, and Carpenter, himself an FRS and by this time a leading pundit on scientific matters in general, must have known it. Crookes was an all-rounder: no scientist of the time had so varied a range of interests. Although Huggins came from a brewing family, his high professional standing as an astronomer was later to be confirmed when his peers elected him President of the Royal Society. The Society's Council felt compelled to pass a resolution condemning the *Quarterly* writer on the ground that the Society did not allow unauthorised accounts purporting to be of its deliberations, but as Carpenter had not put his name to the article, the Society did not need to take any action against him. It was left to Cox to take a neat revenge. Carpenter, he insisted, could not have written it, because no man of his scientific and professional status could 'so far forget the gentleman as, in a purely scientific controversy, to be guilty of the mingled mendacity and meanness that pervade the article in the *Quarterly Review*'.

In private correspondence, Carpenter used to maintain he was not a materialist – the term which by the 1870s scientists were using to describe their rationalist faith. He was even prepared to accept the possibility that the spirits of the dead could excrcise an influence on the living. In public, and in his anonymous contributions to journals, he continued to pretend to be a total sceptic, justified in using tactics which would have been considered disgraceful if he had adopted them against materialists, because in his case they were in a good cause – the fight against resurgent occultism. His peers showed how much they appreciated his work when, the year after he had smeared Crookes, Huggins and Cox, he was elected President of the British Association for the Advancement of Science.

The full extent to which scientists have cheated in order to discredit psychical research will never be known, as few have followed Tyndall's example and boasted about what they have done. Only occasionally has an admission slipped out, as when E.G. Boring, Professor of Psychology at Harvard, was induced to investigate the Boston medium 'Margery' in 1925. Baffled by her ability to move objects at a distance in the seance room, he was relieved when one of her investigators demonstrated how he could obtain the same effects by conjuring tricks. Asked to speak out at the demonstration if he could see how the tricks were done, he said nothing at the time. Later, in an article in *Atlantic Monthly*, he admitted that he had seen through the tricks and should have said so, 'but it never occurred to me to do so'. Only when he had reached home, and thought things over, had he realised that his desire to see the tricks succeed had made him hold his tongue.

There may well have been more such examples. In one recent case, practices carried out in order to discredit certain findings, unwelcome because they could be regarded as promoting occultism, have been exposed – a case in which members of the Committee for the Scientific Investigation of Claims of the Paranormal, commonly known as CSICOP, have been involved.

CSICOP is a cousin of the American Humanist Association. The circumstances of the AHA's conception are illuminating. It was originally formed in 1933, its manifesto leaving no doubt that one of its aims was to overthrow the capitalist system. From 1948 it was largely funded by Corliss Lamont, a dedicated Marxist and fervent admirer of Stalin. On his return from a visit to Russia in 1938, at the height of Stalin's purges and 'treason' trials, Lamont claimed that he had left 'with the definite feeling that its people are well-nigh invincible in an economic, moral and military sense'; as a consequence, 'mankind again forges ahead to conquer new heights of economic and cultural achievement'. The AHA journal, the *Humanist*, inevitably preached dialectical materialism. As at the time parapsychology was condemned in Russia as bourgeois deviationism, it was denounced, along with the profit motive.

In the 1970s the editor of the *Humanist*, Paul Kurtz, Professor of Philosophy at the State University of New York at Buffalo, and himself far from being a communist, became alarmed at the news of a revival of astrology. Twenty years earlier Michel Gauquelin, a French psychologist, had hit upon a surprisingly simple way of testing astrological claims. With his wife he compiled a list of 576 doctors who were members of the Académie de Médecine – in other words, an élite group – and worked out the position of the planets at the hour of their births. To his astonishment, he found that they had been born far more often under Mars and Saturn, while those planets were rising in the sky, than under Jupiter – and far more often than a control group.

Intrigued, he went on to test other groups, finding that sports champions and military leaders tended to be born under Mars 'rising', whereas famous actors were more often born under Jupiter. Similar studies in Belgium produced similar results. The difference between the élites and the rest, acting as controls, was not great, but statistically it was highly significant.

This did not mean, Gauquelin was careful to emphasise, that astrology deserved to be brought back into the scientific fold. It did mean that there were anomalies which pointed to the possibility of some kind of planetary influence, of the kind astrologers had long accepted. But so low had astrology sunk in the estimation of most scientists that when the news of Gauquelin's findings began to spread, in the early 1970s, the general reaction was to damn it. A questionnaire sent out by the *Humanist* in 1975, inviting leading scientists in America and Europe to put their names to a manifesto entitled 'Objections to Astrology', met with a remarkable response.

No fewer than 186 signed, including eighteen Nobel Laureates.

'Scientists in a variety of fields have become concerned about the increased acceptance of astrology in many parts of the world', the manifesto began. The words rang a bell for Paul Feyerabend, echoing as they did the Papal Bull promulgated by Innocent VIII five centuries earlier: 'It has indeed come to our ears, not without afflicting us with bitter sorrow', that in many parts of the world 'persons of both sexes, unmindful of their own salvation, have strayed from the Catholic faith and abandoned themselves to devils.' This was the Bull which provided the Introduction to the notorious *Malleus Maleficarum*, heralding the campaign against witchcraft and heresy which was to destroy hundreds of thousands of lives. The failure of the Papacy to realise that it was not devils who were the threat, but the corruption within the Church, Feyerabend recalled, was to drive young Martin Luther into mounting the campaign which was to split the Church in two.

One well-known scientist, Carl Sagan, refused to put his name to the manifesto on the ground that it was too authoritarian. 'It is simply a mistake', it had stated, 'to imagine that the forces exerted by stars and planets at the moment of birth can in any way shape our future.' Yet though Sagan did not believe that astrology had any validity, the manifesto's assumption that it could be dismissed because there was no known mechanism by which the planets could influence life on earth struck him as unwise. No mechanism was known for the 'continental drift' theory, which had been derided as a consequence; it had turned out to be correct. 'Statements contradicting borderline, folk or pseudoscience that appear to have an authoritarian tone', Sagan concluded, 'can do more harm than good.'

Some damage was in fact done to a number of the Nobel Laureates, who, when asked to appear on a BBC programme to give their views, excused themselves on the give-away ground that they had never studied the subject. For Paul Kurtz, however, the response to the questionnaire had been so gratifying that he hastened to consolidate the rationalist-materialist alliance for which the *Humanist* had been campaigning by inviting well-known scientists and sceptics to form CSICOP. On its stationery appeared such names as Isaac Asimov, Milbourne Christopher, Martin Gardner, Professor Ray Hyman, Laurence Jerome, the Amazing Randi, Carl Sagan, B.F. Skinner and Marvin Zelen. Among the British members were Christopher Evans, Professor Anthony Flew, Eric Dingwall and Professor C.E.M. Hansel. Although they carried less weight than the Nobel manifesto-signers, most of them being better known as publicists and polemicists than for scientific achievements, it was for their polemical capabilities that Kurtz needed them. In 1974 he held a press conference in New York to announce the launching of a campaign to purge the media of occultist leanings. In particular, he pledged that CSICOP would try to ensure that no TV programme dealing with parascience would go out unvetted by the appropriate authorities. He left no doubt that the appropriate authorities should be CSICOP members.

The campaign duly began, and for a time was so intense that producers such as Alan Neuman, who had had a successful American television series on paranormal phenomena and was about to have another, felt they were back in the McCarthy era. The tactics used caused the first split in CSICOP. Among those who resigned was Marcello Truzzi, originally designated CSICOP's co-chairman and editor of the new CSICOP journal. Truzzi, Professor of Sociology at Eastern Michigan University, complained that CSICOP was 'tarring everybody with the same brush'. He thought it unwise to lump together serious parapsychologists, deluded though they might be, with Moonies, believers in the Bermuda Triangle, and reporters of little green men with goggle eyes.

Undeterred, Kurtz went ahead with what was designed to be CSICOP's first major exposure. Gauquelin had found that 23 per cent of sports champions had been born under Mars rising, compared to 17 per cent of non-sports-champions. That 6 per cent difference – soon to be described as the 'Mars Effect' – would have to be challenged. It had in fact already been challenged in the *Humanist* by the science writer, Lawrence Jerome, but that had proved counter-productive, provoking Gauquelin into a devasting riposte and almost into a libel action against Jerome.

In 1976 Marvin Zelen, a colleague of Kurtz in Buffalo, suggested what appeared to Kurtz to be a safer course, because it would hoist Gauquelin with his own petard. Gauquelin would be asked to test for the 'Mars Effect' on ordinary people born about the same time and place as the sports champions (in case regional differences might be shown to account for the earlier differences). The figures were duly produced. They showed that in the new sample the proportion of non-sports-champions born under Mars rising was 16.4 per cent. The Mars Effect, in other words, was even greater than in the earlier trial.

Kurtz was appalled. He could not ignore the result because, without consulting his committee, he had presented the offer to Gauquelin as a formal challenge, promising in the *Humanist* that the outcome would be 'definitive'. He consulted with George Abell, Professor of Astronomy at the University of California, Los Angeles, who had joined the Executive Council of CSICOP, and with Zelen. What could they do?

They were confronted by two alternatives, neither of them palatable. They could accept the new Gauquelin findings, and embark on a search for another natural, rather than astrological, explanation. Or they could challenge the validity of his statistics. The first course would be humiliating. The second would be dangerous, as Gauquelin had easily disposed of such challenges before. They decided against taking either course. Their report in the *Humanist* in the November/December 1977 issue contrived to show that the new test had demolished the case for the Mars Effect. It sounded so convincing that Jerome, grateful for what he took to be retrospective support for his paper, sent his congratulations.

As it was unlikely that any member of CSICOP would want to rally to Gauquelin's defence, that might have been the end of the matter, had it not been for Dennis Rawlins, an astronomer and a member of the inner council. One of CSICOP's hard-liners, his view from the start had been that Gauquelin must have erred, perhaps even unconsciously cheated. If so, what was the point of inviting Gauquelin to do a second test? It would presumably give the same result. When it did, Rawlins felt his warning had been justified.

When he saw Kurtz's contention that the new test had exploded the Mars Effect, Rawlins was astonished. His initial assumption was that a mistake had been made. Only when Kurtz ignored his pleas did it dawn on Rawlins that it had not been a mistake but a decision, taken without consulting him, although he was a council member and an authority on the subject. At least some of his colleagues on the Council, Rawlins assumed, would agree with him that this had been disgraceful. Randi agreed, for one; Kurtz's decision, he thought, had been deplorable. Martin Gardner, too, was unsympathetic, 'chuckling about what an incredibly hilarious foul-up the whole thing had turned out to be'. They declined, however, to take any action. Gardner continued to treat the matter as a joke and Randi, Rawlins eventually realised, had pretended to be sympathetic only to keep him in line. 'When I asked him why, he repeated the tired old alibi that the occultist kooks would whoop it up if Kurtz fell.'

Kurtz made a final appeal to Rawlins for loyalty. He sounded genuinely bewildered, Rawlins recalled. To him it was a political, not a scientific issue. Refusing to be persuaded, Rawlins told the whole story in *Fate* magazine.

He had previously believed, Rawlins explained, that it was simply a figment of the imagination of journals such as the *National Enquirer* that the science establishment would cover up evidence for the occult. Now, no longer. He was still sceptical, 'but I *have* changed my mind about the integrity of some of those who make a career of opposing occultism'. 'They call themselves the Committee for the Scientific Investigation of Claims of the Paranormal', an editorial note in *Fate* commented. 'In fact they are a group of would-be debunkers who bungled their major investigation, falsified the results, covered up their errors, and gave the boot to a colleague who threatened to tell the truth.'

That the cover had been blown in *Fate* gave Kurtz and his associates on the Council the chance to pretend to ignore the onslaught. Although *Fate* had in the past made many damaging exposures of various forms of occultism, it was dismissed by Gardner as 'pulp'. Rawlins, it was put about, had long been a trouble-maker. A letter purporting to correct his mis-statements was circulated privately to CSICOP members by Kurtz and Abell (it simply rehashed their mis-statements, Rawlins complained). To rally the faithful, the *Scientific American*, to which Martin Gardner had long been a regular contributor, printed on the Committee's behalf: 'Who will guard the truth? The answer is CSICOP will!'

Unluckily for this boast, Marcello Truzzi had commissioned an independent survey of the affair from Patrick Curry, a historian of science with a special interest in astrology. It appeared in the *Zetetic Scholar*, which Truzzi had founded after he left CSICOP, and it followed a very different line from CSICOP's *Skeptical Inquirer* or the *Humanist*, giving plenty of space to both sides in any controversy. Curry's concern was with the actual evidence for the Mars Effect. On balance, he concluded, it had been corroborated.

More disturbingly for Kurtz, it was also corroborated by Richard Kammann, a psychologist at the University of Otago in New Zealand. Kammann was highly regarded in CSICOP circles as co-author with David Marks of *The Psychology of the Psychic* – a book which, according to Martin Gardner, 'should have been printed and promoted with trumpets by a major publishing house' – a tribute which in itself was clear evidence of its authors' outright scepticism.

Kammann's initial feeling had been that Rawlins could not have been the single honest person, as in effect he claimed, on a nine-man Council of men of such stature as Martin Gardner and the Amazing Randi. Rawlins, he thought, must have let his anger get the worst of him. When Kammann studied the evidence during seven months of research, he was forced to realise that Rawlins had been right. What made it worse was that a one-page statement in the *Skeptical Inquirer*, signed by the nine members of the Council, with Abell in Rawlins's vacant seat, asserted that there was nothing to hide and no cover-up. Abell was actually smearing Gauquelin with innuendo. Gauquelin, he told *Newsweek*, had no way of proving he had not cheated. This was too much for Kammann. He resigned from CSICOP, sending his report to Truzzi, who published it in the *Zetetic Scholar*. CSICOP, it concluded, 'has progressively trapped itself, degree by irreversible degree, into an anti-Rawlins propaganda campaign, into suppression of the evidence, and into stonewalling against other critics'.

At long last, in the Spring 1983 number of the *Skeptical Inquirer*, Kurtz, Abell and Zelen were smoked out. The issue contained what they euphemistically described as 'A Reappraisal'. 'Apologia' would have been the more appropriate term. They had to concede they had made mistakes. Some they glossed over – they had been wrong to think that the test of the Gauquelin findings would be 'definitive' when 'of course it could not be immune to sample irregularities, such as biased or fudged data'. This was the very point Rawlins had made, which they had ignored. They now came round to it, hinting that Gauquelin might still be caught out. That they had failed to show that the challenge had actually confirmed Gauquelin's findings, they now had to admit, constituted a valid criticism. Kurtz, involved in the administration, and Abell, 'heavily involved with other projects', had 'neglected to examine the manuscript with sufficient care'. This, as Rawlins had shown, was false. Abell *had* examined it six months before it was published as evidence against Gauquelin, with sufficient care to realise that it was actually evidence *for* Gauquelin, and had written to warn Kurtz.

Kurtz and Abell managed to make it all sound as if a few unfortunate errors had occurred which had only come to light later. No reference was made to the fact that Rawlins had drawn their attention to the matter years before. Nor could they leave the subject without yet another thinly disguised attack: 'we should add that there is no clear evidence that the Gauquelins intentionally biased the sample'. No *clear* evidence? There was no evidence of any kind. No apology was made to Rawlins for the attacks on his character and his credibility. No apology was made to CSICOP members for having deceived them for so long. The 'reappraisal' actually concealed the fact that they had managed to maintain the cover-up for over five years.

The heading under which Kammann's account appeared, 'The True Disbelievers', contained an irony which must have been lost on most readers, though not on Kammann himself. In *The Psychology of the Psychic* he had offered a model to account for the persistence of false beliefs, such as the belief in the reality of psi, even when they are undermined by the evidence. 'The model says that once a belief or expectation is found, especially one that resolves uncomfortable uncertainty, it biases the observer to notice new information that confirms the belief, and to discount evidence to the contrary' – an echo of Festinger's theory of cognitive dissonance. 'This self-perpetuating mechanism consolidates the original error and builds up over-confidence in which the arguments of opponents are seen as too fragmentary to undo the adopted belief.'

All that Kammann would have needed to do, in connection with Kurtz and Abell, was add a 'dis' before each 'belief'.

The most depressing aspect of the affair, as Kammann evidently recognised, is not so much that individual scientists should have engaged in unworthy tactics to avoid humiliation, as that their fellow-scientists, when they realised what was happening, should not have manifested their disapproval, either by demanding that the culprits should resign, or by themselves resigning. Only a handful of members quit.

That CSICOP's reaction to the Gauquelin findings was not an isolated example, attributable to the foolishness of the individuals concerned, was shown up by Curry in his *Zetetic Scholar* article, in connection with the very similar reaction of the committee which had been set up in Belgium to investigate Gauquelin's findings. When the Belgian committee also, to its embarrassment, found that its work confirmed Gauquelin's, it rejected the results by claiming Gauquelin must be using the wrong control group level, using this as the excuse to pursue the issue no further. Examining the Comité Para's attempt at a rebuttal of these charges, Curry came to the conclusion that it was deplorably misleading, constituting ample evidence of the committee's unfitness to be entrusted with such an investigation. To find it 'reiterating the same half-truths, untruths and inconsistencies with which we are now familiar', was, to Curry's mind, disturbing.

Wheeler vs Rhine

CSICOP's campaigns can also be held indirectly responsible for another unedifying episode. One of the campaigns a few of its members engaged in during the late 1970s was to try to have the Parapsychological Association thrown out of the American Association for the Advancement of Science; and they had the support of the physicist John Archibald Wheeler of the University of Texas, Austin.

Wheeler had made a name for himself with his far-out speculations about the universe, which he credited 'with an *infinite* number of dimensions', and his liking for vivid similes – 'the space of quantum geometrodynamics can be compared to a carpet of foam spread over a slowly undulating landscape'. To his horror, his ideas were seized upon by parapsychologists as fitting in rather well with their own. At a meeting of the AAAS in 1979 he allowed himself to be made the spokesman for the campaign to, as he described it, 'put the pseudos out of the workshop of science'.

In his paper, Wheeler denounced the Bermuda Triangle, Scientology, flying saucers and so on, without referring to psychical research. Asked why, he replied it was not necessary. He need mention only one experiment conducted by 'the great psychologist McDougall on rats'. McDougall, Wheeler recalled, had put rats through tests designed to discover whether they passed on skills acquired by learning to their progeny. As he had to be away during the summer 'he left the work to his post-doctoral associate'. On his return, when he found that the children of the 'educated' parents had indeed performed better than the controls, McDougall prepared a paper with his associate, giving the statistics. Fortunately, Wheeler went on, the precaution was taken 'thanks to McDougall, to submit the work to Tracy Sonneborne, distinguished both in genetics and in statistics'. Something about the work aroused Sonneborne's suspicions. He went to Duke to discuss it. 'One thing led to another.' It transpired that the associate had been so interested in the success of the children of the educated rats that 'when they made a mistake and went to the wrong outlet where the electric shock was, he pushed down the key a long time and gave them a "lallapallooza" of a shock!' It was no wonder, therefore, that they had learned faster than the controls. 'So the paper was never published.'

At this point Wheeler recalled that he had not mentioned the name of McDougall's associate: 'it was Rhine – Rhine – he started parapsychology that way'. If Wheeler's account was correct, the Parapsychological Association might well have been thrown out of the AAAS. As well as starting parapsychology, in the sense that the term is commonly used in the United States to refer to experimental laboratory studies, Rhine had been, and still was, its leading figure. Nobody at the meeting felt able to rebut the charge, but it was not difficult to go back over the ground to find out what exactly had happened half a century earlier.

That McDougall had carried out experiments with rats to test the neglected Lamarckian hypothesis was not in dispute. It was true, too, that Rhine had helped in the experiments sometimes when McDougall was away. The account, however, was misleading. It had been McDougall, not Rhine, who had obtained the positive results. At no point had Rhine been in a position to tamper with the experimental protocol in a way which could have influenced the findings which were used in the paper.

Sonneborne had published criticisms of the experiments (as McDougall acknowledged) and had visited Duke. So far from criticising Rhine, though, he had praised him for reporting a possible source of confusion. It had been Rhine who had pointed out that unless the length and intensity of the electric shocks were carefully controlled, there might be discrepancies (as indeed there were, when the idea was tested, in both the educated rats and the controls). Far from being suspicious, Sonneborne confirmed he had been impressed by Rhine's 'sincerity and enthusiasm'. And the paper *had* been published.

The most depressing part of the tale was still to follow. *Science* published a letter from Wheeler explaining that at the AAAS meeting he had 'unwisely repeated a second-hand and, as it turned out, incorrect' account of the experiments of Rhine and McDougall. Rather than repeat the 'inaccuracies', he proposed to give references to the literature in which the interested reader could get at the story correctly. Incredibly, he made no apology to Rhine in the letter. As Rhine observed in a dignified rejoinder, Wheeler's letter did not 'identify just *what it is* that he retracts; it could be *any* little thing; he vaguely calls it "inaccuracies" '.

Shabby retreat though it was on Wheeler's part, Rhine was able to point to one benefit. The new President of the AAAS, Kenneth Boulding, asked by the Washington *Star* what he thought about Wheeler's proposal to boot out the parapsychologists, expressed disagreement. 'The evidence of parapsychology cannot just be dismissed out of hand,' he replied. He was 'in favour of keeping them in'.

The Science Journals

In ordinary circumstances the exposure of Kurtz, Abell and Zelen, and the conduct of CSICOP (renamed CSICP in Britain, because of the annoyance of some members at being described as psi cops), and that of Wheeler, could have been expected to find a place in the notes of the science journals, coupled with disapproving editorials. Having relied so heavily on Martin Gardner as its adviser in relation to parapsychology, the *Scientific American* might find it hard to change its tune; but *Science*, as the journal of the American Association for the Advancement of Science, surely had a responsibility to ensure fair play, or at least was expected to expose foul play?

Many years before, *Science* had published the report of trials to find out whether there was any relationship between the brain rhythms of twins in separate laboratories. The findings had revealed a connection so close that it was hard to account for except by some form of ESP (one twin had only to shut her eyes for the other's brain rhythms to alter). The unfortunate editor was deluged with correspondence rebuking him for giving space to so palpably spurious an investigation.

Subsequent editors had fallen back on a simple device. Whenever papers were submitted giving parapsychological findings, one of the referees to whom they were sent would invariably be a sceptic. Invariably, he would advise against the paper. Over a period of forty years up until 1970, a search through the files disclosed, *Science* had accepted only two papers dealing with the subject, one reporting negative results, the other so badly organised that no parapsychological journal would have accepted it.

When the Parapsychological Association was brought in to the American Association for the Advancement of Science, its members' hope was that the editor of *Science*, Philip Abelson, appointed as he was by the AAAS, would realise that the time had come to deal with their papers on their merits. They were soon disillusioned. Some papers received glowing tributes from three referees, but one referee would turn them down without even the pretence of taking them seriously.

Eventually in 1977 the Council of the Parapsychological Association wrote to the President of the AAAS asking for his assistance to persuade Abelson to follow AAAS policy guidelines. The President agreed. 'The doors of science should not be closed to papers on parapsychology,' he wrote. Early in 1978 it was disclosed that 'a major article on parapsychology' was at last in preparation.

It appeared that summer: a denunciation of psychical

research by Persi Diaconis, a statistician working at Stanford University – and an initial member of CSICOP. The main point of the article, the exposure of a flaw in methodology, was itself crucially flawed. Apparently Diaconis had not realised that there had been an earlier examination of the same subject. The rest of the paper was mainly devoted to criticism of informal experiments which parapsychologists themselves agreed were unreliable, and it contained several errors. Among them was a wildly inaccurate account of Eisenbud's research with Serios. Diaconis claimed he had had 'direct experience with more than a dozen experiments'; but his description of the way in which Serios faked his effects, with the help of a tube 'placed on the forehead', suggested his recollection of them was unreliable, as when it *was* used it was *not* placed on Serios's forehead. As Eisenbud tartly pointed out in a letter to the editor, it would 'in any case have been about as much use as a truss placed there'.

This was only one of a number of letters correcting Diaconis's factual mistakes. Abelson told inquirers that he planned to publish them, but they have never appeared.

'*Science*, the foremost scientific periodical in the USA and the official organ of the AAAS, will for the sake of appearances, go through the charade of having a paper refereed; but every parapsychologist knows for a fact that if he claims positive results his paper stands no chance of being accepted, no matter how carefully his experiment was designed or how conscientiously it was executed,' John Beloff lamented at a meeting of the Parapsychological Association. 'Yet this same journal sees nothing incongruous in publishing an article attacking parapsychology even if it appears to be demonstrably misleading, unscrupulous and lacking in scientific objectivity.'

The British science journals have been a little less obstructive, but not much. The then editor of *Nature* was roundly abused for including a paper on the research undertaken with Uri Geller at Birkbeck College, and still more for admitting that it 'created a *prima facie* case for further investigation'. It was his sanity, some readers suggested, which needed to be investigated. When, later, Harry Collins sent a letter to *Nature* relating some research he had undertaken at the University of Bath into 'mini-Gellers', which had had negative results, the

editor accepted it – but intimated to Collins that it would not
have been printed had the findings been positive.

The present editor of *Nature*, John Maddox, has made no
secret of his total scepticism about psi. He has hammered
works which, like Sheldrake's, accept it. The *New Scientist* has
been rather less hostile, sometimes for the pleasure of getting
at *Nature*, but the general tone of the references to psychical
research to be found in it can be illustrated in a review by Jake
Empson, a psychologist not known for his intimacy with the
results of psychical research. Parapsychologists, he urged,
'should have the scientific humility to accept the verdict of
countless experiments showing that people do not have supernatural powers, and that magic is always based on trickery'.

The reluctance to accept unwelcome evidence is not, of
course, limited to excluding papers on parapsychology. The
advocates of unorthodox views about evolution have found it
hard to put them across, as Sir Fred Hoyle and Professor
Chandra Wickramasinghe have found in their campaign to
persuade scientists that life reached (and still reaches) earth
from space. 'We have come to the conclusion that there is no
freedom of speech in science,' Wickramasinghe has complained. 'Very rarely is discussion permitted to take place in
journals. Science journalists have taken on the role of police-
men.' Nevertheless it is parapsychology which has been the
chief victim. Not merely are the researchers deprived of a
hearing for their findings; scientists in general, as they rarely
see the journals of psychical research, are left with the
impression that there is no serious work in progress.

In 1973 a Barnsley doctor, T. Healey, issued a challenge to
healers in *Science*, suggesting that they should submit their PK
powers to controlled trials with bacteria. Six years later he
complained in *World Medicine* that it had never been taken up.
It had. Tests of the kind he had urged, with even more
sophisticated equipment, had been held, with some strikingly
positive results. *Science* had not published the reports.

In *The Psychology of the Psychic* Marks and Kammann,
dismissing the evidence in Matthew Manning's *The Link* for
his psychokinetic powers as of 'minimal scientific value'
because it was autobiographical (ignoring the attestations he
cited), noted that a series of 'learned papers' by scientists
testing him in 1974 had been promised; 'five years later we are

still awaiting these publications with great interest'. Ten years later they would still have been waiting, but not because the tests brought no positive results. Some of the investigators hardly bothered to disguise the fact that they were disconcerted by Manning's powers, which they had assumed to be spurious. Others, though impressed, made no attempt to publish their reports – perhaps fearing the derision of their colleagues. When reports were produced, none of the leading conventional scientific publications would accept them.

In an article in *Science* in 1965 George R. Price, echoing Hume – 'no testimony is sufficient to establish a miracle unless the testimony be of such a kind that falsehood would be more marvellous than the fact which it endeavours to establish' – argued that the results obtained at Duke and elsewhere could be most easily accounted for by the fact that, among the world's inhabitants, there were 'a few people with the desire and ability to produce false evidence for the paranormal'.

Price was taken to task in *Science* by a psychologist, Paul Meehl, and a philosopher of science, Michael Scriven, on the grounds that Price's argument assumed that psi could not exist, which was equivalent to claiming that scientific knowledge is both complete and correct, and that his allegations were irresponsible: 'Price has not made any attempt to verify them (as he admits) despite the unpleasantness they will cause.' Fifteen years later, in a letter to *Science*, Price made belated amends by apologising to Rhine for the smear. The damage had been done.

Scientism's Hit-men

It is understandable, Ray Hyman, Professor of Psychology at the University of Oregon has pointed out, and indeed almost inevitable, that scientists' reaction to psi should be emotional, irrational and sometimes irrelevant, but he fears that this has done great harm. 'The sort of tactics employed by the establishment's "hit men" against the offending claims – blocking access to regular communication outlets, *ad hominem* attacks, mis-representations of claims, dismissal on *a priori* grounds – do succeed in a way', but for the wrong reasons. They serve to discredit the heresy, 'and once it is so tainted, then the establishment scientists feel relieved and ignore it. But "discrediting" is not the same as "disproving" '.

As a founder member of CSICOP Hyman has been in a good position to observe the 'hit-men' in action. They fall into three main categories (with some overlapping): historians, including biographers; science journalists; and stage magicians.

Historians

'The ordinary procedure of the modern historian, even if he admits the possibility of miracle, is to admit no particular instance of it until every possibility of "natural" explanation has been tried and failed', C.S. Lewis noted in his book on miracles. 'That is, he will accept the most improbable "natural" explanation rather than say that a miracle occurred.' Collective hallucination, hypnosis, 'widespread conspiracy in lying by persons not otherwise known to be liars and not likely to gain by the lie – all these are known to be very improbable events: so improbable that except for the special purpose of excluding a miracle, they are never suggested. But they are preferred to the admission of a miracle.'

From the historians' point of view, Lewis thought, this was midsummer madness. Even crazier has been the fact that some historians who cannot accept psi have fallen back on such explanations to demolish the evidence for psi phenomena, such as ESP, which are not generally thought of as miraculous. They have also, where they have felt it to be necessary to their cause, cheated; either by fudging their source material, or by accepting fabrications without bothering to check.

Biographers have been among the worst offenders. Anatole France portrayed Joan of Arc as a credulous girl who had been exploited by wicked courtiers and priests, in order to play down her voices and visions. Andrew Lang, researching for a rebuttal, found that France had shamelessly rigged the evidence to suit his case. The historian Louis Cazamian, an admirer of France, had sadly to agree with Lang. Sometimes, he found, the sources France had quoted did not sustain the point he was making. Sometimes they had actually refuted it.

T.H. Huxley's biographer, C. Bibby, described how Huxley had 'detected gross deception' at a seance he had attended. Huxley had done nothing of the kind; after it had finished he went away and produced a speculative report on how the medium *might* have cheated, incidentally leaving the ugly implication that the respected Hensleigh Wedgwood must have collaborated to the extent of letting the medium out of his control without disclosing it at the time.

Jean Perrin's biographer, Fernand Lot, has described how Eusapia Palladino tried to deceive him and his fellow-investigators, during her tests in Paris, by producing ectoplasmic materialisation under cover of darkness; when the lights were suddenly switched on she was caught cheating. Robert Reid in his biography of Marie Curie tells the same story, presumably taken from Lot; 'with the lights suddenly switched on by one of the scientists, Palladino was revealed, naked of her weighted shoes, waving butter muslin in the air, and with her reputation in that little scientific community in little pieces'. Had either of the authors bothered to refer to the report of the investigating committee, they would have found that this story was simply a malicious invention.

In some cases it is clear that the historian or biographer is chiefly concerned to preserve at all costs the image he or she has of the subject. A good example has been the handling of *An Adventure* written by two Oxford dons, Charlotte Moberly and Eleanor Jourdain, about their experience at Versailles in 1901, when they felt that they had been transported back into the eighteenth century. One of their students, Joan Evans, was bequeathed the copyright of the book, which had continued to sell steadily. This pleased but disturbed her. A formidable personality (her entry in *Who's Who* filled nearly a column), she resented the way in which people she regarded as pipsqueaks in the academic world sneered at Moberly and Jourdain. She greatly admired them both, and was sure they were neither liars nor freaks. Yet she was a staunch rationalist, unable to believe they could have been wafted back in time.

Years later, she found a way to get rid of her cognitive dissonance. In an article in *Encounter* she welcomed new evidence that had come to light which in her view 'provides a rational explanation of the story, with no supernatural element remaining', and at the same time confirmed the integrity of the ladies because it confirmed the accuracy of their observations. Her justification for keeping *An Adventure* in print had been to ensure its availability for people interested in psychical research; 'in my view this reason is no longer valid and I do not propose to authorise a reprint or fresh edition'.

The fresh evidence on which Joan Evans based this autocratic decision was the discovery that Robert de Montesquiou, one of Proust's models for Charlus, had lived for a time in a house at Versailles, and given fancy dress parties there. What the two ladies had seen, a French writer had surmised, was one of them.

For anybody who had studied *An Adventure* with care, this was an unsatisfactory hypothesis. It did not fit much of what Moberly and Jourdain claimed they had seen. Still, if Montesquiou had been giving these fancy dress parties, that, and lapses of memory on their part, would have been hard to reject in favour of retrocognition. *Had* he, in fact, been giving them at the time of the adventure? As Lady Gladwyn, wife of the former British Ambassador to France, wrote to point out, this was the hard evidence Joan Evans needed to support her case, and she had not provided it. The reason she had not provided it was that, as an inspection of the appropriate records eventually revealed, Montesquiou had *not* been giving his parties at the time of the adventure. So anxious had Joan Evans been for a solution to her own problem, she had not cared to undertake research which might have upset it. By the time it had been upset, she was dead.

The extent to which history has been falsified by writers who have been conditioned to accept scientism's rationalist/ materialist faith can only be guessed at. 'When supernatural events begin, a man first doubts his own testimony; but when they repeat themselves again and again, he doubts all human testimony,' W.B. Yeats remarked. 'At least he knows his own bias, and may perhaps allow for it; but how trust historians and psychologists that have for some three hundred years ignored, in writing of the history of the world, or of the human mind, so momentous a part of human experience? What else had they ignored and distorted?' A great deal, it has to be feared. Much of what they ignored may never be known. Still, distortions can be tracked down. Some of the historians of the paranormal have elevated distortion into an art form.

Historians ordinarily are trained, or ought to be, to avoid certain deadly sins. Some of the commandments are obvious: such as 'thou shalt not invent facts'. There are two others which students are particularly enjoined to keep if they are to retain their integrity: thou shalt not indulge in *suppressio veri* – telling the truth, but not the whole truth; and thou shalt not slide into *suggestio falsi*: baseless innuendo. Few of the sceptics who have presented evidence from history have bothered to obey.

The chief characteristic of most of them, from Salverte on, has been a readiness to speculate about the ways in which mediums or investigators or both could have cheated, and if no explanation other than fraud or psi is possible, to leave readers to assume that fraud there must have been.

Frank Podmore was the first real master of the craft. His mistrust of physical mediumship led him to go to great lengths to discredit all those who have been involved in it, though even he could not find any serious flaws in the case histories about Daniel Home. As Podmore accepted mental mediumship, his survey of the historical evidence for it was in general fair. Sceptics who rejected both types of manifestation of psi simply adopted the technique he had used to discredit physical mediums to stigmatise mental mediumship as well: John W. Truesdell in *The Bottom Facts of Spiritualism*, Joseph McCabe in *Spiritualism*, and their successors on up to the present day.

Trevor Hall

Easily the ablest, from the point of view of presenting a well-researched case against individual mediums or psychical researchers, has been Trevor Hall. The research is of a much higher standard than any of his predecessors since Podmore.

In *The Spiritualists*, published in 1962, Hall set out to show that William Crookes, during the years when he was investigating mediums, became infatuated with the young Florence Cook, and joined with her to produce fraudulent materialisations, presumably in order to win or retain her sexual favours. Although for a number of reasons the story was extremely implausible, granted the premise that Crookes was an unscrupulous lecher and Florence a designing hussy it was not difficult for Hall to construct a superficially convincing case, except for one complication – Florence was only seventeen when she met Crookes. For two years before that, she had been demonstrating physical mediumship, including remarkable materialisations. In that time, she had been rigorously tested by researchers – Wallace among them. How could she have become so accomplished a conjuror before she was fifteen years old without anybody knowing?

In the first two pages of his book, Hall settled this issue. 'It is important to try to establish the date of Florence's birth', he claimed, 'since much emphasis has been placed upon her youth in accounts of her early mediumship.' He had accordingly undertaken a search through the files at Somerset House, and found no record of her birth. It had not been registered, or it had been registered under a different name – presumably that of a former lover of her mother's. Either way, this meant that Florence could have been considerably older than she claimed. Furthermore, Hall added, 'as for Florence being "an innocent schoolgirl of fifteen" as Crookes described

her, when she had just started her career as a medium, in
1872, she was teaching at Miss Eliza Cliff's school in Hack-
ney, and 'we know she was asked to leave'.

Two members of the SPR, R.G. Medhurst and Kathleen
Goldney, thereupon went over the same ground as Hall. At
Somerset House they found that Florence Cook's birth *had*
been registered, and that in 1872 she *was* only fifteen. They
also tracked down the letter of dismissal which Miss Eliza
Cliff had sent to Florence's mother. 'I am so grieved at what I
am going to write about that I can scarcely commence,' it
began. Parents of her schoolgirls, apparently, had been object-
ing to Florence's connection with spiritualism, and she had
feared the school would suffer. 'I am so fond of Florrie and I
have such a high opinion of her, that I am sorry to have to say
to you that I am compelled to part with her,' Miss Cliff
concluded, expressing her regret about Florrie's mediumship,
'for she is fitted for something far higher and nobler'.

If any scientist produced a hypothesis based on one crucial
error of fact and an implication, also crucial, combining
suppressio veri and *suggestio falsi*, he would be deluged with
derision. Yet it is Crookes's reputation which remains under a
cloud. The *New Scientist* ran an article in 1978 in which the
writer, taking Hall's work seriously, suggested that Crookes's
mind must have been affected by thallium poisoning (thallium
being the element he had discovered earlier, for which he was
made an FRS). If thallium poisoning played any part in
Crookes's career, scientists ought to consider taking doses of
the stuff. At the same time as he was testing mediums, and
arising out of his research with them, Crookes was doing the
experiments with vacuum tubes which were to pave the way
for the discovery of X-rays and the electron, as well as the
electric light bulb and the television tube. Yet Crookes's
distinguished public life, and his happy family life, have
afforded no protection. 'Who can refute a sneer?' the
eighteenth-century theologian William Paley asked. Who can
refute a smear?

In 1984 *The Spiritualists* was brought out again under a
different title, *The Medium and the Scientist*, the new publisher
being Prometheus Books, Buffalo, New York. Ordinarily a
writer in such circumstances takes the opportunity to slot in
material of interest which has been uncovered since the

original version appeared, and to correct mistakes. Not so, apparently, Trevor Hall.

'During the course of the investigation upon which this book is based, I have tried to make myself acquainted with the very extensive literature relating to the mediumship of Florence Cook,' he wrote in the preface to *The Spiritualists*, 'and I hope that nothing of importance has been omitted.' It was a little unwise of Hall to let that sentence stand in *The Medium and the Scientist* if he proposed to ignore – as he seems to have done – the evidence that the initial premise upon which he based his case against Florence Cook had been exposed by Medhurst and Goldney as false. The sentence 'we may never know when she was born, but we may reasonably assume that it was some time before she said' stays in the new edition, in spite of the discovery not merely that her birth *was* duly registered at Somerset House, but also that it confirmed she was as young as Crookes claimed. Hall has also allowed the damaging innuendo – 'as for Florence being "an innocent schoolgirl of fifteen", we know she was asked to leave her teaching post' – to stand unqualified.

To do him justice, Hall is a most assiduous researcher, and some of his revelations, notably about Harry Price, have been valuable. Yet he has seemed unable to resist innuendo when an opportunity presents itself. His findings in *The Strange Story of Ada Goodrich Freer* did enough additional damage to her never very high reputation without the need for more, in the form of prurient speculation by the eminent psychiatrist Eliot Slater, who wrote the introduction.

In the book Hall had included a letter from a friend of Ada's, saying she would go and 'stroke' Ada sometimes, as she thought it did her good; 'she couldn't stand it if it didn't do her some good'. What could 'stroke' mean? Slater asked. 'It can hardly be doubted, that a sexually-toned contact is intended.' The 'tone' was provided by flagellation. 'The cutaneous nerve supply of the buttock is part of a wider region, including the genitals,' Slater explained. Stimulation can 'give rise to strongly pleasurable sensations' – and so on.

'Stroking' was in fact the name given to a form of hand-healing, which consisted of running the hands down the body of the person being 'stroked' without actually touching it, to 'cleanse the aura'. It was widely practised in the seventeenth and eighteenth centuries, and later by the 'magnetisers', as some practitioners of Mesmer's therapy were known. Among its commonest effects were convulsions, which could be alarming, but were assumed to be a sign that the healing power was working – the precursor of electro-convulsive therapy. It was not surprising that Slater should be unaware of the 'strokers'; behaviourist psychiatrists are not much given to studying the history of unconventional psychiatric techniques. It is hardly conceivable that the erudite Trevor Hall should not have known of their existence.

The research for *The Enigma of Daniel Home*, published in 1984, severely tested Hall, as there are so many accounts by eminent (and eminently sensible) people showing that there was no way in which the phenomena could have been introduced by trickery. Hall gets around this by simply ignoring the accounts, except for one or two in which he thinks he detects a weakness. As the work of a prosecuting attorney, the book could just pass, though mincemeat would be made of it by the defence. As history it is lamentable, displaying, as Stephen E. Braude of the University of Maryland put it in his review, 'an appalling disregard for the canons of historical research'.

Nevertheless, Braude points out, Hall has 'succeeded in performing a minor service to the field'. He has been unable to find any serious flaw in the extensive range of evidence for the genuineness of Home's physical mediumship, to add to the innuendoes and inventions of earlier hatchet-men. In view of Hall's undoubted skill and long practice as a discoverer of skeletons in the cupboards of psychical research, this can be held to be one of the most significant tributes to Home that has yet appeared.

C.E.M. Hansel

Few scientists are likely to have read Hall's books, compared to the number who have read Hansel's *ESP: A Scientific Evaluation* which, Christopher Evans thought when it was published in 1966, heralded the demise of parapsychology.

While he was working at Manchester University, Hansel wrote to Rhine, stating that he was a serious student of psychical research. 'In so doing', according to Gaither Pratt, who was at Duke at the time, 'he made no mention of the fact that he had already written a critical book, then in manuscript form, on the subject.' Rhine's offer of expenses for a visit was repaid, when the book was published, by Hansel's account of how two of the tests at Duke which had given impressive findings might have been obtained by fraud.

Hansel's approach was derived from David Hume. Telepathy and clairvoyance are impossible, he claimed. 'If therefore the statistical data rule out explanations in terms of chance, then the results can only be accounted for by some kind of trick.' Psychokinesis was also ruled out *a priori*.

The evidence about some mediums, such as Home and Ossowiecki, would have presented problems. It would have been difficult for Hansel to show quite how the tricks had been played. He had a simple solution: he left them out of the book.

Where a case could be made for fraud, Hansel felt there was no need to worry whether or not the case was plausible. He did not bother to ask the people involved, if they were still alive, to comment on and if necessary rebut his speculations. It was enough, for him, to offer his hypotheses about the way they might have cheated, and leave it to readers, if they shared his scepticism, to infer that this was how they *had* cheated.

A typical example was his account of the experiments which Pratt had undertaken at Duke with the divinity student Hubert Pearce, to find whether distance made any difference to ESP reception. Pearce was in a library making his guesses, at agreed times, about the cards Pratt was turning up in an office 100 yards away. Pearce, Hansel surmised, could have run round to the corridor past Pratt's room, gone into a room on the other side of the corridor, and there watched Pratt 'with comparative safety by standing on a chair or table and looking through the transom above the door'. For bad measure, Hansel threw in a plan of the rooms and the corridor, to show how it could have been done.

The plan, Hansel admitted, was 'not to scale'. Had a parapsychologist included a not-to-scale plan, Hansel's suspicions would immediately have been aroused. The reason his was not to scale became clear to Ian Stevenson when he checked Hansel's account. Even supposing Pearce had been able to reach the room and use it undetected, he could not have seen the cards because the transoms – 'borrowed-light windows', designed to allow light from the offices to illuminate the corridor – were so high up that nothing that was going on in the offices below was visible.

What Hansel *had* succeeded in doing, Stevenson thought, was finally to destroy the myth of the fraudproof experiment. 'No matter how many precautions and extra witnesses one may introduce, the determined critic of the Hansel type can always find a place where fraud *might* have occurred.' As there was no shortage of imitators, Stevenson wondered whether he should continue to waste his time on them. 'One feels a little like an early settler in the American West. If a settler spent too much time fighting Indians, he would never get his crop planted and so starve. But if he did not spend enough time fighting the Indians he could have his crop and homestead burnt down.'

Stevenson was not the only settler to leave the homestead to take a gun after Hansel. Hansel's accusations of fraud were understandably resented, as was the book's reception in scientific journals, where it was enthusiastically received by Evans in Britain and Martin Gardner in the United States. Evans had one reservation: the historical section was 'somewhat unsatisfactory'.

Unsatisfactory? It was a protracted travesty. In addition to leaving out most of the best of the evidence for psi, Hansel contrived to present weirdly distorted pictures of the careers of some of the more famous mediums, notably Eusapia Palladino. He devoted what for him was considerable space – more than eight pages – to her. This was at first sight surprising, as a great deal of the evidence made it hard for him to sustain the charge that throughout her long career she must have got away with sleight-of-hand. He had to admit that the Paris committee had been 'clearly puzzled by some of the phenomena'. Still, he claimed, they had 'detected many signs of trickery'.

This was incorrect. There had merely been some speculation of how she might have cheated. Even less forgivable was Hansel's summary of the trials by the three members of the SPR sent to Naples to find out just how she played her tricks. Again, he had to admit that the investigators were 'puzzled' by the phenomena. This, he explained, could be accounted for by the fact, among others, that they had 'a strong belief in the supernatural, hence they would be emotionally involved'. Disbelieving sceptics would have approached the investigation 'in quite a different frame of mind'.

Hansel can hardly have been unaware of the reasons why the three men were chosen for the investigation. Dingwall, who knew all three of them well, had described them in detail. Hereward Carrington, one of the ablest investigators in the United States, 'had unrivalled opportunities to examine the host of frauds and fakers who flourished there, and his results had led him to suppose that of the alleged physical phenomena the vast bulk was certainly produced by fraudulent means and devices'. He had described them in detail in his *Physical Phenomena of Spiritualism*, published the year before the Naples investigation. Wortley Baggally had 'for many years studied trick methods, performed them himself, and was almost totally sceptical as to the reality of any supernormal physical phenomena whatsoever'. Everard Feilding was 'a man of vast experience and one of the keenest and most acute critics that this country has ever produced'; although open-minded, 'his scepticism was extreme'.

Hansel had chosen to ignore Dingwall's informed account. He would have been wiser to ignore Eusapia, as he ignored Home. As it was, he could not resist giving space to what clearly delighted him, as he quoted a chunk of it: Münsterberg's 'exposure'. Although Dingwall could not understand why Carrington had wasted time on somebody so 'entirely unfit for such an inquiry' as Münsterberg, he had not realised how Münsterberg had innocently given a striking testimonial to Eusapia's psychokinetic powers. This was precisely the passage Hansel chose to quote.

It was also ill-advised of Hansel to criticise some of the reports of parapsychologists on the ground that they sometimes contained trivial discrepancies which, though unimportant in themselves, were indicative of carelessness. Hansel's work, Stevenson pointed out, was itself 'riddled with errors of detail'. Although they were for the most part trivial, misspellings of names and the like, if Hansel's point was to discredit the researchers, he must believe that to err is human for critics 'but for parapsychologists unforgivable'. In describing the Prague experiments with Stepanek, for example, he had made nine mistakes in twenty-two lines.

Stevenson was in fact being unduly charitable. As para-psychologists with special knowledge of the careers of individual mediums were able to show, Hansel's errors were often far from trivial. 'A good many of the fallacious stories about Mrs Piper put forward by rationalist critics are to be found in C.E.M. Hansel's *ESP*,' Alan Gauld noted. Hansel had made use of one wholly unreliable source, filtered through another. As a result Gauld, quoting verbatim from Hansel's book, was able to insert corrections, often in flat contradiction to Hansel's, in almost every sentence. Yet astonishingly, when Hansel's *ESP and Parapsychology: a Critical Re-evaluation* appeared fourteen years later, the errors remained uncorrected. Hansel blandly claimed that because in the earlier book 'the material was taken in its historical perspective' much of it had been retained, 'since no reason could be found to change what has already been written'.

Hansel could with difficulty allege that he was unaware of the mistakes in the earlier book, or the many misleading statements, such as his reference to Gertrude Schmeidler's sheep/goat work: 'repetition of the test by other investigators did not conform to the original result'. This was the truth – some investigators did not confirm the original result – but not the whole truth: Schmeidler had not conducted only one test – there were several – and several tests by other investigators *had* confirmed her findings. 'Hansel could hardly plead ignorance', the Yale psychologist Irvin Child wrote, reviewing Hansel in the *Journal of Parapsychology*, 'of a body of publications which have had so conspicuous a place in the parapsychological literature.' A reader familiar with parapsychological literature was likely to gain 'an impression of either extreme carelessness or deliberate misrepresentation'.

Hansel was unwise enough to challenge Marcello Truzzi on this issue. Truzzi had commented in the *Zetetic Scholar* that his work was open to counter-criticisms. It was up to Truzzi, Hansel argued, to state them 'or at least give some idea of what they amount to'. Truzzi contented himself with listing a string of reviews, each of which had contained the criticisms. In any case, he pointed out, 'there seems little point in presenting Professor Hansel with new counter-arguments, when he seems to have thus far ignored most of the ones already available for him'.

Ruth Brandon

The latest recruit to the ranks of purveyors of history from the sceptics' viewpoint is Ruth Brandon, whose *The Spiritualists* appeared in 1983. It is characterised by a range of *suggestio falsi* and *suppressio veri* worthy of Hall and Hansel, of whose works she has made extensive use. Even the title is appropriated from Hall's – and is less justified, as there is little in the book about the spiritualists, except in their capacity as mediums in connection with psychical research.

Typical of the trust Brandon obviously reposes in Hall is her blanket acceptance of Hall's version of the relationship between Crookes and Florence Cook, that the seances were an excuse for a liaison, giving Florence a hold over Crookes 'which would ensure that he never betrayed her but helped, and would continue to help, her career'. Apart from the fact that Crookes did not continue to help her career, as he abandoned psychical research, Brandon can hardly have been unaware that the basis for Hall's allegation had been undermined by Medhurst and Goldney. She actually mentions their contribution. Nevertheless she claims that there are 'very good grounds' for believing Hall's argument. 'It is soundly based on evidence; it explains all the facts; and it feels right.'

Confronted by the problems of how to discredit Daniel Home, Brandon falls back on gossip which was shown to be false at the time, or has since been exploded. Not merely does she cite Sir David Brewster's recantation of what he witnessed as if she believed it – 'there was no one less likely to be taken in by trickery', she claims, 'and indeed he was not taken in' – she does not mention the letter in which Brewster's duplicity was exposed when it was published by his daughter, though if Brandon had read the books listed in her bibliography she must have known about it.

She repeats, too, the rumours which went around when Home left Paris, where he had been giving seances for the Emperor Napoleon III and his Court. Had his mediumship, she asks, been shown up as fraudulent? 'The fact remains that he did leave Paris very abruptly; if this was not the reason', Brandon asks, 'what was it?' Another reason given at the time was that he had been arrested for homosexual practices in Lyons, but released and expelled for fear he might spread scandal about the Court. 'Was this true?' she asks. Again, if she consulted the sources she gives in her bibliography she would have known that both stories were fabrications. Home had left Paris to visit the United States, there to pick up his young sister, whose education the Empress had promised to take care of, as she did. When they returned, Home resumed his former cordial relations with her, and with the Emperor.

Brandon's treatment of Richet is another example of *suppressio veri*. As her book purports to be about spiritualism she might have been expected to make it clear that Richet did not believe in spirits, and devoted much of his energies to seeking a materialist explanation for ectoplasm and other manifestations of psi. Of all the psychical researchers of that time, he had been the hardest to convince of the reality of the physical phenomena, materialisations in particular. He was actually to apologise for the ridicule he had poured on Crookes and others for their reports. Yet Brandon claims that he was deluded 'by the strength of his will to believe, and his disinclination to accept any unpalatable contrary indications'.

To reinforce her shaky case, Brandon contrasts Richet's research with that of the Curies. Theirs, she argues, was principally 'hard, hard labour', involving 'constant repetition of processes, testing of materials, infinite refining down'. Richet's was a vain attempt to demonstrate the reality of psychic phenomena; 'that was where the Curies began – with the reality'.

True – but it is not the whole truth. Brandon omits to mention the Curies' involvement in psychical research in the Paris investigations of Eusapia. They witnessed, and were clearly impressed by, the 'reality' of the phenomena. As for her comment about 'the tedium of many of the texts of parascience. They are merely repetitious', so are the Curies' research papers!

Journalists

For some reason, no well-known science journalist in Britain has specialised in savaging psychical research. Things have been very different in the United States, particularly since the setting up of CSICOP. The doyen of the sceptics' establishment is unquestionably Martin Gardner, who has used the position he has won as a science writer to conduct a forceful campaign against the parapsychologists. Whereas Hansel ignores critics who try to set him to rights, Gardner revels in controversy, answering them in detail – or pretending to, giving casual readers the impression that he has really been in the right even when shown up to have been in the wrong.

Giving Hansel's *ESP* an enthusiastic welcome in the *New York Review of Books*, Gardner concentrated on his account of the Pearce-Pratt trials, repeating Hansel's hypothesis. Pearce could have left his cubicle, 'sneaked back across the campus, entered a vacant room across the corridor from Pratt's office, stood on a chair and peeked through the transom and a clear-glass hallway window' to get a good view of the cards. Anyone who has read the accounts of the Pearce-Pratt tests, by Rhine and Pratt, Gardner admitted, would have been impressed 'by the lengths to which Rhine went to rule out collusion between Pratt and Pearce', but 'the one thing neither Pratt nor Rhine ruled out was the possibility that Pearce did not stay in his cubicle'.

The one thing? Pratt wrote to the *Review* to chide Gardner. Why had its readers not been told that the plan Hansel had shown in his book was not to scale, as Hansel had admitted, and that if it *had* been to scale, it would have revealed 'that the supposed peeking was impossible?' Gardner's riposte was characteristic. The exact floor plan, he replied, was 'now seen to be amusingly irrelevant' ('amusingly' is a term he employs in the sense Oliver Lodge had in mind when he warned that any attempt to convince sceptics by controlled tests 'could be permeated with a sort of humorous doubt, and holes picked in the record with the help of jokey asides such as "Ah ha! What was the assistant doing?" '). Granted it might have been impossible for Pearce to peek from across the corridor, Gardner argued, there was nothing in Pratt's 'clumsy experimental design' to prevent Pearce 'from standing on a chair in the corridor'.

Oh, but there was, Pratt wrote in reply. He was glad, he noted, to see that the editorial space restriction under which he had had to labour must have been removed for Gardner, because Gardner 'had admirably used more than half of his reply admitting to a number of errors in his review'. The exact floor plan, Pratt agreed, was irrelevant – for the evaluation of

the experiment. But it was 'extremely relevant for the evaluation of the objectivity shown by Professor Hansel in making
his "scientific" evaluation of ESP'. Was Gardner seriously
suggesting that Pearce would have risked being seen 'on a
chair in a busy corridor peeking at me through my own
transom?' Even Hansel had not contemplated suggesting
'such a daily public display of cheating' or he would not have
had to resort to his inaccurate plan.

'No one is now interested in what Pratt has to say about
those old tests,' Gardner loftily protested – using another
favoured device to get himself off a hook. More to the point
was what Pratt's subject would have to say. 'A full report by
the Reverend Hubert Pearce', he urged, 'on his sensational,
unrivalled ESP work when he was a student at Duke, would
make a dramatic book. Since scientific truth is also God's
truth, it seems to me that such a report would serve both God
and man. But my precognition tells me that Pearce will never
write it.'

Pearce had already written it. Had Gardner been familiar
with the reviews of Hansel's book he would have seen it. Stung
by Hansel's innuendo, Pearce had gone to a notary public to
testify 'that at no time did I leave my desk in the library
during the tests, that neither I nor any person whom I know
(other than the experimenter or experimenters) had any
knowledge of the order of the targets prior to my handing the
list of calls to Dr Pratt or Dr Rhine, and that I certainly made
no effort to obtain a normal knowledge by peeking through the
window of Dr Pratt's office – or by any other means.' Yet
having asked for the avowal, Gardner declined to accept it.
After the news of Pearce's death he actually commented 'we
are unlikely to know whether Pearce cheated'.

Gardner evidently does not feel it is always necessary to
check 'facts' which happen to suit his purpose. When conjurors explained how Ted Serios could have faked putting his
mental images on film, Gardner claimed 'Serios lost his power
and faded from the psi scene'. Precautions had in fact been
taken to prevent Serios from using the method which the
conjurors – Randi was one of them – claimed he had used.
Randi had been invited to come and see a demonstration. He
had declined.

Most disturbing of all has been Gardner's role in the

publicising of Wheeler's diatribe against Rhine. Worried by the parapsychologists' use of the indications which quantum physics was producing for nuclear particles communicating at a distance, Gardner had claimed that there was 'not the slightest evidence' for it. He enlisted Wheeler as an ally. Urging at the AAAS 1979 meeting that the 'pseudoscientists' should be expelled, Wheeler insisted that the experiment which had confirmed Bell's proposition should not be used 'to claim that information can be transmitted faster than light, or to postulate any "quantum interconnectedness". Both are baseless. Both are mysticism. Both are moonshine.' Gratefully, Gardner set out his views in an article entitled 'Quantum Theory and Quack Theory' in the *New York Review* (it was not clear what it had to do with literature; but Gardner has used the *Review* as his public convenience), along with a couple of curious squibs Wheeler had composed: 'Drive the pseudos out of the workshop of science' and 'Where there's smoke, there's smoke'.

Wheeler himself could hardly have invented the story about Rhine. He had got it, he claimed, at second hand. Obviously somebody put him up to it, knowing that what he would have to say at the AAAS meeting would carry weight. In other words, he was the fall guy. Gardner must have realised this, accepting as he did Rhine's reputation for integrity, and knowing that the version of the McDougall trials was rubbish. Gardner did not include Wheeler's story about Rhine in the *Review* but, in view of the fact that Wheeler's paper attacking parapsychology had been associated with a misapprehension, Gardner might well have refrained from publishing the paper altogether.

Even if Gardner's credibility had not been challenged before, his conduct during the Gauquelin affair would have exposed the shallowness of his reputation as the Robespierre, the sea-green incorruptible of scepticism. Gardner knew that the evidence from the tests Kurtz had arranged had confirmed Gauquelin's findings; that the *Skeptical Inquirer*'s pretence that they had not confirmed those findings was false; and that Kurtz and Abell were engaging in a cover-up to avoid disclosing what they had done. Yet when appealed to by Rawlins, he had dismissed it as 'a hilarious foul-up'. When Kammann expected him to stand up and be counted among those CSICOP members who refused to be parties to such conduct, Gardner remained firmly seated.

Conjurors

The magician, no less an authority than Martin Gardner has asserted, 'is a consummate liar'. His principles may be borrowed from physics and psychology, but they are permeated 'through and through with deliberate falsification'. The accuracy of Gardner's diagnosis can be judged from the record of the attitudes of conjurors past and present to psi.

Robert-Houdin, the first to make an international reputation, accepted the existence of clairvoyance, having witnessed Alexis Didier demonstrating it. John Maskelyne, the first stage magician to make a name in Britain, detested spiritualist mediums and did his best to expose them as fraudulent, but was convinced that table-turning was genuine. A number of his contemporaries, testing mediums, accepted psi, as did Harry Kellar and Harry Houdini – though towards the end of his life Houdini became ambivalent on the subject, largely because of his growing mistrust of spiritualism.

Houdini had a number of experiences which, he did not dispute, might have been psychic. When standing by the grave of an old friend and fellow magician he said, flippantly, 'Lafayette, give us a sign you are here' (presumably a reference to Charles Stenton's 'Lafayette, we are here' when the American troops landed in Europe in 1917, a tribute to the illustrious Marquis who had served under Washington in the War of Independence). Hardly had Houdini spoken when two pots of flowers which he had brought with him promptly fell over. They fell again and broke, after he set them upright. 'All very strange' he could not help thinking, though he blamed the wind blowing at the time.

Houdini did not deny that mediums could produce manifestations, 'impulsive, spasmodic, done on the spur of the moment' which he knew he could not duplicate by any conjuring trick; but the failure of spiritualist mediums to bring him into communication with his dead mother, whom he had adored, at first saddened and later infuriated him, and in particular he loathed some of the physical phenomena. 'Nothing has crossed my path', he claimed, 'to make me think that the Great Almighty will allow emanations from the human body of such horrible, revolting, viscous shapes, which like "genii from the bronze bottle", ring bells, move handkerchiefs, wobble tables and do other "flap-doodle" stunts.'

Towards the end of his life Houdini became paranoid on the subject. Convinced that mediums who produced materialisations must be fraudulent, he did not hesitate to cheat to 'expose' them. According to his assistant, he left a telescopic ruler in the box he had constructed to encase the Boston medium 'Margery', so that if he found she could still move objects at a distance he would have an excuse to say that she had used it to move them. On this occasion, he was caught out – by 'Margery's' spirit 'control' who denounced him. He nevertheless claimed to have exposed her – falsely, as two of the members of the committee who were investigating her with him felt bound to report, though they were almost as anxious to expose her as he was.

One of them was his friend Walter Franklin Prince. Although Prince ran the American Society for Psychical Research, and accepted the evidence for mental mediumship, physical mediumship repelled him. To the end of his life he could not bring himself to accept it. A member of the American Society of Magicians, he shared Houdini's assumption that 'Margery' must be an accomplished trickster, and hoped Houdini would find out how she played her tricks.

Greatly though Prince admired Houdini – 'the world seemed poorer when his big heart and eager brain were stilled' – he was acutely embarrassed by *A Magician Among the Spirits* when it was published in 1924. It was the prototype of many that have followed, blandly presenting Houdini's prejudices as if they were historical facts. He described how 'Eva C.' had achieved her effects by swallowing material and regurgitating it, ignoring the fact that when he himself had attended a session with her, he had witnessed the precautions which were taken to detect regurgitation, if she tried it, and had admitted that in spite of them she had produced a materialisation in a way he could not account for.

This was not one of the inaccuracies Prince listed in *The Enchanted Boundary*. There were plenty without it. He felt compelled to warn those who relied on Houdini's book that it was 'strewn with blunders', devoting a couple of pages to listing some of them before excusing Houdini on the ground that bias is less reprehensible in a professed polemic than in a history. This was over-indulgent of him. It was not just bias that disfigured Houdini's book, but a string of fabrications.

Joseph Rinn's *Searchlight on Psychical Research* was, if possible, even more misleading. Yet the palm must go, in this context, to the Amazing Randi, for his books, articles and speeches.

Randi was one of the founder members of CSICOP, and has been one of the most active since. He has had the widest exposure of any of them, as he gives demonstrations to scientific societies and to student bodies. Most of them are designed to show how foolish it is to pay attention to parapsychologists, who have allowed themselves to be the easy dupes of the likes of Geller. Imitation spoon-bending has been one of Randi's stand-bys. Yet anybody who has had the opportunity to compare his version with Geller's would realise that Randi carefully makes no attempt to do what Geller did in the same conditions. Randi has always shrewdly avoided submitting himself to controlled tests of the kind Geller undertook.

Randi owes his reputation chiefly to Geller. As a run-of-the-mill magician, for a time he suffered severely from the public's greater interest in Geller. In one year, he recalls, he lost $15,000 of college lecture bookings when people backed out of contracts saying openly that the students preferred to watch Geller. Randi retaliated by becoming one of the first to cash in on Geller imitations, emerging as the most accomplished of the bunch. (His leading rival in Britain at the time, Romark, was unwise enough to claim he could drive through London blindfolded, as Geller had done. He had hardly started when he ran into the back of a car. It turned out to be a police car.) With the help of a vigorous campaign to discredit Geller, physical mediums, parapsychologists, and their dupes, Randi has remained in the news ever since.

Randi has never pretended to be anything but an entertainer who has happened to find an extremely lucrative market for his wares. 'I'm a charlatan, a liar, a thief and a fake altogether,' he admitted on television in 1982. 'There's no question of it, but I'm an actor playing a part, and I do it for purposes of entertainment.' Those whom he has maligned find it less amusing than his audiences. In his books, articles and

TV programmes, he has accused mediums and researchers of deception. Going through Randi's account of the Stanford Research Institute tests in *The Magic of Uri Geller*, Harold Puthoff and Russell Targ found that Randi had devoted twenty-eight pages to it, in which he had made twenty-four factual errors. He had claimed that Geller had been allowed to bring a confederate with him; that no magician had been consulted about precautions; that Geller, though in a 'Faraday cage' to ensure he was properly insulated, had been able to put his arm out of it. 'Having examined the book carefully', they concluded, 'we find that in every instance Randi, in his efforts to fault the SRI experiments, was driven to hypothesise the existence of a loophole condition that did not, in fact, exist.' Yet this was a book which Carl Sagan had called 'Splendid!' and Christopher Evans 'unarguably definitive'. 'Every blow', Martin Gardner had claimed, 'is a blow for sanity.'

Thus encouraged, Randi produced fresh indications of his inventiveness. Puthoff and Targ, he claimed in *Flim-Flam*, had pretended that a videotape was of actual tests when it was a reconstruction. The cameraman, Zev Pressman, had been annoyed at their pretence. 'I have examined the evidence', Randi boasted, and had come to the conclusion that Targ and Puthoff's claim was 'a blatant misrepresentation'. Randi had not bothered to consult Pressman, who replied that Randi's revelations were 'pure fiction'. The tape had been made during the actual experiments. 'Nothing was restaged or specially created.'

The accounts which Randi has provided of his activities as an investigator often vary markedly from those provided by the people he has investigated. Before his facial features, in particular the burst-horsehair-sofa beard, became too well known, he used to pretend that he was psychic, and would play his tricks to prove it, to soften up parapsychologists prior to finding ways to trip them up. Or he would claim to be an interested journalist, as he did when he visited John Hasted at Birkbeck College to find out what Geller had done in tests there. Geller had been reported as getting 'pulses' which showed up on a Geiger counter. It had clearly not occurred to Hasted, Randi wrote afterwards, that Geller's brother-in-law Shipi, or even Geller himself, could have obained the same effect, as Randi himself claimed to have done, simply by a well-aimed kick. 'Try it,' he told Hasted. 'It works.'

Shipi, Hasted replied, had not been present. Geller had not been within kicking reach of the recorder. Even if he had been, the 'pulse' could not have been effected with a kick. 'I'm sure that the manufacturers will not mind if I say that I have been unable to get an observable pulse even with a blow of a hammer.'

Randi's technique as an investigator has been to make certain, if he can, that he will not be confronted with evidence which he cannot account for, or which his CSICOP advisers cannot demolish. Thus he wrote to Dr A.R.G. Owen, who had been investigating Matthew Manning in Toronto, putting a series of searching questions about the trials, saying that he was preparing a report on Manning for his new book. Owen was able to show that defects in the trial, which the questions were clearly designed to show up, had been avoided. Randi was then reduced to an allegation of fraud on Manning's part. In connection with a nationwide ESP test conducted in Britain, Manning, he said, must have gone round Britain writing in the answers on postcards. Perhaps Randi was warned that this allegation would make him a laughing stock. The report on Manning was not included in his book.

One of Randi's accomplishments has been his ability to rewrite history. In 1973 the *New York Magazine* ran an article by Andrew Tobias containing an account of how Ted Serios was supposed to have cheated in his 'thoughtography'. Randi, Tobias recalled, had appeared with Serios on a TV programme and duplicated the feat. 'After the show, Randi says, Serios told his mentor, Eisenbud, that the jig was up; that his method had been found out. But Eisenbud, says Randi, by now a fervent believer in Serios's psychic powers, grabbed Serios by the shoulders and said, on the verge of tears, "What do you mean, Ted? You can do it; I know you can!" '

What had actually occurred can be reconstructed from the correspondence between Randi and Eisenbud at the time of the TV show, six years earlier. The show had been sparked off by an 'exposure' of Serios in *Popular Photography*, purporting to show how Serios put his 'mental' pictures on film. Eisenbud agreed that Serios *could* have faked them in the way the writers alleged, if he had been allowed to; but the control conditions prevented it. If any conjuror was able to duplicate Serios's effects in the same conditions, Eisenbud promised in a letter to the editors, he would allow them to publish his picture in a dunce's cap, and devote his spare time to 'selling door to door subscriptions to this amazing magazine'.

Only one conjuror had replied: Randi. Before they went on the air, Eisenbud wrote to Randi, agreeing to meet him to discuss how to proceed if Randi accepted the challenge. Randi duly did, on the TV show, 'with a great flourish', giving a demonstration to the studio audience of the way he thought Serios did the trick. So childishly obvious was Randi's conjuring that Eisenbud was able to tell how he did it; far from bemoaning the fact that he had been let down by Serios, he could look forward with delight to watching Randi's effort to make good his challenge. But Randi backed down.

'The mischief caused by public unsupported claims such as those made by *Popular Photography* and the Amazing Randi can be boundless,' Curtis Fuller, editor of *Fate*, warned in an article in which he related the story, quoting from the correspondence and confirming just how misleading both the initial 'exposure' and Randi's later description of the TV show episode had been, and citing articles which had been appearing in European as well as American journals based on the assumption that Serios really had been discredited. To this day, Eisenbud has kept reminding Randi of the challenge, without eliciting any response. Yet to this day, too, articles have been continuing to appear following the Randi line (it has also found its way into Martin Gardner's *Science, Good, Bad and Bogus*, dedicated to, among others, Randi).

Randi's most effective gimmick has been his $10,000 challenge. That sum, he says, will be given to anybody who can demonstrate psi under controlled conditions. Houdini warned magicians against making such challenges. 'Notwithstanding the fact that innumerable exposures have been made', he argued, 'such fact is no proof that any investigator, legerdemain artist or otherwise, is fully capable of fathoming each and every effect produced.' He cited a performance by Samuel C. Hooker 'which included the levitation of a life-sized head of an animal, possessed of life-like movement while in a state of suspension', with no visible means of support; 'on one occasion a dozen or more of the most expert professional magicians were in attendance, but no one could offer a satisfactory solution'.

Randi, however, has so arranged matters that he has nothing to fear. According to his friend Dennis Rawlins, Randi told him, 'I always have an out.' Randi denies this, but from time to time he has refused to accept conditions which appear to be perfectly fair to both sides.

In his capacity as a founder member of CSICOP, Randi has not hesitated to use more direct means of discrediting parapsychology. The action which has won him the most publicity recently has been 'Project Alpha', orchestrated with two youths, Michael Edwards and Steven Shaw, to show them how they could fool investigators by offering their services as potential mini-Gellers to the McDonnell Laboratory for Psychical Research. According to Randi's account at a triumphant press conference, the 'MacLab' 'investigators had allowed themselves to be duped into accepting that Edwards and Shaw had genuine powers'. As a result, 'scientific papers containing spurious data have been published by several parapsychologists'.

What actually occurred has been set out by Michael Thalbourne in a paper, 'Science vs Showmanship: the case of the Randi Hoax'. Towards the end of his career Rhine had recommended a two-stage procedure in tests. Initially, 'free exploratory conditions were to be allowed to see what the subjects could do, and how best to develop their abilities; better controlled conditions can then be introduced when the stage is reached at which it is worth while and important to increase the precautions against counter-explanations'. The 'MacLab' investigators had adopted this course. Dr Peter R. Phillips, its Director, had in fact explained that he would, when the laboratory was first set up.

As Thalbourne points out, parapsychologists are not the only people to have taken this course. It has also been recommended by Professor Neal Miller in connection with animal experiments designed to explore learning theory. It was adopted when Edwards and Shaw offered to demonstrate. The fact that they had shown promise was reported at the annual convention of the Parapsychological Association, and was therefore included among the 'research in progress' abstracts in the annual publication *Research in Parapsychology*.

It was this, presumably, which Randi had in mind in his reference to publication of spurious data in 'scientific papers'. They were not. Nor were they intended to be. They were simply a work-in-progress report.

At the meeting, parapsychologists who watched videotape made of the experiments were critical. For the next stage of the investigation, the procedures were tightened up. From this time on Edwards and Shaw began to find it impossible to obtain positive results. This did not at first arouse suspicion, as it could be attributed to decline-effect. Eventually it was decided that they were of no further use in experiments, and they were told their services were no longer required.

At this point their usefulness to Randi ceased, too. He called his press conference in New York to disclose 'Project Alpha' which he claimed, had been undertaken with a sociological purpose, to show that parascientists were incapable of setting up reliable test procedures. Needless to say, he did not refer to the fact that the trials in which his accomplices had succeeded had not been in test conditions. Nor did he make it clear that at no point had the investigators claimed anything more than that the results had been promising. The Randi hoax received massive publicity in the media, across the country, from the *New York Times* to the *San Francisco Chronicle*, on television and on radio, the impression being given that Randi had done a public service.

Had he? Münsterberg, of all people, had given the answer over half a century before. 'If there were a professor of science who, working with his students, should have to be afraid of their making practical jokes or playing tricks on him, he would be entirely lost,' Münsterberg had observed in his article on his 'exposure' of Eusapia Palladino. Everything must be done in good faith 'and there is perhaps no profession which presupposes the good faith of all concerned so instinctively. The scientist lives in the certainty that everyone who enters the temple of science considers truth the highest godhead.'

A few commentators have echoed Münsterberg. 'If Mr Randi were a psychologist', William Broad observed in the *New York Times*, 'the hoax might have landed him in hot water,' a verdict which the Director of the Ethics Office of the American Psychological Association confirmed. Randi accordingly changed his tack. Edwards and Shaw had not been 'planted', he insisted on a British TV programme; 'I would never with a scientist get together to deceive or embarrass somebody.' What, it may be wondered, were Edwards and Shaw doing, if they were not first deceiving and then embarrassing their 'MacLab' hosts? They so far succeeded, in fact, that 'MacLab' has since been closed down.

It would have been interesting to have seen how the scientific establishments would have reacted had the hoax taken a different form. A parallel case would be if an anthropologist were to discover one of the missing links in the Darwinian chain. He could expect immediate fame, and in due course a Nobel Prize. What would then be the reaction of scientists if his assistant, who had helped him find the 'link', disclosed that he was a Creationist, and that the link was a hoax designed to show how untrustworthy scientists are when dealing with evidence which fits their preconceptions – and, incidentally, designed also to reassure Creationists that they need not take 'scientific' evidence too seriously? Scientists, and not only those in the anthropological field, would surely be outraged, and rightly. Yet the initial reaction to the Randi hoax – even, incredibly, among a few parapsychologists – was that it had indeed performed a valuable service.

Randi has since confessed that what he divulged at his press conference was misleading. Both he and his two accomplices have conceded that when formal conditions were imposed, they were unable to cheat. Randi has actually since admitted to the 'MacLab' investigators that they passed the test. Had he really been anxious to perform a sociological service, he would have ascertained this before giving his press conference. As it is, all that the public remembers, if anything, is that 'Project Alpha' showed up parapsychology as nonsense, and parapsychologists as gullible asses.

Only one serious criticism can be levelled, in retrospect, at the 'MacLab' investigators: they were naive. In an information letter circulated to members of the Parapsychological Association Peter Phillips has recalled that in 1979, soon after his appointment as Director, he heard from Randi, 'who inquired about our plans and offered his assistance in checking protocol' – offers he repeated frequently in the months following, even sending his list of rules to prevent cheating. As the investigators were not, at that stage, particularly concerned with preventing cheating, they neither accepted his help nor followed his advice, though later they enlisted it.

Timeo Danaos . . . Even a casual familiarity with Randi's work and attitudes, more especially after acquaintance with Rawlins's CSICOP article in *Fate* magazine, should have made it apparent that if Randi was being helpful, it was not for love of parapsychology.

At the 1983 Convention the Council of the Parapsychological Association adopted a resolution welcoming collaboration with magicians 'who by their past behaviour and membership in respected organisations, have maintained high standards of professionalism and have adhered to the ethical code of the fraternity'. Although such individuals may be found, and could be useful in devising stratagems to prevent or detect fraud, the historical record suggests that even if experienced magicians vet projects, and give the seal of their approval, it will bring little benefit.

A long line of conjurors, all celebrated in their day and some still remembered, have testified to the genuineness of psi phenomena, or individual mediums. Samuel Bellachini, Court conjuror to the Emperor Wilhelm I of Germany, wrote that what he had witnessed Slade doing in full daylight could not be explained by prestidigitation. 'I am satisfied there was no trickery', John Maskelyne admitted after participating in a table-turning session, adding that Faraday's explanation could not account for the movements of so heavy a table; 'I believe, in my mind, that it must have been some psychic force which passed from our own bodies and neutralised the laws of gravity.' When Harry Kellar tried to prevent the medium William Eglinton from levitating, he had to admit he had found himself carried up with Eglinton to the ceiling.

Wortley Baggally was unable to detect any fraud in the course of the investigation, with Carrington and Feilding, of Eusapia Palladino. Howard Thurston, who had been Kellar's assistant, wrote to the *New York Times* after the reports of Palladino's 'exposure' to say that although throughout his career he had always been able to show how mediums cheated, his tests with her had convinced him she was genuine.

As chairman of the Atlanta Society's Occult Investigation

Committee, Artur Zorka went with a colleague Abb Dickson in 1975 to test Geller. They had witnessed ESP and PK effects, they reported; 'there is no way, based on our present collective knowledge, that any method of trickery could have been used to produce these effects under the conditions to which Uri Geller was subjected'.

Zorka could hardly be regarded as inadequately qualified. He was a past Vice-President of a division of the International Brotherhood of Magicians, and ten years earlier had been voted Magician of the Year by his Atlanta peers. Now, appalled by his report, a committee of his peers rejected his findings as 'totally inconclusive, being merely opinions of relatively inexperienced investigators'. Any magician unwise enough to testify on Geller's behalf in that period would have met with the same response from his colleagues. They simply could not afford to admit that Geller might be genuine.

Ironically, they were even forced back on the argument which previously they had used to scoff at scientists. 'Geller flatly refuses to operate when there are known magicians present,' Bernard A. Juby, President of the British Magical Society and a member of the Inner Magic Circle, complained in 1976. When he was gently reminded of the investigation by Zorka and Dickson, he replied that he was well aware of it, but 'it is a well-known fact that some magicians can fool the pants off other magicians'.

Without realising it, Juby had made nonsense of his contention, so often echoed by conjurors, that only conjurors are qualified to investigate mediums. His attitude also helps to explain why Geller realised he was wasting his time undergoing tests of any kind. There were always going to be excuses to ignore or reject the results.

The New Inquisition

Half a century ago Walter Prince listed the reasons for not reposing any trust in any commentary on psychical research written by a professional sceptic. They are still valid today. The writers do not face the real evidence; they 'either avoid the great evidential cases altogether, or they make a travesty of them'. They are 'frequently guilty of absurd blunders in matters of fact' which they could easily have checked. They give evidence of not having read the original sources. They are prone to emotional judgments. They entrench themselves behind 'supposed scientific maxims which beg the very questions of fact in dispute'. And 'they exchange argument for technical Billingsgate, applying to their opponents expressions of which the shorter and plainer equivalents are "cranks" and "simpletons" '.

All these are applicable to the CSICOP stable, along with one or two additions. The lack of acquaintance with the original sources is now commonly masked by a proliferation of impressive-looking source references. Only when these are more closely examined does it become clear that most of them are secondary sources – almost invariably also the work of sceptics. This applies even to some of the relatively well-informed critics, such as James E. Alcock in his *Parapsychology: Science or Magic?* It becomes more difficult to take it seriously when, excusing himself for not going into the evidence about Pavel Stepanek, Alcock refers readers to Hansel for information on the subject.

Contributing to Ludwig's symposium, George R. Price praised the 'careful studies of men like Podmore and Houdini'. Hansel has described Hall as 'the most systematic, thorough and reliable contemporary investigator of the early history of psychical research'. Martin Gardner's source references are commonly secondary authorities, such as Truesdell and Houdini – even Randi. Sceptics take in each other's dirty linen.

Some of them are even more unscrupulous in their personal attacks than they were in Prince's time. 'I know of no other branch of science past or present, other than parapsychology, where innuendoes and accusations of fraud are allowed to appear in print and go unpunished unless the charges are substantiated', Ian Stevenson remarked, reviewing Hansel's *ESP*. 'No one would think of accusing me of fraud for my work in conventional psychiatry, but obviously I lose this immunity when I work in parapsychology. Why?' It is all too obvious why. Too many scientists, threatened more than they care to admit by psi, are prepared to accept support against it from any quarter without worrying whether it should be trusted.

Why can't the maligned mediums or researchers sue? In theory they can, but the vagaries of the laws of libel in the

United States and the legal precedents from court cases in
Britain are discouraging.

Giving judgment against the medium Henry Slade in 1876
the magistrate said that if Slade claimed that he was not using
sleight-of-hand when moving objects at a distance, he must be
guilty of false pretences, because 'according to the well-known
course of nature' there could be no other explanation. Order-
ing Daniel Home to return some money to a woman who had
given it to him, the judge explained that although she had
made 'mis-statements on oath so perversely untrue that they
embarrassed the court to a great degree and quite discredited
her testimony', the gift would have to go back to her, 'for as I
hold spiritualism to be a delusion, I must necessarily hold the
plaintiff to be the victim of delusion'. These precedents have
been adhered to in several cases since; in fact it was only in the
1950s that 'fortune telling' ceased to be an indictable offence.
Anybody seeking damages after being accused of cheating
would almost certainly be required to show the jury that he
had not cheated. As he would probably not be allowed to give
a demonstration in court, this would be difficult.

The way has consequently been clear for rationalists to do
unto anybody in psychical research what the church used to
do to them. 'They treat independent thought as the inquisitors
treated free thought in days gone by,' Joseph Maxwell
lamented. They could no longer deliver the heretic up to the
executioner, 'but they excommunicate him, in their fashion'.
The archpriests had become 'the Carpenters of science',
Stainton Moses observed, 'who have run away with the
cast-off clothes of medieval priestcraft'. They are still worn
today – even in Russia; 'Priests in the shrine of the progress of
science have become priests of conservatism', A.P. Dubrov
and V.N. Pushkin claim in their *Parapsychology and Contemporary Science*. 'Now, they raise barriers to the further advancement of human knowledge.'

Although only a minority of scientists are active heresy
hunters, the silent majority, Ardrey felt, must be included in
the indictment because they are responsible for maintaining
the 'temple psychology' which suffuses science, conditioning
students to obedience; they have to accept current dogmas 'or
suffer excommunication'. The sad consequence is that many
young scientists who are prepared to concede that there is a

case for psi (replies to questionnaires show that many do) are unwilling to stand up to be counted. Even sadder is the result: that the reputations of many honourable scientists, past and present, remain tarnished by the sceptics' smears.

The Uses of Psi

I have tried to show how, and why, scientism has had so destructive an influence over scientists, with particularly unfortunate consequences for psychical research. One question remains to be answered. Granted, for argument's sake, that psi is a reality, is it really all that important?

Ordinarily the search for new forces, or the phenomena associated with them, is considered of fundamental importance. Huge sums have been and are being spent at CERN and elsewhere pursuing elusive nuclear particles, identifying those which are discovered and giving them curious names – 'quarks', 'strangeness', 'charm'. A familiar force which has remained inexplicable is the one responsible for action and communication at a distance. This is precisely the area in which psychical research has been most deeply involved, and has most to offer. As Jule Eisenbud has argued, it is no longer a question of whether science can find a niche into which psi can conveniently be slotted. The question scientists should be asking themselves is what clues psi can provide, which will help them to fill the chasm left by their inability to cope with the evidence for action and communication at a distance.

The demonstrations that nuclear particles enjoy 'non-locality', as it has come to be called, have prompted David Bohm, Professor of Theoretical Physics at Birkbeck College and internationally respected for his seminal *Wholeness and the Implicate Order*, to explore ways by which psi can be established within that 'order'. Non-locality, he told the audience at the presentation of the first Gardner Murphy award for services to parapsychology, is basically foreign to classical physics. It necessitates a new concept of information as 'something that need not belong only to human consciousness but that may indeed be present, in some sense, even in inanimate atoms and electrons' – as in a silicon chip – bringing the mental and the material together as 'two sides of one overall process'. ESP, Bohm surmises, can be regarded as a method of conveying information directly through psycho-kinesis. A more detailed mathematical theory, he admits, is needed before psi can be incorporated in the quantum struc-ture. As the eminent and entertaining physicist Richard Feynman won his Nobel prize for a demonstration that nuclear particles can move backwards in time, this may not be so difficult as has been thought.

Recent advances in other disciplines have been demonstrat-ing non-locality. Ilya Prigogine, also a Nobel Laureate, has told an interviewer 'the amazing thing is that each molecule knows in some way what other molecules will do at the same time'. All the experiments Wilder Penfield undertook over a period of fifty years 'were built on the principle that the brain generates the mind, and that mind is completely dependent on brain', he wrote at the close of the career which had won him international renown as a neurophysiologist. 'They were all designed to prove it. All of them proved exactly the opposite.'

Psi could help to fill that gap, and many others. Psychical research, William James thought, was 'restoring continuity to history'. It can also restore a measure of credibility to religions by demonstrating that some, at least, of the 'miracles' periodi-cally reported in Catholic countries, and of the phenomena which feature every week in Spiritualist journals, may be genuine – even if the interpretations put upon them may owe more to the beliefs of the witnesses than to detached assess-ment. Doubtless many manifestations are fraudulent, and others promoted by mass hysteria, leading to hallucinations; but to dismiss them all because some are spurious is a symptom of rationalism's inability to face uncomfortable facts.

How can scientists and academics in general be persuaded to accept that far from being a nagging nuisance, acceptance of psi could actually help to solve hitherto insoluble problems? Clearly further work of the kind parapsychologists have been engaged in for the past half century is unlikely to convert them. There appears to be 'an irrational layer of the psyche that cannot be removed by rational arguments alone, includ-ing experimental data with impeccable statistics and high significance levels', Rhea White warned in her Presidential address to the Parapsychological Association in 1985. 'If so, we cannot break the deadlock by doing still more research.' The members of the academic establishment cannot be expected to change their attitude in the foreseeable future unless pressure of a different kind is brought to bear on them.

There is one encouraging precedent. The realisation of the powers of the mind over the body, which have been revealed in experiments with hypnosis and bio-feedback, coupled with the growing realisation that the dangerously close relationship between the medical profession and the pharmaceutical industry has been producing too high a rate of disastrous side-effects to be tolerated any longer, has led growing numbers of patients to transfer from conventional to alternative medicine. Although this has as yet had relatively little impact on hospitals, where the consultants are insulated against its consequences, it has been compelling general practitioners to explore acupuncture, herbalism, homeopathy, and other forms of therapy which until recently were dismissed with derision, and convincing some of them that unconventional treatments can be more effective and safer than the medicine they were taught.

The public cannot exert so direct an influence on the scientists, but if indirect persuasion can be brought to bear, the seedy, spooky image that scientism has imposed upon psi can gradually be removed.

This will not be easy. 'The human mind is in the grip of an unconscious urge which makes it cling desperately to the world of familiar things,' G.N.M. Tyrrell, one of the shrewdest of psychical researchers, pointed out – 'an urge which resists all that threatens to tear it away from its moorings'.

A telling demonstration of the strength of this urge has been provided by Arthur Ellison, Professor of Engineering at the City University in London, and a past President of the Society for Psychical Research. In the course of a lecture given on one of the University's 'open days', to a mixed audience, he announced that he was going to try to cause a bowl of flowers to levitate. It would be necessary, he explained, to obtain the psychic support of the audience and, for this to be effective, he suggested that all those present should join him in making the sound 'Ommmm . . . ', which he would reinforce with the help of a loudspeaker. The audience responded, and the bowl duly rose an inch or two above the table on which it had been resting.

Ellison had called for six volunteers to watch the bowl closely, and to raise their hands if it floated. One raised a hand; the others claimed they had seen no movement. Ellison thereupon explained that the 'levitation' had been obtained by a concealed electromagnetic device, and that the 'Ommmm . . . ' had been necessary only to ensure that the noise which the device would make when he switched it on would not give the show away. Yet the five (and probably many members of the audience), conditioned to regarding levitation as impossible, had refused to accept (or at least to admit) the evidence of their eyes.

The resistance to recognising psi is all the stronger because of the fear that 'dabbling in the occult' can be dangerous. Mending an electrical appliance can be, too, if the necessary skill is lacking. Yet electricity has been tamed for use in the home. Psi could also be domesticated, as Émile Boirac, Rector of Dijon Academy (a sceptic until, to his amazement, a table which he had facetiously beckoned to come towards him at a table-turning session obeyed him, though nobody was touching it), foresaw in 1908 in his *Psychology of the Future*. If the mystery of second sight were solved 'it would not be too daring to say that there will be found in man an organ of communication which can be compared with telegraphy'. It could be used to detect criminals, or to give warning of attackers. It was already being used to detect underground streams. If psychokinesis could be brought under control, we might be able to provide our own heat and light without the need to tap other sources. Utopian? Perhaps, Boirac admitted; yet when Galvani, experimenting with electricity, was watching the contractions of the frogs' legs dangling above his balcony, who could have foreseen 'that the force which manifested itself under his very eyes, in effects so puerile, would one day in human hands send thought, light and motion round the world?'

Some progress has been made in bringing Boirac's prognostications to fruition. Although the mystery of second sight has not been solved, the experiments in remote viewing at the

Stanford Research Institute and elsewhere have lent confirmation to its reality, and have shown that many of us who have not previously thought we had any psychic capabilities may find we can 'see' distant locations, or foretell events, if we can achieve the appropriate relaxed frame of mind – a matter of trial and error – and have the confidence to try. In *The Mind Race*, which Targ wrote with Keith Harary and published in 1984, the chapter on 'what you can do with psi' offers an intriguing range of possibilities, including

* Remote viewing one's car and intuiting dangerous mechanical defects
* Being in the right place at the right time for worthwhile opportunities
* Understanding and becoming aware of the psi content of dreams and making use of it.

Perhaps the most valuable benefit from precognition is advance warning of danger. Targ describes how a premonition saved him from what would have been a serious accident. A similar gut feeling prompted his wife to break up a dinner party, insisting she must go home, where she found her young son 'quietly choking to death'. There are scores of accounts of individuals who have saved themselves or others by obeying hunches of this kind; and all too many of individuals who, like W.T. Stead, refused to obey them, with fatal consequences. He went down on the *Titanic*.

Of Boirac's other notions, progress has also been made in the detection of crime, as Whitney S. Hibbard and Raymond W. Worring, two private investigators from Montana, have shown in their *Psychic Criminology*. Much depends, they insist, upon establishing mutual respect between psychics and police. Too often it has been lacking. Often, too, psychics are not called in until conventional methods of detection have failed. By this time their main value – suggesting directions for the investigators to explore – has been squandered. Except where a really gifted psychic such as Gerard Croiset, who gave much useful material to the police in Holland and other countries, has established a reputation, the record has been erratic. Yet it would require no more than one correct lead to the police out of every ten given – if they have the confidence to follow up each lead – to reduce the crime rate in a district. Should that proportion of criminals be detected and jailed, the rest would surely be less inclined to take the risk.

Psychokinesis of the kind which influences the dowser's hazel twig may turn out to be related to PK of the kind which many sportsmen have reported, leaving them under the impression that they have been temporarily taken over, for their own benefit, by some force beyond themselves. The subject is surveyed by Michael Murphy and Rhea White in *The Psychic Side of Sports*, with descriptions by, among others hardly less famous, Muhammed Ali, Roger Bannister, Jack Nicklaus, Sugar Ray Robinson and Babe Ruth.

Not far removed is the psi component of 'green fingers'. Here, as with dowsing, experimentation around the home is relatively easy. Members of the Association for the Scientific Study of Anomalous Phenomena (ASSAP) in Britain have the benefit of a do-it-yourself experiment project explaining how to conduct a controlled trial with seeds in pots, requiring the expenditure of only a little time each day, to find if 'positive thoughts' about those selected for benefit eventually have the desired effect.

Healing

One of the most valuable of all the contributions which exploitation of psi can make is in the promotion of health and the prevention of illness; where these fail, in the diagnosis and treatment of disorders.

The value of meditation, or auto-hypnosis, is now well established. Its usefulness, the Australian psychiatrist Ainslie Meares believes, lies in the fact that it promotes 'atavistic regression'. We revert to a state of mind that preceded consciousness, allowing instinct to come through and take on the task of keeping us healthy, or getting rid of symptoms. In such states, some individuals enjoy psi. They can 'see' what is the matter with them or with other people, by the equivalent of remote viewing.

This form of clairvoyance was often reported by the early mesmerists. The report of the investigating committee of the French Academy of the Sciences described in 1831 how a girl, 'Céline', had been carefully tested, and had shown she could 'see' what was the matter with patients, and prescribe what were taken to be appropriate remedies, though she had no medical knowledge. In one case where they thought she had been wrong, the patient died when treated for a different disease. An autopsy revealed she had been right.

Mesmer's assumption that there is a healing force coming from the planets, akin to magnetism, has long been derided. Yet the existence of *a* healing force of the kind he and his followers believed in has now been amply confirmed. Following Grad's experiments with mice, a number of trials have been held to find out if the force can be detected in laboratory conditions. In one trial, reported in 1981, sixty college students not known to be psychically gifted were asked to see if they could influence the growth of the bacterium *E. coli* in test-tubes. Some were to try to promote it; some to inhibit it; some to act as controls by not trying to influence it either way. The hypothesis that the growth would be greater in the promoted tubes than in the inhibited tubes or in the controls was confirmed. Although there was no difference in the results between the inhibited tubes and the controls, the general outcome of the trial was confirmation of the existence of paranormal influencing of the bacteria.

This trial was held in the United States. Confirmation came from an unexpected source: Russia. In the Stalinist era somebody practising as a psychic healer could have expected prosecution and a jail sentence. Realising this, Djuna Davitashvili decided to qualify as a paramedic. When she secured a post as a senior researcher at a medical research institute, she was able to interest her fellow-scientists in what she was careful to describe as 'information-energy interaction with living organisms' through 'contact and non-contact (bio-energy) massage': in other words, the laying on of hands to transmit the healing force. Persuaded that this lay within Marxist/Leninist guidelines, her colleagues set up laboratory tests which convinced them that her information-energy interaction with frogs could alter their pulse rates, and with humans, their blood pressure. The risk that zealous party liners might unmask her ruse was substantially reduced when first, trade union executives, then politicians, and eventually President Brezhnev asked her for treatment.

Although there are more healers in Britain than all the

practitioners of other forms of alternative medicine put together, many people still feel that to visit a healer is to give way to superstition. This is illogical, considering how well the existence of a healing force is now attested. The most recent development has been a revival of a combination of traditional 'stroking' and the laying on of hands, known as therapeutic touch. Nurses have been trained to provide it by Dolores Krieger, Professor of Nursing at New York University. Not merely do patients enjoy the attentions; controlled trials have shown that the condition of their blood cells improves.

Emotional health, too, could be improved by a better understanding of the effects of psi communications, when they leak through into consciousness. People who 'see things' or 'hear voices', who now go to a psychiatrist and are commonly treated with drugs or sent to a mental hospital, ought to be encouraged to listen to their voices, and to try to interpret their visions – not with the intention of obeying the instructions, but of assessing their usefulness. Serious psychiatric illness can be caused by paranormal promptings which have not been recognised or have been repressed, the Scots psychiatrist James McHarg has found. In *Cosmic Factors in Disease* and other books Arthur Guirdham has given case histories of people with psychosomatic disorders from the same cause. Recognised and exploited, psi information leaking its way through into consciousness can be converted from a menace into an asset.

Survival

When the Society for Psychical Research was formed, the chief hope of many of its founder members was that light would be thrown on what, to them, seemed the most important issue of all: is there life after bodily death?

Ironically, as Alan Gauld has shown in his *Mediumship and Survival*, although there is an impressive amount of evidence for survival, 'what we know stands in proportion to what we do not know as a bucketful does to the ocean. Certainty is not to be had.' Perhaps Arthur Koestler – whose *Janus* remains the most telling of all the indictments of scientism for, among other failings, its refusal to accept psi – can be left with the last word. In the moving suicide note he composed when the

combination of Parkinson's disease and leukemia was about to
render him helpless, he reassured his friends that he was
leaving them in a peaceful frame of mind 'with some timid
hopes for a de-personalized after-life beyond due confines of
space, time and matter and beyond the limits of our compre-
hension'. This, surely, is the most for which anybody who is
not a believer in the immortality of the soul can live in – timid
hope.

Postscript

Just as I had completed the typescript of *The Hidden Power*, serendipity (or synchronicity) confronted me with an apologia William McDougall made in the symposium held at Clark University in 1927, published in *The Case For and Against Psychical Belief* (ed. C. Murchison).

What then of my dabbling in psychical research? What is my apology for such 'pandering to superstition'? I was led to make some study of this field by my desire to know the truth. Here, it seemed to me, was a body of ancient beliefs all of which Science seemed utterly to deny. Yet the ground of such denial was plainly inadequate. It was in the main an inference from the assumption that the universe is a strictly mechanical system. Here were phenomena alleged to occur in all times and places, an allegation supported by a body of strong testimony. And Science frowned upon it all and said: 'Such things cannot happen'. As usual I was thrown into rebellion against this orthodoxy. Further, I saw in the Society for Psychical Research a body of earnest seekers after truth, conscientiously using methods which might reveal truth.

I am sure McDougall was right in his judgment; and I would like to think that if *The Hidden Power* does nothing else, it will do something to restore credit to those researchers, maligned in their lifetimes, and since derided or forgotten.

Acknowledgments

My thanks to John Beloff, Professor Eric Laithwaite, Professor Robert Morris, Guy Playfair, Ann Shearer, Rupert Sheldrake, Professor Ian Stevenson, Michael Thalbourne, Joanna Trevelyan, Marcello Truzzi, Lyall Watson and Ruth West for reading the typescript, or segments of it, and offering comments, criticisms and corrections; to Jule Eisenbud for information and encouragement; to Eleanor O'Keeffe and Nick Clark-Lowes for their help at the Society for Psychical Research; to Renée Haynes and Bernard Levin, acting again in their capacity as readers and critics (in Bernard's case, caustic) of the proofs; to Douglas Matthews, for the helpful index; and to Tony Colwell and Mandy Greenfield of Cape, for their patience.

I would also like to thank the following for permission to include copyright photographs and figures: Ken Batcheldor – no. 7; BBC Hulton Picture Library – nos 3, 4 and 5; William Collins, Sons & Co., Ltd – figs 1 and 3 (from Sir Alister Hardy's *The Living Stream*); Jule Eisenbud – no. 11; The Illustrated London News Picture Library – no. 15; Michael Manni Photographic – no. 13; The Marconi Research Company – no. 6; The Mary Evans Picture Library – no. 19; The Mary Evans Picture Library/Harry Price Collection – no. 17; The Mary Evans Picture Library/The Society for Psychical Research – no. 21; Methuen and Co., Ltd – no. 6, inset diagram (from Sir Eric Eastwood's *Radar Ornithology*); *News of the World* – no. 14; Guy Lyon Playfair – nos 8 and 10; the estate of Upton Sinclair – fig. 6 (from Upton Sinclair's *Mental Radio*); Russell Targ – no. 12.

Source References

In the following references the words or names in parentheses refer to a subject in the text. The source is identified by the author, date and page number(s) of the book, which will be found in the bibliography. (p.c. indicates a personal communication.)

The *Journal of the American Society for Psychical Research* is commonly known to its readers as *JASPR*, pronounced 'Jasper', so I have used that as the abbreviation, differentiating it from the British society's publication, *SPR Jnl*. *Procs* are the society's Proceedings. IEEE refers to the Institute of Electrical and Electronic Engineers.

Page

THE MENACE OF SCIENTISM
1   McClenon, 1984, 2, 131.
      Feyerabend, 1978, 73.
2   Medawar, 1985, 98.
3   McGlashan, 1976, 9.
      Wallace, 1905, i, 236.
      Wallace, 1905, i, 335.
4   Flammarion, *Des forces naturelles inconnues*, 1866.
      Hazlitt, 'Essay on Genius'.
5   Aristotle, cited by Heisenberg in Wilber, 1984, 59.
      Ducasse, *Jnl Philosophy*, 1954, li, 810-23.
6   (polls), *The Times*, December 20, 1980: Audience
          Selection, January 1981.
      Duncan, p.c.

PHYSICS
9   Hume, 1875, 103.
      (Newton), cited Easlea, 1980, 181-2.

10   (quantum), de Broglie, *Physics and Metaphysics*, cited
      Jahn, 1984, 38.
      (quantum and psi), Pauli, *Essays and Lectures on
      Physics*, cited Jahn, 1984, 29-30.
      Goethe, *Autobiography*, 1897, i, 433.
      (Einstein/Bell), Zukav, 1979, 297-323.
      Koestler, 1978, 256-9.
11   (Chew), Pedler, 1981, 168-70.
      (de Beauregard), cited Ingo Swann, *Star Fire*, 1978,
      9-10.
12   Sheldrake, 1981, 105-7; *Nature*, September 24, 1981,
      245-6.

      BOTANY
13   (Bose), Tompkins/Bird, 1974, 81-6.
14   Plotinus, *Works*, 1918, 531.
      Fechner, 1946, 207.
      (Bose), Tompkins/Bird, 1974, 87-96.
15   Backster, *International Jnl Parapsychology*, winter
      1968, 329-48; Kmetz, *JASPR*, April 1977, 158-69;
      Dubrov/Pushkin, 1982, 102-3.
16   Francé, 1926, 40.
      Eiseley, 1978, 148.
      (Bogoraz), R.G. Wasson, *Soma*, 1968, 275.
17   *New Scientist*, August 16, 1984, 72.
18   Sinel, 1927, 24-8.
      New Scientist, January 8, 1981, 72.
      Wardlaw, cited Denton, 1985, 226.
19   Tomkins/Bird, (Bird, p.c.).
20   Weyers, *New Scientist*, May 17, 1984, 9-13.
      Schrödinger, 1956, 3.

      ETHOLOGY
21   Thorpe, 1979, 90.
      Hardy, 1965, 229-31.
23   'Pop ethology' used by Stephen Jay Gould about
      the works of Ardrey, Desmond Morris and
      others.
      Thomas, 1974, 14.
24   Marais, 1937.

24   (Riley), Callahan, 1977, 134-5.
25   Wheeler, 'The Ant Colony as an Organism', *Jnl Morphology*, 1911, xxii, 307-25.
          (pheromones), Edward O. Wilson, *Scientific American*, May 1963, 100-14; Thomas, 1974, 16-17.
26   Thomas, 1974, 12-13.
28   Eisenbud, 1983, 177-81.
29   Sinel, 1927, 128-9.
          (Murie), Ardrey, 1967, 122.
          Newland, 1916, 126.
30   (albatrosses), Ardrey, 120, 151-2.
31-2   (homing pigeons), Pratt, 1964, 182-207; CIBA, 1956, 165ff.; (Matthews), CIBA, 156ff.
32   Rushton, p.c. (letter dated May 20, 1971).
          (magnetic sense), Walcott *et al.*, 'Pigeons have magnets', *Science*, September 7, 1979, xxv, 1027-9.
33   (olfactory sense), *New Scientist*, May 19, 1977, 395.
          (salmon), Droscher, 1969, 112-13.
          (infrasound), *The Times*, March 26, 1981; *Jnl Comparative Psychology*, 1981, cxli, 153.
          Newland, 1916, 187-9.
34   Williams, 1958, 131.
          (Sauer), Droscher, 1969, 256-60.
35   Cherfas, *New Scientist*, December 10, 1981, 732.
          (Baker), *New Scientist*, November 9, 1978, 453.
36   Fabre, cited Sinel, 1927, 28-31.
          Fabri, cited Vasiliev, 2nd edn 1976, 196-7.
36-8   Callahan, 1977, 115-45; Laithwaite, *The Entomologist*, 'A Radiation Theory of the Assembling of Moths', June 1960, 113-17; July 1960, 133-7; April 1961, 95-9.
39   Thorpe, 1979, 30-3; Selous, 1931, 9-12.
          (flock brain), Selous, 42-61.
40   Newland, 1916, 106-7.
          Burton, p.c. (letter dated April 13, 1967).
41   *Nature*, 1984, cccix, 344; *New Scientist*, August 2, 1984, 37.
          Boring, in Hansel, 1966, xiv.
          Nature, 1968, ccixx, 482.
42   ('angels'), Eastwood *et al.*, 'Radar Ring Angels', *Procs Royal Society*, B, 1962, clvi, 242-67.

VITALISM REVISITED

43   Carington, 1945, 96.
Tinbergen, cited Broad, 1953, 159.
Hardy, 1965, 174.
44   Schrödinger, 1956, 22-3.
Denton, 1985.
45   (Grassé), cited Koestler, 1978, 182.
Hardy, 1965, 207-8.
46   Waddington, *Listener*, February 13, 1952.
Hardy, 1965, 234-61.
47   Selous, 1901, 119-28.
New Scientist, February 21, 1985, 44.
48   McDougall, 1911, 349-79.
Monod, cited Koestler, 1978, 173.
49   Schrödinger, 1956, 13.
Thouless, *Procs SPR*, 1942, xlvii, 16-17.
50   Marais, 1937, 40-6.

SHAMANISM

51   van der Post, 1958.
Unaipon, *Melbourne Harbinger of Light*, August 1914.
52   Callaway, *The Religious System of the Amazulu*, 1868,
338.
53   Tylor, 1871, i, 134-41.
54   Frazer, 1890, i, 52.
Kingsley, Mary, *Travels in West Africa*, 1897, 435.
55-7   Lang, 1898; (Cock Lane) 1894.
57   Frazer, *The Belief in Immortality*, 1913, i, 14-15.
Hawkes, *Punch*, December 18, 1963, 874.
van der Post, (p.c.).
(Howitt), Marett, *The Threshold of Religion*, 1914,
151(n.).
58   Eliade, *Myths, Dreams and Mysteries*, 1968, 88.
(anthropologists), Van de Castle, in Wolman, 1977,
668.
Van de Castle, *Procs Parapsychological Association*,
1970, vii, 97-102.
59   (Castaneda), de Mille, 1976, 72.
(Lévi-Strauss), Sturrock, 1979, 19.
Culture and Curing, ed. Morley/Wallis, 1979.
60   Lodge, *Observer*, March 3, 1980.

Feyerabend, 1978, 77.
61   (Arigo), Playfair, *The Flying Cow*, 1975, 130-43.
      (Philippines), G. Meek, *Healers and Healing* (Los
         Angeles, California), 1966.
62   Playfair, 1985, 94-8.
      Eliade, 1964, 335; David-Neel, 1967, 227-9.
63   Melland, 1923, 229.

HISTORY
66-7 (megaliths), Wilson, 1977, 141-2.
      Ivimy, 1974, 110-21; Hitching, 1978, 58-64.
68   Dodds, 1971.
69   Eliade, *Myths, Dreams and Mysteries*, 1968, 86.
      Huxley; cited Haynes, 1961, 126.
70   St Teresa, 1870, 144.
      (Joseph), Dingwall, 1947, 9-27.
      Cicero, *On Divination*, 1876 edn.
      (Socrates), Myers, 'The Daemon of Socrates', *Procs
         SPR*, 1888-9, v, 522-47.
71   (Joan), Lang, 1908; 'The Voices of Jeanne d'Arc',
         Procs SPR, 1895, xi, 198-212; Warner, *Joan of Arc*,
         1983, 139.
      Johnson, *A Journey to the Western Isles*, 1925, 160-3.
72-3 (Pomponazzi, Sennert), Hutchison, *Isis*, 1982,
         lxxiii, 233-53; *History of Science*, 1983, xxxi, 297ff.
74   Montaigne, *Essays* (ed. Cohen), 1958, 87.
      (meteorites), Krinov, 1960, 9-13. Polanyi, *Personal
         Knowledge*, 1958, 138(n.); Koestler, 1978, 322.
75   (Angélique), Figuier, 1860, iv, 160-80.
76   (Fox sisters), Capron, *Modern Spiritualism*, 1855.
77   (Jewish sect), Barrett, 1920, 22.
77-8 (Brewster), M. Brewster, 1869, 254-5; Macaulay,
         Life, 1909, 560.
78   (Victoria), Longford, *Victoria*, 1964, 339.
      (von Humboldt), Reichenbach, *The Odic Force*,
         1968, xiii.
      de Gasparin, 1857.
79   Donkin, 'A Note on Thought-reading', *Nineteenth
         Century*, August 1882.
80   Faraday, 'Experimental Investigation of Table-
         moving', *Athenaeum*, July 2, 1853.

80   Salverte, 1846.

81-5   (Brewster), Home, 1863, i, (appendix).
Home, 1863; Julie Home, 1888, 1890. Jenkins, 1982; Hall, 1984; Inglis, 1977, 225-314; (Tolstoy), Home, 1888, 162.

86   Lodge, 1931, 305.
Barrett, *Procs SPR*, 1920, xxx, 334-7.

87   Smith, *Procs SPR*, 1920, xxx, 306-33.
(Batcheldor), Playfair, 1985, 172-200.
Lodge, 1931, 306.
Crookes, 1874, 87.

PSYCHICAL RESEARCH

88   Barrett, *Procs SPR*, 1903-4, xviii, 323-50.

89   James, *Psychology Review*, July 1898, 421-2.

90   Leonard, 1931; Smith, 1964.

91   Crookes, 1874; Richet, *Annals Psychic Science*, October, November 1905.

92   (Palladino), Lombroso, 1909, preface; *Annals Psychic Science*, 1907-9; Feilding, *Sittings with Eusapia Palladino*, 1963; *Jnl SPR*, November 1894.

94   Münsterberg, 'Report of a Sitting with Eusapia Palladino', *Metropolitan*, February 1910.

95   (Krebs), Flournoy, 1911, 85-6; Hyslop, *Contact with the Other World*, 1919, 350-1.

96   (Béraud), Schrenck-Notzing, 1920; Bisson, 1914; Geley, 1927.

97   Eisenbud, 1983, 209.
Geley, 1927, 180.

98-9   Rhine, 1934, 1937, 1965; Mauskopf/McVaugh, 1980, 71ff., Rao, 1982, 192-212; Eysenck, 1957, 131-2.

100   (Skinner), Mauskopf/McVaugh, 259-61.
Whately, cited Crookall, *Intimations of Immortality*, 1965, 14.

101   (Langdon-Davis/Dingwall), CIBA, 1956, 111-13, 122.

102-4   (Rosenheim), Bender, *Procs Parapsychological Association*, 1969, 93-5; Karger/Zicha, *Procs Parapsychological Association*, 1968, v, 33-5,

105   (bottle-tops), Pratt, 1964, 80-115.

106   Vogt/Hyman, 1959, 121-52.
          Kaufman, *Parapsychology Review*, January, 1971.
107   Bird, 1979.
          Elliot, 1977.
          Lodge, 1933, 273.
108   Evans, *New Scientist*, September 13, 1966.
108-10 (*Guardian* and others), November/December 1973.
111   Dixon, *World Medicine* October 22, 1975.
          Gardner, 1983, 99.
112   Randi, *New Scientist*, April 6, 1978, 12.
          Hasted, 1981.
          (nitinol), Panati, 1976, 67-74; Randall, *SPR Jnl*,
             October 1982, 368-73.
113   (conjurors), Panati, 157-68.
114   Lang, 1898, 77.
115   Myers, 1903, xvii-xviii.
          Johnson, cited Boswell, *Life*, 1906, i, 251.
          ('Hinch'), Fuller, 1979, 37-8.
116   James, *Principles of Psychology*, 1891, ii, 115.
          (Dessoir), Lang, 1898, 35.
117   (Mirabelli), Dingwall, 'An Amazing Case', *JASPR*,
             1930, xxxlv, 296-306.
          (Fenwick), Schatzman, 1980, 270-84.
118   Geley, 1920, 48-73.
          (surveys), Sidgwick, *Procs SPR*, 1923, xxxiii, 23ff.;
             JASPR, 1962, 3-47; Green/McCreery, 1975.
118-20 Puthoff/Targ, 1977 (Geller), 135-65; (Swann), 1-4;
             (Price), 46-80; (Gardener), 179-82; (Randi), 182-
             6; *Procs IEEE*, March 1986, lxiv, 329-54.
120   *Nature*, August 17, 1978, cclxxlv, 680-1; (Tart),
             March 13, 1980, cclxxxiv, 191.
          (Hammid), Targ/Harary, 1984, 75-82.
          (Congressional Committee), Targ/Harary, 4.
121   Vasiliev, 1963, 108-56 (appendix D); Pratt, *JASPR*,
             October 1970, lxiv, 385-43.
          (Russian research), Dubrov/Pushkin, 1982.
122   (Swann), Targ/Puthoff, 1977, 18-25.
          (Rose), McCrea, *Omni*, April 1984, 60-3.
123   *Psi Research*, June 1984, iii, 66-73.
          (inter-continental trial) *San Francisco Examiner*,
             October 10, November 23, 1984.
          Dubrov/Pushkin, 1982.

THE FOUR COUNTS

127   Richet, 1923, 343.
128   Hume, 1875, 101-3.
        Lang, 1898, 17.
        Flew, in Ludwig, 1978, 148.
        Hansel, 'Experiments on Telepathy', *New Scientist*,
            1959, 457-61.
129   Ornstein, *The Psychology of Consciousness*, 1972, 220.
        Myers/Gurney, *Procs SPR*, 1882, i, 118.
        Wallace, 1905, ii, 278-84.
130   Schiller, *Procs SPR*, 1903-4, xviii, 419.
        Price, *Science*, August 1955, cxxii, 367; January
            1972, clxxii, 359.
        Sidgwick, *Procs SPR*, 1882, i, 12; Hansel, *New
            Scientist*, 1959, 457-61.
        Sargent, *Omni*, November 1979.
131   Ehrenwald, *JASPR*, January 1984, lxxviii, 71.
132   Heywood, 1964, 80.
        (Ossowiecki), Geley, 1927, 42-65; Barrington, 'The
            Mediumship of Stefan Ossowiecki' (paper pre-
            sented at the SPR centenary conference, Cam-
            bridge, August 16-21, 1982); Richet, 1931, 145.
        (Stepanek), Pratt, in Beloff, 1974, 95-121.
133   McClenon, 1984, 12-13, 89-91.
        Ehrenwald, *JASPR*, January 1984, lxxviii, 29-39.
        (Boring), Ludwig, 1978, 146.
134   Podmore, 1910.
        Snow, cited Schmeidler, 1967, 53.
        (Ptolemy *et al.*), Broad/Wade, 1982, (appendix).
135   (Haeckel), Hitching, 1982, 202-8; (tooth), 212.
        (Gould), Broad/Wade, 1982, 85.
        (Thomas), Broad/Wade, 195-6.
136   Kefauver, 87th Congress, Report no. 448 on Ad-
            ministered Prices, Drugs; Hamblin, *World Medi-
            cine*, March 21, 1984.
        Cargill, *World Medicine*, October 1984.
        (fraud), Broad/Wade, 1982, 22-3; (Soal), Mark-
            wick, *Procs SPR*, 1978, lvi, 250-80.
        (Price), Gregory, 1985.
137   (Sidgwick), Holroyd, 1976, 44; Merchant, *Wallace*,
            1916, 204.
        James, 1961, 29.

Salverte, 1846, introduction.
138   Festinger, 1957.
       (SORRAT), Richards, 1982.
139   (Eva C.), Geley, 1927; (German critics), Verrall,
          Procs SPR, 1914-15, xxxii, 336-43; (Houdini),
          Doyle, *The Edge of the Unknown*, 1930, 60-1;
          Houdini, 1924.
       Richet, 1923, 510.
140   Dingwall, *Procs SPR*, 1926-8, xxxvi, 1-33; Mann,
          1932; *Encounter*, April 1976.
141   (Richet/Marthe), Flournoy, 1911, 221.
142   Flournoy, 1911, 248-9.

       THE SIGNIFICANCE OF PSI EFFECTS
143   Rosenthal, 1976, 378-9.
144   Rhine, 1937.
       Schmeidler, *ESP and Personality Patterns* (with R.A.
          McConnell), 1958; *Parapsychology Review*, Septem-
          ber 1983.
       Carington, 1945, Thouless, *SPR Jnl*, December
          1978, 965-8.
145   Sidgwick, *Procs SPR*, 1924, xxxiv, 28-9, 35.
       (Warcollier), Targ/Harary, 1984, 50-1.
146   (Lacan), Sturrock, 1979, 118.
       Howell, *Tatler*, May 1980 (I was a witness on the
          occasion).
147   (Galton), Pearson, *Francis Galton*, 63-6.
       (de Morgan), Wallace, 1905, ii, 284.
148   (Sidgwick), James, 1961, 309.
       Crookes, cited Medhurst/Goldney, *Procs SPR*, 1964,
          liv, 91(n).
       Murphy, *Procs SPR*, 1949, xlii, 1-15.
149   Fisk/West, *SPR Jnl*, November-December 1953,
          185-97; July 1954, 330; March 1960, 219-37;
          March 1973, 21-30; CIBA, 1956, 19, 49.
150   Eisenbud, *International Jnl Parapsychology*, summer
          1963.
151   Heywood, p.c.
       Journal, 1973, 298-322.
152   Manning, *Procs SPR*, 1982, lvi, 353-60.
       Lodge, 1933, 273.

153   Hasted, 1981, 175.
       (Manning), Mishlove (ed.) 'A month with
          Matthew Manning' (Washington Research Cen-
          ter, San Francisco), 1977, 56; and p.c.
154   de Morgan, *From Matter to Spirit*, 1863.
       Playfair, 1980.
       Maxwell, 1905, 65.
155   ('Philip'), Owen, 1976.
       Flammarion, 1900, 194-5.
156   Tuckett, Ivor, *Evidence for the Supernatural*, 1932 edn,
          84-5.
       (*Titanic*), Eisenbud, 1983, 187-207.
157   Richet, 1923, 282.
       Koestler, *The Invisible Writing*, 1959 edn, 452-3.
158   Flammarion, 1900, 192-5.
       (Paine), Prince, *Noted Witnesses*, 1928, 219.
159   (Guinness), Koestler, 1972, 172-3; (tube train),
          170-2.
       Maeterlinck, 1914, 142.
160   Rhine, in Wolman, 1977, 45.
       Beloff, *Parapsychology Review*, November/December
          1983; Blackmore, January/February 1984.
       Stanford, *JASPR*, January 1981, 69.
161   Broughton/Miller, *Parapsychological Review*, January
          1979.
       (Pauli), Hardy *et al.*, 1972, 177-8.
       Collins/Pinch, 1982.
162   (Thompson/McConnell), McClenon, 1984, 56-9.
163   Rosenthal, *Behavioral Science*, 1963, viii, 183-9.
       (Miller), McBeath, in *Research in Parapsychology*,
          1983, 47-8.
164   Josephson, Collins/Pinch, 1982, 78.
165   Pratt, in McConnell, 1981, 135-6.
167   Lodge, 1933, 270-3.
       Ehrenwald, *Science*, September 30, November 4,
          1977; Grattan-Guinness, 1982, 332-3.
       Ducasse, cited Eisenbud, 1982, 31.

       DOGMAS IN DECLINE
171   Tyndall, 1874.
       Wundt, *Popular Science* 591, September 1879.

Whitehead, 1934, 13-19.
172 Heisenberg, in Wilber, 1984, 73.
Conant, cited McConnell, 1981, 93.
Kuhn, 1970, x-xi, 74-5.
Schumacher, 1978, 12-13.
173 Koestler, *The Invisible Writing*, 1959 edn, 359-60.
Heisenberg, cited Zukav, 1979, 211.
Maslow, cited Schumacher, 1978, 70.
174 Goethe, cited Eckermann, *Conversations with Goethe*,
1901 edn, 47-8.
Jahn, *Research in Parapsychology*, 1983, 131.

FESTINGER'S SYNDROME
176 (Browning), Jenkins, 1982, 37-49.
Wundt, *Popular Science Monthly*, September 1879;
Report of the Seybert Commission, Philadelphia,
1920, 104-5.
177 Wallace, 1905, ii, 315-21.
178 Eisenbud, 1983, 111-29.
(Sarfatti), Collins/Pinch, 1982, 165-6.
179 Hasted, *SPR Jnl*, September 1978, xlix, 902.
Taylor, *Nature*, November 2, 1978, 64-7; LeShan,
Light, spring 1985, 19.
180 Alexander, 1871.
Schiller, in Murchison, 1927, 215-18.
(Taylor), Collins/Pinch, 1982, 253-4.

POLANYI'S SYNDROME
181 Thomas, 1971, 579.
Polanyi, *Personal Knowledge*, 1958, 286-94, 358; *The
Logic of Liberty*, 1951, 15.
182 Braid, 1843, 21-37; Carpenter, *Principles of Mental
Physiology*, 1874, 550-1.
(Lehmann), Tischner, 1925, 35; (subconscious),
cited Paul Tabori, *Companions of the Unseen*, 1968,
30.
183-4 Murray, *Procs SPR*, xxix, 46-63; (Sidgwick), *Procs
SPR*, 1924, xxxiv, 212ff., 356ff.; *The Times*, December 13, 1924; Dodds, *Procs SPR*, 1971, lv,
371-42; Dingwall, *Procs SPR*, 1973, lvi, 21-39.
184 Rayleigh, *Procs SPR*, 1938-9, xlv, 1-18.

185   Thouless, *Procs SPR*, 1942, xlvii, 2-3.
        Coleridge, 1956 edn, 65-6.
186   Lang, 1898, 324; Prince, 1930, 117-18.
187   (Milligan), Keyes, 1983.
        Roberts, *New Scientist*, February 2, 1984, 12-14.
188   Sigerist, *A History of Medicine*, 1951, i, 187.
        Hume, 1875, 101-3; Adare, *Experiences with Home*,
          1869, 178-9; Crookes, *Procs SPR*, 1890, 98ff.;
          (Schwartz), Greens, Elmer and Alyce, *Beyond
          Biofeedback*, 1977, 236; *Brain/Mind Bulletin*,
          December 4, 1978.
189   Salverte, 1829, i, 321.
        Frazer, 1900, iii, 308.
        (Hocken), Lang, 1901, 277ff.
        (epidermis), Fairlie, 1978, 232.
190   Carpenter, *Mesmerism, Spiritualism*, etc., 1877, 67.
        Coe, *Psychological Record* (Wichita University),
          October 1957.
        New Scientist, June 6, 1985; London fire-walk, *Sunday
          Times*, June 16, 1985.
191   Stowell, *SPR Jnl*, June 1928, xxiv, 278-82.
        Despatures, cited Thurston, 1952, 186-9.
        La Salamandre, Mathieu, 1864, 223ff.
192   Thomson, *South Sea Yarns*, 1894, 195-207.

        MEDAWAR'S SYNDROME
193   Medawar, *The Future of Man*, 1959, 62.
        von Hartmann, *Philosophy of the Unconscious*, 1884
          edn, 108-9.
        Thomas, 1974, 12.
194-5   ('Clever Hans'), Pfungst, *Clever Hans*, 1911;
          Maeterlinck, 1914, 203-26; Richet, 1923, 240-4;
          (Mackenzie), Sudre, 1960, 383; (Bekhterev), *Jnl
          Parapsychology*, 1949, xiii, 166-76.
196   Hediger, cited Watzlawick, 1976, 33-6.
197   Barrett, 1920, 156.
        Beloff, cited Broad, 1953, 158.
        (Duke), *Jnl Parapsychology*, xxvi, 1-22.
        ('Tony'), Pratt, 1964, 160-1.
198-9   (McDougall/Agar), Sheldrake, 1981, 186-91; *Nature*
          (Speransky), Playfair, 1985, 156-8.

200   Hitching, 1978, 20-3.
       Harrison, 1976, 27-30.
201   (Widnes case), *Mail on Sunday*, February 24, 1985;
          Fortean Times, summer 1985.
202-3   (Abrams), Horder, *British Medical Journal*, January
          24, 1925.

THE GREGORY/MAYO SYNDROME
204   Mayo, 1851, 7-16.
205   ('higher phenomena'), Dingwall, 1967; Playfair,
          1985, 203-4.
206   (Hall), *Lancet*, December 28, 1843; March 1, 1851.
207   Gregory, 1851, 33-5.
208   ('Mme B.'), Ochorowicz, 1891, 44ff.
209   (Delboeuf), Playfair, 1985, 10.
210   (Ewin), Playfair, 9-11.
211   (Royal Free), *Postgraduate Medical Jnl*, November
          1978, liv, 709-77; Inglis, *The Times*, April 12,
          1982.
212   Carington, 1945, 160-4.

THE LID-SITTERS
213   McDougall, *Procs SPR*, 1920, xxxi, 105-23.
       McClenon, 1984, 138-48.
214   Greenwell, *Zetetic Scholar*, 1982, x, 137.
       McConnell, 1982, 71-116.
       Seybert Committee Report, 1887.
215   Gibbs-Smith, cited Koestler, 1978, appendix iv.
216   Faraday, *Life*, 1870, 207ff.; Tyndall, *Fragments of
          Science*, 1892, i, 447-52; Huxley, *Life*, 1900, i,
          419-23.
217   Carpenter, *Quarterly*, October 1871; Crookes, 1874,
          73ff; Cox, *Spiritualism Answered by Science*, 1871, 56;
          Home, 1888, 308-9.
218   Boring, *Atlantic*, January 1926, 81-7.
219   (CSICOP), Rockwell *et al.*, 'Irrational Rationalists',
          JASPR, January 1978, lxxii, 23-34; Gauquelin,
          1983.
220   Feyerabend, 1978, 91-2.
221   (campaign on media), *New Scientist*, August 18,
          1977; *Daily Mail*, August 12, 1977; Neuman, p.c.

221   Truzzi, *New York Times*, June 25, 1978.
222-3   Rawlins, *Fate*, October 1981.
         Scientific American, February 1982.
224   Curry, *Zetetic Scholar*, March 1982, ix, 34-52.
225-6   Kammann, *Zetetic*, December 1982, x, 50-65;
         (Royce) *Zetetic*, 1983, xi, 15-21.
227   Wheeler, tapes of AAAS session, Houston, January
         8, 1979; *New York Review of Books*, April 13, 1979;
         R.R. Rao, *J.B. Rhine: on the Frontiers of Science*,
         1982, 203-10; McClenon, 1984, 119-21.
229   (*Science*); (twins), Ardrey, 1967, 153; (device),
         JASPR, April 1975, 146.
230   Diaconis, *Science*, July 1978, cci, 131-6.
         Beloff, *Encounter*, January 1980, 86-7; McClenon,
         1984, 114-18.
         Nature, 1974, 251, 559-60, 602-7.
         Collins, in Wallis, 1979, 259.
231   Maddox, *Nature*, January 24, 1970, cclv, 313.
         Empson, *New Scientist*, September 1, 1977, 541-2.
         Wickramasinghe, *Guardian*, February 2, 1985.
         World Medicine, November 17, 1979, January 12,
         1980.
         Marks/Kammann, 1980, 153.
232   Price, *Science*, 1965, cxxii, 359-67; cxxiii, 14-15;
         1972, clxxv, 359.

SCIENTISM'S HIT-MEN
233   Hyman, in McConnell, 1982, 157-8.
         Lewis, 1947, 121-3.
234   Cazamian, *Andrew Lang and the Maid of France*, 1931,
         10-16.
         Bibby, T.H. Huxley, 1959, 251.
         Lot, *Perrin*, 1963, 101-2.
         Reid, *Madame Curie*, 1974, 141.
235   (*An Adventure*), MacKenzie, 1982, 124-55.
         Yeats, *Autobiographies*, 1980, 264.
238   Medhurst/Goldney, *Procs SPR*, 1964, liv, 48, 62.
         New Scientist, August 10, 1978, 392-4.
         Paley, *Moral Philosophy*.
239   ('stroking'), Inglis, in *Quarto*, September 1980.
240   Braude, *SPR Jnl*, February 1985, liii, 40-6.

241   (Rhine), Pratt, 1964, 217.
        ('Hume-derived'), *British Jnl Statistical Psychology*,
            xiii, 175-8; Burt, in van Over, 1972, 336; Hansel,
            1966, 19.
        (Pearce), Hansel, 1966, 71-85.
242   Stevenson, *JASPR*, July 1967, 254-67.
        Evans, *New Scientist*, September 15, 1956; Gardner,
            New York Review of Books, May 26, 1966.
243   (Palladino), Hansel, 1966, 209-17; Dingwall, 1950,
            201-2, 211.
        Stevenson, *JASPR*, 1967, 254-67.
244   Gauld, 1968, appendix B.
        (Schmeidler), Child, *Jnl Parapsychology*, December
            1984, xlviii, 358-61.
        Zetetic, 1980, vii, 5.
245-6   Brandon, 1983 (Hall), 122; (Brewster), 57-9;
            (Paris), 65-7; (Richet), 135; (Curies), 162-3; *SPR
            Jnl*, October 1983, 209-12.
247-9   Gardner, 1983 (Pearce), 225-31; Lodge, 1933, 271;
            (Serios), 103; *New York Review of Books*, April 13,
            1979.
250   (magician), Gardner, 1983, 91.
        (Robert-Houdin), Delaage, *Le Sommeil magnétique*,
            1856, 122-3; (Maskelyne), *Pall Mall Gazette*, April
            20, 1885; Zöllner, 1882, appendix C.
        Houdini (experiences), 1924, 25-6; (Lafayette),
            Christopher, 1969, 159; Houdini, 1924, 179.
251   (assistant), Christopher, 1969, 193-4.
        Prince, 1930, 148-50; (Eva C.), Houdini, 1924,
            166-73.
252   (Rinn), Dale, *JASPR*, April 1951, 77-83.
        Randi (Geller), 1975; (charlatan), *PM Magazine*,
            July 1, 1982, Channel 15 TV, Madison, Wiscon-
            sin.
253   Puthoff/Targ, p.c.
        (Sagan/Evans/Gardner), Randi, 1975, blurb.
        Pressman, correspondence in SRI International,
            Documentation Report (Puthoff), August 17,
            1981.
        Hasted, p.c. (letter dated April 19, 1983).
        Manning, p.c.

254   (Serios), Curtis Fuller, *Fate*, August 1974, 65-74; *JASPR*, 1975, lxix, 94-6.

255   Houdini, 1924, 244.

256   Rawlins, *Fate*, October 1981, 1-32.

            Münsterberg, *Metropolitan Magazine*, February 1910, 561.

257   Broad, *New York Times*, February 15, 1983.

258   (MacLab), Michael Thalbourne, 'Science versus Showmanship: the Case of the Randi Hoax', Washington University, 1983.

259   (conjurors), Bellachini, cited Zöllner, 1882, 260-1; Maskelyne, Zöllner, appendix C; Kellar, *North American Review*, January 1893; (Baggally), Feilding, *Palladino*, 1963; Randall, 1982, 126-7, 190-1.

260   (Zorka), Panati, 1976, 157-67.

            Juby, *World Medicine*, September 22, 1976, (and following issues).

            Prince, 1930, 19.

261   Alcock, 1981, vii.

            Price, in Ludwig, 1978, 145-71.

            Hansel, 1980, 73.

            Stevenson, *JASPR*, 1967, lxi, 254-67.

262   (Slade), *The Times*, November 1, 1876.

            Home, 1888, 252ff.

            Maxwell, 1905, 394.

            Moses, *Carpenterian Criticism*, 1877, 14.

            Dubrov/Pushkin, 1982, 20.

            Ardrey, 1970, 13.

THE USES OF PSI

264   Eisenbud, 1983, 38.

            Bohm, 'A New Theory of the Relationship of Mind and Matter', 1985.

265   (Prigogine), *Omni*, May 1983, 90.

            Penfield, cited LeShan, *Light*, summer 1985, 53.

            James, *Procs SPR*, 1896-7, 2-10.

266   White, 'The Spontaneous, the Imaginal and Psi', 1985.

            Tyrrell, 1951, 45.

            (Ellison), Eric Laithwaite, p.c.

267   Boirac, 1919, 1-13.

268   Targ/Harary, 1984, 154-62.
      Hibbard/Worring, 1982; W.H.C. Tenhaeff, 'Psychoscopic Experiments on Behalf of the Police', *Procs 1st International Conference on Psychological Studies*, 1958.
269   Meares, 'Atavistic Regression', *Medical Jnl of Australia*, 1977, ii, 132-3.
      Grad, in Schmeidler, 1976, 76-81.
270   (*'E. coli'*), Nash, *Research in Parapsychology*, 1981, 61-4.
271   McHarg, in Grattan-Guinness, 1982, 316-24.
      Gauld, 1982, 261.

Bibliography

The books listed below are those referred to in the text (except where the reference is in passing, to a work not concerned with psi). In addition, I have included a selection of more important general works, old and new, on the subject. The place and date of publication refer to the edition I have consulted: if the first edition was several years earlier it is put in parenthesis. Where books have been translated into English, the English publication is listed.

Abell, George, and Barry Singer, *Science and the Paranormal*, London, 1982.

Agee, Doris, *Edgar Cayce on ESP*, New York, 1969.

Aksakov, Alexander, *Animisme et spiritisme*, Paris, 1906.

Alcock, James E., *Parapsychology: Science or Magic?*, Oxford and New York, 1981.

Alexander, Patrick P., *Spiritualism*, Edinburgh, 1871.

Ardrey, Robert, *The Territorial Imperative*, London, 1967.

—— *The Social Contract*, London, 1970.

Ashby, Robert, *Guidebook for the Study of Psychical Research*, London, 1972.

Barrett, Sir William, *On the Threshold of the Unseen*, London, 1920.

—— and Theodore Besterman, *The Divining Rod*, London, 1926.

Beloff, John (ed.), *New Directions in Parapsychology*, London, 1974.

Bergson, Henri, *Creative Evolution*, London, 1964 (1911).

Bird, Christopher, *The Divining Hand*, New York, 1979.

Bird, J. Malcolm, *'Margery' the Medium*, Boston, 1925.

Bisson, Juliette, *Les Phénomènes de Matérialisation*, Paris, 1914.

Blake, Henry, *Talking with Horses*, London, 1975.

Bloch, Maurice, *Marxism and Anthropology*, Oxford, 1983.

Bohm, David, *Wholeness and the Implicate Order*, London, 1980.

Boirac, Émile, *The Psychology of the Future*, London, 1919.

Bowler, Peter J., *Evolution: the History of an Idea*, Berkeley, California, 1984.

Bozzano, Ernesto, *Polyglot Mediumship (Xenoglossy)*, London, 1932.

Braid, James, *Neurypnology*, London, 1899 (1843).

—— *Magic, Witchcraft, Animal Magnetism*, London, 1852.

Brandon, Ruth, *The Spiritualists*, London, 1983.

Braude, Stephen E., *ESP and Psychokinesis: a Philosophical Examination*, Philadelphia, 1979.

Brewster, Sir David, *Letters on Natural Magic*, London, 1832.

Brewster, Margaret, *The Home Life of Sir David Brewster*, Edinburgh, 1869.

Broad, Charlie Dunbar, *Religion, Philosophy and Psychical Research*, London, 1953.

—— *Lectures on Psychical Research*, London, 1965.

Broad, William, and Nicholas Wade, *Betrayers of the Truth*, London and New York, 1982.

Burt, Sir Cyril, *Psychology and Psychical Research*, London, 1968.

—— *ESP and Psychology*, New York, 1975.

Callahan, Philip S., *Tuning in to Nature*, London, 1977.

Callaway, Bishop Henry, *The Religious System of the Amazulu*, Cape Town, 1868.

Capra, Fritjof, *The Tao of Physics*, Boulder, Colorado, 1975.

—— *The Turning Point*, New York, 1983.

Carington, Whately, *Telepathy*, London, 1945.

Carlson, Rick J., *The Frontiers of Science and Medicine*, London, 1975.

Carrington, Hereward, *The Physical Phenomena of Spiritualism*, New York, 1907.

—— *The American Seances with Eusapia Palladino*, New York, 1954.

Castaneda, Carlos, *The Teachings of Don Juan*, London, 1970.

Cavendish, Richard (ed.), *Encyclopaedia of the Unexplained*, London, 1974.

Cazamian, Louis, *Andrew Lang and the Maid of France*, Oxford, 1931.

Christopher, Milbourne, *Houdini: the Untold Story*, New York, 1969.

CIBA Foundation, *Symposium on ESP*, Boston, 1956.

Collins, Harry M., and T.J. Pinch, *Frames of Meaning: the Social Construction of Extraordinary Science*, London, 1982.

Conant, James B., *On Understanding Science*, Oxford, 1947.

Coxhead, Nona, *Mindpower*, London, 1976.

Crawford, W.G., *Experiments in Psychic Science*, London, 1919.

Crookes, Sir William, *Psychic Force and Modern Spiritualism*, London, 1871.

—— *Researches in the Phenomena of Spiritualism*, London, 1874.

David-Neel, Alexandra, *Magic and Mystery in Tibet*, London, 1967.

de Gasparin, Agénor, *A Treatise on Turning Tables*, London, 1857.

de Mille, Richard, *Castaneda's Journey*, Santa Barbara, 1976, and London, 1978.

de Morgan, Mrs ('C.D.'), *From Matter to Spirit*, London, 1863.

Denton, Michael, *Evolution: A Theory in Crisis*, London, 1985.

Dingwall, Eric J., *Some Human Oddities*, London, 1947.

—— *Very Peculiar People*, London, 1950.

—— (ed.), *Abnormal Hypnotic Phenomena* (4 vols), London, 1967-8.

Dodds, E.R., *Supernormal Phenomena in Classical Antiquity*, London, 1971.

Douglas, Alfred, *Extra-sensory Powers*, London, 1976.

Doyle, Arthur Conan, *The History of Spiritualism*, London, 1926.

Driesch, Hans, *Psychical Research*, London, 1933.

Droscher, Vitus P., *Mysterious Senses*, London, 1964.

—— *The Magic of the Senses*, London, 1969.

Dubrov, A.P., and V.N. Pushkin, *Parapsychology and Contemporary Science*, New York, 1982.

Dunne, J.W., *An Experiment with Time*, London, 1927.

Easlea, Martin, *Witch-hunting, Magic and the New Philosophy*, London, 1980.

Ebon, Martin, *Psychic Warfare: Threat or Illusion?*, New York, 1983.

Ehrenwald, Jan, *The ESP Experience*, New York, 1978.

Eiseley, Loren, *The Star Thrower*, London, 1978.

Eisenbud, Jule, *The World of Ted Serios*, New York, 1967.

—— *Paranormal Foreknowledge*, New York, 1982.

—— *Parapsychology and the Unconscious*, Berkeley, California, 1983.

Eliade, Mircea, *Shamanism*, New York and London, 1964 (1951).

Elliot, J. Scott, *Dowsing: One Man's Way*, Jersey, 1977, and London, 1979.

Espinas, Alfred, *Des Sociétés animales*, Paris, 1878.

Eysenck, Hans, *Sense and Nonsense in Psychology*, London, 1957.

—— and Carl Sargent, *Explaining the Unexplained*, London, 1982.

Fairlie, Peter, *The Conquest of Pain*, London, 1978.

Fechner, Gustav, *Religion of a Scientist*, New York, 1946.

Ferguson, Marilyn, *The Aquarian Conspiracy*, Los Angeles, 1979.

Festinger, Leon, *A Theory of Cognitive Dissonance*, Evanston, Illinois, 1957.

Feyerabend, Paul, *Science in a Free Society*, London, 1978.

Figuier, Guillaume, *Histoire du merveilleux* (4 vols), Paris, 1860.

Flammarion, Camille, *The Unknown*, London, 1900.

—— *Death and its Mystery* (3 vols), Paris, 1922.

Flournoy, Theodore, *From India to the Planet Mars*, New York, 1901.

—— *Spiritism and Psychology*, New York, 1911.

Fodor, Nandor, *Encyclopaedia of Psychic Science*, London, 1934.

Francé, Raoul, *Plants as Inventors*, London, 1926.

Frazer, Sir James, *The Golden Bough*, London, 1900 (1890).

Fuller, John G,. *The Airmen Who Would Not Die*, London, 1979.

Gardner, Martin, *Science, Good, Bad and Bogus*, Oxford, 1983.

Gauld, Alan, *The Founders of Psychical Research*, London, 1968.

—— *Mediumship and Survival*, London, 1982.

—— and A. Cornell, *Poltergeists*, London, 1979.

Gauquelin, Michel, *The Truth about Astrology*, Oxford, 1983.

Geley, Gustave, *From the Unconscious to the Conscious*, London, 1920.

—— *Clairvoyance and Materialisation*, London, 1927.

Geller, Uri, *My Story*, New York, 1976.

Glanvil, Joseph, *Sadducismus Triumphatus*, London, 1689.

Gooch, Stan, *Creatures from Inner Space*, London, 1984.

Grattan-Guinness, Ivor (ed.), *Psychical Research*, London, 1982.

Green, Celia, and Charles McCreery, *Apparitions*, London, 1975.

Gregory, Anita, *The Strange Case of Rudi Schneider*, Metuchen, New Jersey, 1985.

Gregory, William, *Letters on Animal Magnetism*, London, 1851.

Grimble, Arthur, *Pattern of Islands*, London, 1952.

Gris, Henry, and William Dick, *The New Soviet Psychic Discoveries*, London, 1979.

Guirdham, Arthur, *Cosmic Factors in Disease*, London, 1963.

Gurney, Edmund, F.W.H. Myers and Frank Podmore, *Phantasms of the Living* (2 vols), London, 1886.

Hall, Elizabeth, *Possible Impossibilities*, Boston, 1977.

Hall, Trevor, *The Spiritualists*, London, 1962.

—— *The Search for Harry Price*, London, 1978.

—— *The Enigma of Daniel Home*, London, 1984.

—— *The Medium and the Scientist*, Buffalo, 1984.

Hansel, C.E.M., *ESP: A Scientific Evaluation*, New York, 1966.

—— *ESP and Parapsychology: A Critical Re-evaluation*, London, 1980.

Hardy, Sir Alister, *The Living Stream*, London, 1965.

—— Robert Harvie and Arthur Koestler, *The Challenge of Chance*, London, 1972.

Harrison, Michael, *Fire from Heaven*, London, 1976.

Hasted, John, *The Metal Benders*, London, 1981.

Haynes, Renée, *The Hidden Springs*, London, 1961.

—— *The Society for Psychical Research*, London, 1982.

Heywood, Rosalind, *The Sixth Sense*, London, 1959.

—— *The Infinite Hive*, London, 1964.

Hibbard, Whitney S., and Raymond W. Worring, *Psychic Criminology*, Springfield, Illinois, 1982.

Hitching, Francis, *Pendulum: the Psi Connection*, London, 1977.

—— *World Atlas of Mysteries*, London, 1978.

—— *The Neck of the Giraffe*, London, 1982.

Holroyd, Stuart, *Psi and the Consciousness Explosion*, London, 1976.

Home, Daniel D., *Incidents in My Life*, London, 1863.

—— *Lights and Shadows of Spiritualism*, London, 1877.
Home, Julie, *D.D. Home*, London, 1888.
—— *The Gift of D.D. Home*, London, 1890.
Houdini, Harry, *A Magician Among the Spirits*, New York, 1924.
—— *'Margery' the Medium Exposed*, New York, 1924.
Howitt, A.W., *The Native Tribes of S.E. Australia*, London, 1904.
Hume, David, *Essays* (2 vols), London, 1875.
Hyslop, James, *Enigmas of Psychical Research*, London, 1906.
Inglis, Brian, *Natural and Supernatural*, London, 1977.
—— *Science and Parascience*, London, 1984.
—— *The Paranormal: an Encyclopaedia of Psychic Phenomena*, London, 1985.
Ivimy, John, *The Sphinx and the Megaliths*, London, 1974.
John, Robert G., and Brenda J. Dunne, *On the Quantum Mechanics of Consciousness*, Princeton University School of Engineering, 1984.
James, William, *On Psychical Research* (ed. G. Murphy and R.O. Ballou), London, 1961.
Jenkins, Elizabeth, *The Shadow and the Light: D.D. Home*, London, 1982.
Kerr, Howard, and Charles L. Crow (eds), *The Occult in America: New Historical Perspectives*, Chicago, 1983.
Keyes, Daniel, *Minds of Billy Milligan*, New York, 1983.
Koestler, Arthur, *The Roots of Coincidence*, London, 1972.
—— *Janus*, London, 1978.
—— *The Challenge of Chance*: see Hardy.
Krinov, E.L., *Principles of Meteorites*, London, 1910.
Krippner, Stanley (ed.), *Advances in Parapsychological Research*, (series), New York, 1977.
Kuhn, Thomas, *The Structure of Scientific Revolutions*, Chicago, 1970.
Lang, Andrew, *Cock Lane and Common Sense*, London, 1894.
—— *Modern Mythology*, London, 1897.
—— *The Making of Religion*, London, 1898.
—— *Magic and Religion*, London, 1901.
—— *The Maid of France*, London, 1908.
Langdon-Davis, John, *Man: the Known and Unknown*, London, 1960.
Leeds, Martin, and Gardner Murphy, *The Paranormal and the Normal*, Metuchen, New Jersey, 1980.
Leonard, Gladys Osborne, *My Life in Two Worlds*, London, 1931.
Leroy, Olivier, *La Raison primitive*, Paris, 1927.
—— *Les Hommes salamandres*, Paris, 1931.
LeShan, Lawrence, *The Medium, the Mystic and the Physicist*, Esalen, California, 1974.
—— and Henry Margenau, *Einstein's Space and Van Gogh's Sky*, Brighton, 1983.

Lévi-Strauss, Claude, *The Savage Mind*, London, 1966.
—— *Structural Anthropology*, London, 1968.
Lewis, C.S., *Miracles*, London, 1947.
Lodge, Oliver, *Survival of Man*, London, 1909.
—— *Past Years*, London, 1931.
—— *My Philosophy*, London, 1933.
Lombroso, Cesare, *After Death, What?*, London, 1909.
Long, Max Freedom, *The Secret Science Behind Miracles*, Vista, California, 1948.
Ludwig, Jan (ed.), *Philosophy and Parapsychology*, London, 1978.
McCabe, Joseph, *Is Spiritualism Based on Fraud?*, London, 1920.
McClenon, James, *Deviant Science: the Case of Parapsychology*, Philadelphia, 1984.
McConnell, R.A., *Encounters with Parapsychology*, Pittsburgh, 1981.
—— *Parapsychology and Self-Deception in Science*, Pittsburgh, 1982.
—— *An Introduction to Parapsychology in the Context of Science*, Pittsburgh, 1983.
McCreery, Charles, *Science, Philosophy and ESP*, London, 1967.
McDougall, William, *Body and Mind*, London, 1911.
—— *The Group Mind*, Cambridge, 1920.
—— *The Riddle of Life*, London, 1938.
McGlashan, Alan, *Gravity and Levity*, London, 1976.
MacKenzie, Andrew, *Hauntings and Apparitions*, London, 1982.
McRae, Ronald M., *Mind Wars*, New York, 1984.
Maeterlinck, Maurice, *The Unknown Guest*, Paris, 1914.
Mann, Thomas, *Three Essays*, London, 1932.
Manning, Matthew, *The Link*, London, 1974.
—— *In the Minds of Millions*, London, 1977.
Marais, Eugène, *The Soul of the White Ant*, London, 1937.
Marks, David and Richard Kammann, *The Psychology of the Psychic*, Buffalo, 1980.
Maskelyne, J.N., *Modern Spiritualism*, London, 1876.
Mathieu, P-F., *Histoire des miracles et des convulsionnaires de St Médard*, Paris, 1864.
Mauskopf, Seymour H., and Michael R. McVaugh, *The Elusive Science*, Baltimore, 1980.
Maxwell, Joseph, *Metapsychical Phenomena*, London, 1905.
Mayo, Herbert, *Letters on the Truths Contained in the Popular Superstitions*, London, 1851.
Medawar, Sir Peter, *The Limits of Science*, London, 1985.
Medhurst, R.G., K.M. Goldney and M.R. Barrington, *Crookes and the Spirit World*, New York, 1972.
Melland, Frank, *In Witchbound Africa*, London, 1923.
Mesmer, Franz, *Mesmerism*, London, 1948 (1779).

Michell, John, and J.M. Rickard, *Phenomena*, London, 1977.

Mitchell, Edgar D., *Psychic Exploration*, New York, 1976.

Moberly, C.A., and E.F. Jourdain, *An Adventure*, London, 1955 (1911).

Moore, R. Lawrence, *In Search of White Crows*, New York, 1977.

Morley, Peter, and Roy Wallis, *Culture and Curing*, London, 1979.

Moses, Stainton, ('B.A. Oxon'), *Carpenterian Criticism*, London, 1877.

Moss, Thelma, *The Probability of the Impossible*, London, 1977.

Münsterberg, Hugo, *Psychology and Life*, London, 1899.

Murchison, Carl (ed.), *The Case for and against Psychical Belief*, Clark University, 1927.

Murphy, Gardner, *The Challenge of Psychical Research*, New York, 1961, and London, 1979.

Murphy, Michael, and Rhea White, *The Psychic Side of Sports*, Reading, Mass., 1978.

Myers, F.W.H., *Human Personality and its Survival after Bodily Death* (2 vols), London, 1903.

Nelson, Geoffrey K., *Spiritualism and Society*, London, 1969.

Newland, C. Bingham, *What is Instinct?*, London, 1916.

Nichols, Beverley, *Powers that Be*, London, 1966.

Ochorowicz, Julian, *Mental Suggestion*, New York, 1891.

Oppenheim, Janet, *The Other World*, Cambridge, 1985.

Osterreich, T.K., *Occultism and Modern Science*, London, 1923.

Osty, E., *Supernormal Faculties in Man*, London, 1923.

Owen, A.R.G., *Can We Explain the Poltergeist?*, New York, 1964.

Owen, I., and M. Sparrow, *Conjuring Up Philip*, Ontario, 1976.

Panati, Charles (ed.), *The Geller Papers*, Boston, 1976.

Pedler, Kit, *Mind Over Matter*, London, 1981.

Pfungst, O., *Clever Hans*, New York, 1965 (1911).

Pitman, Michael, *Adam and Evolution*, London, 1984.

Playfair, Guy Lyon, *The Flying Cow*, London, 1975.

—— *This House is Haunted*, London, 1980.

—— *If This Be Magic*, London, 1985.

Plotinus, *Works* (ed. Guthrie), London, 1918.

Podmore, Frank, *The Newer Spiritualism*, London, 1910.

Polanyi, Michael, *The Tacit Dimension*, London, 1967.

Pollack, Jack H., *Croiset the Clairvoyant*, New York, 1965.

Pratt, J. Gaither, *Parapsychology*, London and New York, 1964.

Price, Harry, *Fifty Years of Psychical Research*, London, 1939.

Price, Henry H., *Perception*, London, 1932.

Prigogine, Ilya, *Order out of Chaos*, London, 1984.

Prince, Morton, *The Dissociation of a Personality*, Oxford, 1978 (1905).

Prince, Walter Franklin, *The Enchanted Boundary*, Boston, 1930.

—— *The Case of Patience Worth*, Boston, 1964 (1929).

Randall, John, *Parapsychology and the Nature of Life*, London, 1975.
—— *Psychokinesis*, London, 1982
Randi, James, *The Magic of Uri Geller*, New York, 1975.
—— *Flim-Flam*, London, 1980.
Rao, K. Ramakrishna (ed.), *J.B. Rhine: On the Frontiers of Science*, Jefferson, North Carolina, 1982.
Rhine, J.B., *Extra-Sensory Perception*, Boston, 1934.
—— *New Frontiers of the Mind*, New York, 1937, and London, 1973.
—— *et al.*, *Parapsychology from Duke to F.R.N.M.*, Durham, North Carolina, 1965.
Rhine, Louisa, *Hidden Channels of the Mind*, London, 1962.
—— *ESP in Life and Lab.*, New York, 1967.
—— *Mind Over Matter*, New York, 1970.
—— *The Invisible Picture*, Jefferson, North Carolina, 1981.
Richards, John T., *SORRAT: a History of the Neihardt PK Experiments*, Metuchen, New Jersey, 1982.
Richardson, Mark W., *et al.*, *Margery – Harvard – Veritas*, Boston, 1925.
Richet, Charles, *Thirty Years of Psychical Research*, London, 1923.
—— *Our Sixth Sense*, London, 1930.
—— *L'Avenir et la prémonition*, Paris, 1931.
Richmond, A.B., *A Review of the Seybert Commissioners' Report*, Boston, 1880.
Rinn, Joseph, *Searchlight on Psychical Research*, New York, 1954.
Robins, Don, *Circles of Silence*, London, 1985.
Rosenthal, Robert, *Experimenter-Effects in Behavioral Research*, New York, 1976.
St Theresa of Avila, *Life*, London, 1870.
Saintyves, P., *La Force magique*, Paris, 1914.
Salter, W.H., *Ghosts and Apparitions*, London, 1938.
Saltmarsh, H.F., *Foreknowledge*, London, 1938.
Salverte, Eusebe, *The Occult Sciences* (2 vols), London, 1846 (1829).
Sardina, Maurice, *Where Houdini was Wrong*, London, 1950.
Schatzman, Morton, *The Story of Ruth*, London, 1980.
Schmeidler, Gertrude (ed.), *Extra-Sensory Perception*, New York, 1967.
—— (ed.), *Parapsychology: Its Relation to Physics, Biology, Psychology and Psychiatry*, Metuchen, New Jersey, 1976.
Schrenck-Notzing, Baron, *Phenomena of Materialisation*, London, 1920 (1913).
Schrödinger, Erwin, *Mind and Matter*, Cambridge, 1956.
Schumacher, E.F., *A Guide for the Perplexed*, London, 1978.
Seabrook, William, *Witchcraft*, New York, 1934.
Selous, Edmund, *Thought Transference, or What? in Birds*, London, 1931.

Shallis, Michael, *On Time*, London, 1982.

Sheldrake, Rupert, *A New Science of Life*, London, 1981.

Sinclair, Upton, *Mental Radio*, New York, 1930, and London, 1951.

Sinel, Joseph, *The Sixth Sense*, London, 1927.

Smith, Susie, *The Mediumship of Mrs Leonard*, New York, 1964.

Smythies, J.R. (ed.), *Science and ESP*, London, 1967.

Soal, S.G., and F. Bateman, *Modern Experiments in Telepathy*, London, 1954.

Stevenson, Ian, *Twenty Cases Suggestive of Reincarnation*, Charlottesville, Virginia, 1966.

Stobart, Mrs St Clair, *Ancient Lights*, London, 1926.

Sturrock, John (ed.), *Structuralism and Since*, Oxford, 1979.

Sudre, René, *Treatise on Parapsychology*, London, 1960.

Targ, Russell, and Harold Puthoff, *Mind-Reach*, London, 1977.

—— and Keith Harary, *The Mind Race*, New York, 1984.

Tart, Charles, *Altered States of Consciousness*, New York, 1969.

Taylor, John, *Superminds*, London, 1975.

—— *Science and the Supernatural*, London, 1980.

Tenhaeff, W.H.C., *Telepathy and Clairvoyance*, Springfield, Illinois, 1965.

Thakur, S. (ed.), *Philosophy and Psychical Research*, London, 1976.

Thalbourne, Michael A., *A Glossary of Terms used in Parapsychology*, London, 1982.

Thomas, Keith, *Religion and the Decline of Magic*, London, 1971.

Thomas, Lewis, *The Lives of a Cell*, New York, 1974, and London, 1980.

Thorpe, William, *Animal Nature and Human Nature*, London, 1974.

—— *The Origins and Rise of Ethology*, London, 1979.

Thouless, Robert H., *Experimental Psychical Research*, London, 1969.

—— *From Anecdote to Experiment in Psychical Research*, London, 1972.

Thurston, Herbert, *Modern Spiritualism*, London, 1938.

—— *The Physical Phenomena of Mysticism*, London, 1952.

Tischner, Rudolf, *Telepathy and Clairvoyance*, London, 1925.

Tompkins, Peter, and Christopher Bird, *The Secret Life of Plants*, London, 1974.

Truesdell, John W., *The Bottom Facts of Spiritualism*, New York, 1887.

Tylor, Edward B., *Primitive Culture* (2 vols), London, 1871.

Tyndall, John, *Fragments of Science for Unscientific People*, London, 1871.

Tyrrell, G.N.M., *Science and Psychical Phenomena*, London, 1938.

—— *Apparitions*, London, 1942.

—— *The Personality of Man*, London, 1946.

—— *Homo Faber*, London, 1951.

van der Post, Sir Laurens, *The Lost World of Kalahari*, London, 1958.

—— and Jane Taylor, *Testament to the Bushmen*, London, 1984.

van Over, Raymond (ed.), *Psychology and Extra-Sensory Perception*, New York, 1972.

Vasiliev, L.L., *Experiments in Distant Influence*, London, 1963.

de Vesme, Caesar, *Primitive Man*, London, 1931.

Vogt, Evon Z., and Ray Hyman, *Water-Witching USA*, Chicago, 1959.

Wallace, Alfred Russel, *On Miracles and Modern Spiritualism*, London, 1896 (1875).

—— *My Life* (2 vols), London, 1905.

Wallis, Roy (ed.), *On the Margins of Science*, Henley, 1979.

Warcollier, René, *Experiments in Telepathy*, London, 1939.

Watson, Lyall, *Supernature*, London, 1973.

—— *Lifetide*, London, 1979.

Watzlawick, Paul, *How Real is Real?*, London, 1976.

West, Donald J., *Psychical Research Today*, London, 1962 (1954).

Wheeler, William Morton, *The Social Insects*, New York, 1928.

White, Rhea, and Laura Dale, *Parapsychology: Sources of Information*, Metuchen, New Jersey, 1973.

Whitehead, Alfred North, *Science and the Modern World*, London, 1975 (1925).

—— *Nature and Life*, Cambridge, 1934.

Wilber, Ken, *Quantum Questions*, Boulder, Colorado, 1984.

Williams, C.B., *Insect Migration*, London, 1958.

Wilson, Colin, *The Occult*, London, 1973.

Wilson, E.O., *The Insect Societies*, Cambridge, Mass., 1971.

—— *Sociobiology*, 1975.

Wilson, Frank A., *Crystal and Cosmos*, London, 1977.

Wolman, Benjamin (ed.), *Handbook of Parapsychology*, New York, 1977.

Yates, Frances A., *The Occult Philosophy in the Elizabethan Age*, London, 1979.

Zohar, Danah, *Through the Time Barrier*, London, 1982.

Zöllner, Johan, *Transcendental Physics*, London, 1882.

Zukav, Gary, *The Dancing Wu Li Masters*, London, 1979.

Zusne, Leonard, and Warren H. Jones, *Anomalistic Psychology*, Hillsdale, New Jersey, 1982.

Periodicals

In addition to the publications of the established psychical research societies, I have consulted *Brain/Mind Bulletin*, *Fate*, *Fortean Times*, *Nature*, *New Scientist*, *Parapsychology Abstracts International*, *Science*, *Scientific American*, *Skeptical Inquirer*, and *Zetetic Scholar*.

Index